Back to the Drawing Board

Back to the Drawing Board: African-Canadian Feminisms

Edited by

Njoki Nathani Wane,

Katerina Deliovsky

& Erica Lawson

SUMACH

PRESS

WOMEN'S ISSUES PUBLISHING PROGRAM

SERIES EDITOR BETH MCAULEY

NATIONAL LIBRARY OF CANADA CATALOGUING IN PUBLICATION

Back to the drawing board: African-Canadian feminisms /
[edited] by Njoki Nathani Wane, Katerina Deliovsky and Erica Lawson.

Includes bibliographical references.
ISBN 1-894549-17-1

1. Black Canadian women. 2. Feminism — Canada.
I. Wane, Njoki Nathani II. Deliovsky, Katerina III. Lawson, Erica, 1967-

HQ1457.B32 2002 305.48'896071 C2002-904624-6

Edited by Beth McAuley

*Sumach Press acknowledges the support of the Canada Council
for the Arts and the Ontario Arts Council
for our publishing program.*

Printed in Canada

Published by

SUMACH PRESS
1415 Bathurst Street, Suite 202
Toronto ON Canada M5R 3H8
sumachpress@on.aibn.com
www.sumachpress.com

Contents

Part III:
THE SOCIAL GAZE

Acknowledgements

The editors of *Back to the Drawing Board* would like to acknowledge the contributors who have made invaluable contributions towards a more inclusive feminism(s). Without them there would be no book. We would also like to acknowledge and thank Beth McAuley, editor at Sumach Press, for her tireless devotion to this project. Her expertise and endless patience brought this book to another level. We would also like to honour the spirits of those who came before us who have struggled for a better world. May this book be a part of the struggle.

To the many women who shared their stories with me, may you continue to tell your stories and may this be just the beginning of your writing and publishing achievements. To Aziz and Sein, the book is done, and I thank you for your enthusiasm and support. To Amadou, *A jarama* for being there all the time and for your continued assistance and support of my academic endeavours.

— NW

I want to specifically acknowledge Tamari Kitossa, my partner in love and life. No words can capture the extent of his contributions to this project. I would also like to thank Njoki Wane and Erica Lawson for allowing me to enter and share their "space."

— KD

I would like to thank Wendy, Lorraine, Karen, Rachael and Roslyn for sharing their insights into Black women in the media and popular culture. My contribution to this book would not have been possible without their input. I would also like to thank my dearest friend Philip and my mother for their support.

— EL

FOREWORD

THROUGHOUT the history of Canada, Black women have contributed to the country's development — most, in ways that were common to all women of the times; but some, through exceptional acts made necessary by the harshness and the deprivation of their lives. None of our stories, not even in wide sociological groupings, appears in the texts from those periods.

Wanting to see our reflection in the texts, we have been forced to attempt identity-transpositions from white-Canadian women's stories or to rely on the oral histories of our mothers. Immigrant women or daughters of immigrants were subtly encouraged to identify with their own or their mothers' immigrant pasts. Such definitions were almost demanded by multiculturalism, which overtly allowed us to celebrate our cultures but often covertly tied us to a past we respected but sometimes barely knew. Frustrated by the absence of real information about our own stories in North America, Black-Canadian women reached across the border to borrow and incorporate stories of Black women and movements in the United States as part of the wider circle of our own herstories.

Having suffered the omission of our true histories, been assigned a hyphenated label to include our qualified Canadian status and having acquiesced to the borrowed American banner that carries an ill-fitting cultural identity, Black-Canadian feminists now want to define and describe ourselves and to tell our own stories. Neither the definitions nor the descriptions will be monolithic, for we are many and varied in background. Such diversity influences our views and enriches our deliberations.

Back to the Drawing Board encourages a dialogue about Black-Canadian feminism and focuses on key topics that are important issues in the discussion. For those readers who are not Black-Canadian feminists, I believe this book will provide an introduction to and a guide towards achieving a better understanding of who we are and what we think. For those readers who are Black-Canadian feminists, it is my hope that you will see some part of you in these pages and resolve to document in some other publication those parts of you that are not reflected here. For who we are and what we think has for too long been omitted from public record or left to others to write. *Back to the Drawing Board* is an important step in the process of putting ourselves into the feminist picture.

ZANANA AKANDE

Introduction

Njoki Nathani Wane, Katerina Deliovsky
and Erica Lawson

THE EMERGENCE OF BLACK FEMINIST THOUGHT arose in response to the unavailability of space within White women's feminism and Black men's articulation of Black Nationalism. In the words of Black feminist Gloria T. Hull, "No other ostensibly progressive movement has ever considered [Black women's] specific oppression as priority or worked seriously for the ending of that oppression."[1] With that in mind, Black feminists in the United States articulated their experiences of "double oppression,"[2] "multiple jeopardy/multiple consciousness"[3] and the "dialectic of Black womanhood."[4] In agreement, Black feminists the world over have theorized that there is indeed a uniqueness to being Black women. Out of this theorizing and the articulation of a unique but diverse standpoint, Black feminists have sought to give expression to a multiplicative Black feminist standpoint. Indeed, attesting to the particularity of this experientially grounded politics and theorizing, Patricia Hill Collins argues that a precondition for producing a Black feminist standpoint is living life as African-American women.[5] However, during the 1970s in Britain, the term "Black" was used as a politically unifying terminology for women of colour who were not necessarily of African ancestry. In naming the shared space of marginalization, women of colour in Britain consciously constructed a political identity shaped by shared experiences of racialization and its consequences.[6]

In recent years, the word "African" has been embraced by Diasporic African peoples to more accurately reflect their cultural and political affinity to the continent (e.g., African Canadian and African American).[7] In this book, we use the term "Black" and "African" interchangeably with specific reference to women of African ancestry. In doing so, we acknowledge that both "Black" and "African" are political and cultural identities. Some women may have more affinity for one term over the other. In the same vein, the use of upper case or lower case for "Black" and "White" reflects a similar definition of politics. Each author in this text has her/his unique orientation to the usage of Black or African, and upper or lower case Black and White. Allowing for this kind of diversity is one of the strengths of *Back to the Drawing Board*, as it tries to capture the political diversity of African women's politics. In addition, it tries to articulate a coherency and unity through these differences of perspective and politics. Having said that, the central task of *Back to the Drawing Board* is to explicate the particular sets of historical, material and social conditions of African women's lives regardless of the politics involved.

While we believe there are experiences that are particular to being Black women, it is equally important to acknowledge that these experiences vary according to class, sexuality, geography and national origin. Any feminist research that tries to explicate a diverse range of women's stories must attend to the contextual and historical intersections of race, ethnicity, class and gender. In light of this, it is important to highlight that the Black community in Canada consists of a number of groups, including those who have been in Canada for over two hundred years: African Caribbean and Afro-Latinas/Latinos, continental Africans and Black Canadians. Their histories and cultures have produced a rich and diverse tradition of Black feminist theory both within and outside the academy.[8] This multiplicity of Black feminism reflects the reality that being "Black Canadian" is a contested and heterogeneous identity. Thus, the Black feminisms found in this text are the convergence of many journeys to a central place by people who are located differently in terms of class, sexuality, language and ethnicity yet who share similar histories of oppression resulting from slavery, colonialism and racism. This makes it possible to speak of shared perspectives on Black feminist thought, even though they may be differently defined.[9]

Over the last two decades a small but important body of literature by Black feminists in Canada has been edging towards an explicit theory of Black feminist thought. Few books, however, have taken the concreteness of a Black feminist standpoint as the basis from which to develop Black feminist thought as a mode of theorizing the diverse experiences of Black women. *Back to the Drawing Board* attempts to provide a framework for Black/African-Canadian feminist thought through a collection of essays that examine the historical and cultural realities that have influenced Black-Canadian feminist theory. This collection is not exhaustive and we recognize that most of the contributors are Ontario based; nonetheless, it does offer an opportunity to initiate a dialogue based on historical and contemporary feminist theorizing.

Through a process of collaboration, we hope to advance a body of feminist theory that is informed by a practice that closely reflects the daily realities of African-Canadian women and their communities. We also hope to engage our allies in a broader discussion about feminist theorizing that challenges racist violence, both spiritual and physical, in the lives of African-Canadian women and that critically analyzes its debilitating impact on all of us. Much of the literature informing Black-Canadian feminist thought, however, originates in the United States and the United Kingdom. *Back to the Drawing Board* is therefore a project that aims to carve out critical space in which we can theorize, interrogate and dialogue about issues relevant to African-Canadian women. It is our intent to build a body of work that is dynamic, theoretical and practical.

The idea for this book arose out of the scarcity of scholarly writing on African-Canadian feminist thought. This scarcity was particularly apparent to Dr. Njoki Wane when she proposed to teach a course on Black feminist thought and found that there were few appropriate materials available. While it is important to acknowledge that during the last two decades there has been a considerable amount of writing by and about Black women in Canada (and the authors wish to acknowledge those who have laid the foundation), it is still carried out predominantly in piecemeal fashion. It became apparent that in order to build on previous work and to advance the rich heterogeneity of Black-Canadian women's experiences, a more unified Black feminist text was needed.

To embark on this project, Njoki Wane decided to make the project a collective effort and invited Erica Lawson and Katerina Deliovsky to team up with her. Erica and Katerina are doctoral students of Jamaican and Macedonian ancestry, respectively, who participated in Njoki's Black feminist course. While we were aware that we occupied different locations and identities and thus perspectives, we felt these differences would offer a unique richness and depth to the book. These diverging views helped to bring the voices, concerns and issues of African-Canadian women and other marginalized women "back to the drawing board." Embracing and theorizing the diversity of African-Canadian women's lives meant expanding the boundaries of how we connected and related to one another's location and knowledge production. Understanding how these connections speak to African-Canadian feminisms is the most important aspect of this book. The contributors to this text, who come from various racial, ethnic and gender backgrounds, enhance these voices and connections. To capture this diversity, *Back to the Drawing Board* is divided into four thematic sections: Theorizing Feminisms, Education and Activism, The Social Gaze and Indigenous Connections.

Theorizing Feminisms

In the first chapter of this collection, "Black-Canadian Feminist Thought: Drawing on the Experiences of My Sisters," Njoki Wane explores Black feminism(s) and why it is necessary to have a Black-Canadian feminist theory. She invites readers to engage in an open dialogue about what constitutes Black-Canadian feminist theory and the ways in which Black women's histories and present experiences inform this theory. In this chapter, Wane emphasizes the importance of creating spaces where Black women can articulate their feminist ideas, be it through writing or community or scholarly work, in a language that represents their own perspectives. Wane also advances the importance of working with an ideology that decolonizes the mind, and she attempts to anchor her theory in a framework that embraces her African-Canadian work. "It has been crucial for me," she writes, "to find and articulate a feminism that speaks to my historical and contemporary experiences — a multi-layered feminism that incorporates the ideologies of African, African-American and White feminisms and that places Black-Canadian women in the centre."

In chapter 2, "The More Things Change ... Rethinking Mainstream Feminism," Katerina Deliovsky argues that White feminists have not made theoretical advances that provide the ideological basis for a liberatory struggle. The superficial accommodation of race as an integral and meaningful feminist category of analysis suggests reluctance to give up a White feminist hegemony. To effectively provide an epistemology with a liberatory praxis, there needs to be a serious reconceptualization of two fundamental concepts integral to White feminist analysis: gender and patriarchy. Deliovsky's contention is that these concepts currently rest on universalized and narrow parameters of what constitutes women's oppression.

Tamari Kitossa argues in chapter 3, "Criticism, Reconstruction and African-Centred Feminist Historiography," that feminist historiography represents the struggle to write women into history as agents of their own making and as members of social collectives. Yet, in spite of women's heterogeneity, feminist historiography in Canada is equated with White women. Consequently, the feminist movement in Canada has been represented as a correlate of the social and political activism of White women. Through an African-Canadian centred approach to history and historiography, Kitossa examines the ways in which racism consistently negates the significant contributions that African-Canadian women have made to feminist consciousness in Canada.

Afua Cooper's excerpted essay in chapter 4, "Black Women and Work in Nineteenth-Century Canada West: Black Woman Teacher Mary Bibb," concludes this section by exploring the life of Mary Bibb, who was born in 1820 in Rhode Island and eventually settled in southwestern Ontario. By examining Mary Bibb's life as a teacher and an activist, Cooper illustrates how Black women participated in the building, education and empowerment of their communities. Freed from slavery, Bibb devoted her life to educating Black people, believing that education would offer her community a measure of self-sufficiency. She achieved this against great odds since there were scarcely any schools in the early eighteenth century designated for Black children. Although Mary Bibb may not have called herself a feminist, her activities are representative of early Black feminist theorizing and practice.

Education and Activism

This section opens with Dolana Mogadime's essay "Black Women in Graduate Studies: Transforming the Socialization Experience," in which she questions the limited number of Black women faculty in higher education. She argues that an understanding of this limitation might shed more light on the socialization processes that discourage minority women from pursuing academic careers. Based on interviews with five Black women in graduate school, Mogadime explores why there are so few Black women and women of colour in the academy and how their participation can be increased. Drawing on Stanley James's argument that Black women's theorizing is informed by their experiences, Mogadime's essay provides insight into Black feminist theories as they unfold through the lived realities of Black women in the academy.

Chapter 6, "Reconceptualizing Our Classroom Practice: Notes from an Anti-Racist Educator" by Grace Mathieson, provides practical strategies for integrating Black feminist theory into curriculum development and teaching practices. Mathieson's essay points to the necessity of rethinking what and how we teach in order to rupture pervasive colonial perspectives. Drawing on Aboriginal and Black writers, she elaborates on the importance of interrogating colonial education for the purposes of pedagogical transformation, and challenges White educators to engage in active and responsible educational transformation.

Njoki Wane takes up issues highlighted in Mogadime's and Mathieson's essays and presents an analysis of the complex and challenging positions faced by African-Canadian women in chapter 7, "Carving Out Critical Space: African-Canadian Women and the Academy." She argues that African-Canadian women need to create a critical space from which they can theorize and concludes with some suggestions and recommendations for promoting a liberatory education in the academy.

The Social Gaze

This section opens with Erica Lawson's "Images in Black: Black Women, Media and the Mythology of an Orderly Society." In this essay, she examines historical and contemporary socially constructed images of Black women and the ways in which these images are used to sustain racism and sexism in a capitalist society. Lawson argues that there is a dissonance between the caricaturization of Black women as objects in subordinate roles and the everyday lives of Black women as embodied subjects engaged in multiple roles. In particular, the hyper-sexualized representations of Black women in mainstream media and the invisibility of Black women in "spaces that matter" work in tandem to perpetuate Black women's exclusion and to undermine their personal and professional authority. Drawing on her interviews with five African-Canadian women, Lawson explores the ways in which these women interpret contemporary exploitative images.

Chapter 9, "Spirit-Murdering the Messenger: The Discourse of Fingerpointing as the Law's Response to Racism" by Patricia J. Williams, illustrates the effects of accumulated pain that comes from negative racial imagery and depiction. Williams explains that there is a slow death, a mutation that takes place within the individual as a result of this pain. She names these deeply painful and assaultive experience of racism as "spirit-murder" and advocates that it be elevated to the conceptual level of a capital moral offence. In making her argument, she analyzes the language of lawmakers, officials and the public to illustrate how the law is used to deflect responsibility in the creation and perpetuation of spirit-murder. She stresses that spirit-murder is a cultural cancer that is wreaking spiritual genocide on "blacks, whites, and the abandoned and abused of all races and ages."

Katerina Deliovsky explores the experiences of six White women in interracial relationships with Black men in chapter 10, "Transgressive Whiteness: The Social Construction of White Women Involved in Interracial Relationships with Black Men." Her essay focuses on how the socially constructed hegemonic representations of whiteness, blackness and gender impinge and determine the life experiences of these women. While class and age assume an important role in the context of their interracial relationships, race and gender appear to be the primary "relations of ruling"[10] that affect the quality of their lives. Deliovsky's work contributes to the body of knowledge about White women whose actions symbolically and literally transgress the boundaries of the White racial order. Her work further illustrates how Black feminist thought can be used by White feminists to open critical spaces in which White women can address the intersections of class, gender and race.

Adrien Wing's "Brief Reflections toward a Multiplicative Theory and Praxis of Being" concludes this section in chapter 11. For Wing, an important element in the desire to name the spirit-murder articulated by Patricia William springs from the need to define the unique experiences of Black women. She specifically addresses the multiple levels of consciousness that characterize Black women's experiences, experiences that cannot be reduced to a simple addition problem: racism plus sexism. Wing stresses that Black women must be seen as a "multiplicative, multilayered, indivisible whole, symbolized by the equation one times one, not one plus one." This knowledge is important in order to create empowering programs and services that deal with the fact that Black women are the victims of spirit-murder no matter their social location.

Indigenous Connections

This section explores the ways that Indigenous knowledge is theorized and practised by Black/African and Aboriginal women. Indigenous knowledge is defined as the cultural traditions, values, belief systems and world views in any indigenous society that are imparted to the young generation by community elders.[11] Such knowledge constitutes an informed epistemology, crucial for the survival of society; the unique, traditional, local knowledge existing within and developed around the specific conditions of an Indigenous people within a particular geographical area. These are based on collective understandings and interpretations of the social, physical, and spiritual worlds,[12] and include the concepts, beliefs, perceptions, and experiences of local peoples in their natural and human-built environments. Claiming indigeneity is a way African and Aboriginal women can create a space in which to celebrate their ways of knowing and teaching.

The three essays in this section explore Indigenous stories of creation, spiritual practices and connections to the land. Chapter 12 is an excerpt from Njoki Wane's essay "African Women and

Spirituality: Harmonizing the Balance of Life." Rather than offering any concrete definitions, Wane defines spirituality as something essentially intangible and indefinable. To explore this, she draws on her interviews with the Embu rural women of Kenya and explores the potential of African women's spirituality to inform human relations.

In chapter 13, "Living Well Within the Context of Indigenous Education," Brenda Firman shares her experiences as a pupil among First Nations people and how doing so has taught her to acknowledge her privilege as a White woman. As a grandmother of two children who live in an Anishnabe community, she understands the importance of providing the right education for children. She argues that children have a right to learn with, from and about their own people, in their own language.

The spiritual knowing explored in Wane's paper resonates in Barbara Waterfall's "Reclaiming Identity: Native Wombmyn's Reflections on Wombma-Based Knowledge and Spirituality." Her position is that women's spiritual knowledge originates from their wombs, which she refers to as wombma spirituality and which she celebrates as sacred knowledge. Waterfall also shows how the collaboration of Native and Black women can be a very powerful endeavour in reclaiming identity and space in feminisms. She emphasizes the importance of creating healthy connections with others and, by drawing on the works of Black women writers, illustrates the similarities between the teachings of African-Canadian and Native women.

♦

NJOKI WANE: Reading Patricia Hill Collins's *Black Feminist Thought: Knowledge, Consciousness and the Politics of Empowerment* challenged me. Although the book focuses on African-American women, I was inspired by it and felt there was a need to build on the works of Black-Canadian feminists who base their theorizing on Black-Canadian writers — Sylvia Hamilton, Annette Henry,

Nourbese Philip, Linda Carty, Wanda Bernard, Peggy Bristow, Dionne Brand, Afua Cooper and Agnes Calliste, to name just a few. Women's Studies and Gender Studies have made great strides in ensuring that women's realities and gender issues are integrated into the academy, thereby providing the means for a fuller understanding of how society functions. However, the experiences of Black-Canadian women have not been given enough attention within these fields, and if they are included, they have not been sufficiently drawn upon. The importance of documenting my reality and articulating feminisms that speaks to my be-ing as an African-Canadian woman compelled me to initiate this project. Although there are many texts that provide insights into African-Canadian women's lives, I have not yet come across a book whose central theme is Black-feminist thought from a Canadian perspective. *Back to the Drawing Board* is the first step in filling this vacuum.

KATERINA DELIOVSKY: Although I always believed this book to be a vitally important and exciting project, I was reluctant to be a part of this project. My reluctance centred on my not wanting, as a European woman, to step into a space that was not mine. While I am aware that as a Macedonian woman with two mixed-race children from an interracial relationship with an African Jamaican I am stigmatized by my choices, I am also aware (through the contributions of Black feminist thought and anti-racist scholarship) that I am privileged by my whiteness. I did not want this race privilege to alter or impose a different set of dynamics than was originally intended. Women of African descent have been relegated to the margins for so long and I did not want my whiteness to hijack or distort a project that meant to place African women in the centre. After much thought and discussion with my partner, I decided to become involved. I then had to ask myself, What will be my part? I, like Njoki and Erica, believe White feminists need to engage in committed anti-racist feminist work. As such, my contribution to this project is to call attention to the White feminist hegemony that has participated in a form of "spirit-murder," which is highlighted in this collection. In addition, my work tries to illustrate that through physical and psychological violence, the privilege and surreptitious sense of superiority White people experience as White people has come at the expense of racialized people. For the betterment of human relations it needs to stop. I hope that this project can advance these goals.

ERICA LAWSON: Some books are like my family. They tell me who I am and where I have been. They let me know about the people I belong to and the journeys that we have taken together. They connect me to the past and help me to make sense of the present. They also give me a glimpse into the future. One of the most important books in my life is *Lionheart Gal: The Life Stories of Jamaican Women*, produced by the Sistren Collective with Honor Ford-Smith. It is the only book, to my knowledge, that captures narratives about Jamaican women in our language. It is feminist, political, anti-colonial and powerful. *Lionheart Gal* speaks to the necessity, indeed the urgency, of telling stories about Black women from where we live and about the conditions that shape our realities. I wanted to contribute to a book about African-Canadian women because Canada is where I live. And it is from this place that I need to critique the invisibility of Black women and challenge the injustices to which we are subjected. Just as *Lionheart Gal* "draws on the legacy of tale telling which has always preserved the history of Caribbean women,"[13] so too must this book document and interpret the historical and contemporary realities of African-Canadian women.

Notes

1. Gloria T. Hull, "The Combahee River Collective," in Gloria T. Hull, Patricia Bell Scott and Barbara Smith, eds., *All the Women are White, All the Blacks Are Men, But Some of Us Are Brave* (New York: Feminist Press, 1982), 15.

2. J. Beale, "Double Jeopardy: To Be Black and Female," in Tone Cade Bambara, ed., *The Black Woman: An Anthology* (Toronto: New American Library of Canada Ltd., 1973).

3. Deborah King, "Multiple Jeopardy, Multiple Consciousness: The Context of a Black Feminist Ideology," *Signs: Journal of Women in Culture and Society* (1988); Brenda Eichelberger, "Voices of Black Feminism," *Quest* (Spring 1977), 17–33. Eichelberger's article is based on two questions she asked eight women: Why are so few Black women in the feminist movement? Is there a need for Black feminism? The answers are varied; however, most women see the need for a movement that is initiated by Black women, controlled by Black women, for the purposes of Black women.

4. Bonnie Thornton Dill, "Race, Class and Gender: Prospects for an All-Inclusive Sisterhood," *Feminist Studies* (1983).

5. Patricia Hill Collins, "The Social Construction of Black Feminist Thought," in N. Tuana and R. Tong, eds., *Feminism and Philosophy* (Boulder: Westview Press, 1995), 539.

6. Heidi Safia Mirza, "Black Women in Education: A Collective Movement for Social Change," in Heidi Safia Mirza, ed., *Black British Feminism: A Reader* (London: Routledge, 1997); Njoki NathaniWane, "Black Feminist Thought: In Search of a Black Canadian Feminist Framework," paper presented at the Race, Gender and Class Conference, New Orleans, October 18 to 21, 2001.

7. For example, Sylvia Hamilton notes that while the term Black is most commonly used to identify people of African origin in Nova Scotia, Afro-Nova Scotian has come into contemporary use to identify people of African descent who live in that province. "Our Mothers Grand and Great: Black Women of Nova Scotia," *Canadian Woman Studies* (Spring 1991).

8. Wane, "Black Feminist Thought: In Search of a Black Canadian Feminist Framework."

9. Ibid.; A. Calliste and George Dei, eds., *Anti-Racist Feminism: Critical Race and Gender Studies* (Halifax: Fernwood Publishing, 2000).

10. Dorothy Smith, *The Everyday World As Problematic: A Feminist Sociology* (Boston: Northeastern University Press, 1987).

11. George Dei, Budd Hall and Dorothy Rosenberg, *Indigenous Knowledge in Global Contexts: Multiple Readings of Our World* (Toronto: University of Toronto Press, 2000); Louise Grenier, *Working with Indigenous Knowledge: A Guide for Researchers* (Ottawa: International Development Research Centre, 1998).

12. Wane, "Black Feminist Thought: In Search of a Black Canadian Feminist Framework."
13. Honor Ford-Smith and the Sistren Collective, *Lionheart Gal: The Life Stories of Jamaican Women* (Toronto: Sister Vision Press, 1987), 3.

Part I

Theorizing Feminisms

Chapter One

Black-Canadian Feminist Thought:

Drawing on the Experiences of My Sisters

Njoki Nathani Wane

> We and you do not talk the same language. When we talk to you we use your language: the language of your experience and your theories. We try to use it to communicate our world of experience. Since your language and your theories are inadequate in expressing our experiences, we only succeed in communicating our experience of exclusion. We cannot talk to you in our language because you do not understand it. So the ... facts [are] that we understand your language and that the place where most theorizing about women is taking place is your place, both combine to require that we either use your language and distort our experience not just in speaking about it, but in living of it, or that we remain silent.
>
> — Maria C. Lugones and Elizabeth Spelman, "Have We Got a Theory for You!"

Maria Lugones and Elizabeth Spelman are speaking to theorists who refuse to acknowledge that the formulation of theories is a prerogative not only for scholars in the academy but also for community members who combine theory and practice in their everyday experiences. Many Black women leave feminist theorizing to feminist scholars who contextualize theory in scholarly terms, but many of these women articulate the fundamentals of Black feminist theory in their everyday lives and within their communities.

We have examples throughout our history of how Black-Canadian women have struggled for equality and dignity. Their tenacious spirit has been the strongest and most constant ally for Black-Canadian women.[1] Many have taken it upon themselves to educate community children, create programs for them and organize activism to resist oppression. For instance, in 1787, Catherine Abernathy, taught a class of twenty children in a log schoolhouse that was built by the community. Abernathy established a tradition of Black women teachers that continues to the present day. In more recent memory, Dr. Miriam Rossi, a medical practitioner and professor at the University of Toronto, co-founded a successful University of Toronto Summer Mentorship Program for Black children. Through this summer program, many Black children have been encouraged to seek a higher education. Dr Rossi and others may not identify themselves with Black feminist theory, but their actions inform their theory. Another dedicated Black women educator is former Ontario MPP, Zanana Akande. Through speeches and various activities she continues to tirelessly champion education of interest to Black Canadians. In these particular instances, I would define these women's actions through a Black-Canadian feminist lens.

I am writing as a feminist scholar who works in the academy, but the core of this chapter relies on the voices of Black women both in the university and in the community who articulate Black feminist thought from a Canadian perspective. As Black Canadian women, it is important that we create spaces where we can articulate our feminist ideas, be it through writing or community or scholarly work, in a language that represents our own voices and theory.

In this chapter I invite readers to participate in a dialogue that focuses on the following questions: What is Black feminist thought? What does it constitute? Can Black-Canadian women[2] theorize their experiences using a Black feminist framework? If they can, will they be told that they are mimicking African-American or middle-class White feminisms? Is it necessary for us to develop a specific feminism for each category of Black women living in Canada or would a general category be sufficient as a theoretical framework? Is Black feminist thought no more than White mainstream feminism with a prefix? Black-Canadian women, what do you want to call your feminisms?

I ask these questions as a woman who understands that the framework of African feminist thought was in existence before the emergence of Black feminisms as they are articulated now. I use a qualified Black feminist thought as an entry point for my work as an African woman living in Canada. However, as an African woman I see things through an African woman's eyes.[3] What I remember most are how the experiences of my mothers, grandmothers and aunties — women who worked tirelessly to provide the basic needs for their families and to sustain their communities — engaged in feminist practice and theory. Would I have called them feminists if I had not engaged myself in the search for what is feminism? A quick overview of African feminism will clarify what I am referring to.

African feminism evokes the power, not paralysis, of African women and accounts for their triumphs without underestimating the gravity of their circumstances. The feminist spirit that pervades the African continent is very complex. The majority of African women do not hesitate to articulate their feminism, they just do it. This notion of an action-oriented type of feminism is clearly articulated by Obioma Nnaemeka and Juliana Makuchi Nfah-Abbenyi, among others.[4] Nnaemeka and Nfah-Abbenyi have written extensively on issues of African women and feminism, and African women's writing. According to them, African women believe that what they do and how they do it is what matters the most and it is this that provides the framework for their gender-centred awareness. Some African women claim that feminism is not an African ideology, that what exists is a Western feminism that educated African women have embraced. Many African women have rejected this feminism because they feel that it aligns them with white middle-class feminism. Others dismiss feminism because they interpret it as an ideology imported into Africa to ruin good African women. Still others claim that African feminism is in its infancy, while some argue that feminism is indigenous to Africa and that African women were feminists long before there was a Western feminism. They might not have called it feminism, but African women have a long history of gendered consciousness,[5] and many attribute this consciousness to the long lineage of women in their families.[6]

As you can see, African feminism is complex, and even I have found it difficult to identify with and engage in. In fact, at the beginning of my PhD program at the University of Toronto, I announced to everybody in my feminist class that I was not a feminist. However, after further dialogue with my colleagues and my professor, I agreed my activism was feminist in nature but I had refused to call myself a feminist because of the negative connotation I had attached to the word feminism. As an educator who teaches Black feminist thought, I need to work with an ideology that decolonizes my mind, anchors my theory in my ancestors' knowledge and creates a framework that embraces my work. It is has been crucial for me to find and articulate a feminism that speaks to my historical and contemporary experiences — a multi-layered feminism that incorporates the ideologies of African, African-American and White feminisms and that places Black-Canadian women in the centre. While White feminisms do offer some important contributions, they do not fully include Black feminist thought as articulated by Black women. In their critique of White mainstream feminisms, Black women have come to terms with their absence and have critically responded to the ways in which White feminisms have made them visible only when it is convenient.

Black-Canadian feminist thought has been shaped by theorists, activists and feminists from the United States who speak to the experiences of African-American women and whose works[7] draw on earlier Black feminist founders and scholars, including Sojourner Truth, Zora Neale Hurston, Harriet Tubman, Harriet Wilson, Mary Shadd, Mary Stewart, Michelle Wallace, Barbara Smith and The Combahee River Collective. While we acknowledge the contributions African-American women have made, we must continue to develop a Canadian-focused Black feminist theory.

How, then, can we create a Black-Canadian feminist thought that speaks to all of us and reflects all our experiences and histories? Black women in Canada come from Africa, Asia, Britain and the Caribbean and it will be difficult to articulate a common feminist thought because our experiences and histories are too numerous and too varied.[8] I cannot, therefore, attempt to represent the voices of all Black women; however, I would like to open the dialogue so that we can work towards building a feminist thought that includes and acknowledges our range of experiences. Students and women from the community all seem to have different views on what constitutes Black-Canadian feminist thought. In this essay, I look at some of the writings that influence our theorizing and draw on conversations and interviews with Black-Canadian women who have expressed their perspectives on what Black-Canadian feminist thought means to them. These women were students in a course I have been teaching since 1999.

Drawing on the Experiences of My Sisters

In the summer of 1999, I initiated a graduate-level course at the Ontario Institute for Studies in Education of the University of Toronto (OISE/UT) that was called Black Feminist Thought:

Sociological Research in Education. I wanted this course to build a dialogue around the questions I posed at the beginning of the chapter and to place Black women's experiences at the centre of our interpretations. I introduced concepts and perspectives of Black feminisms — Black feminist thought, mothering by Black women, media representation and the social construction of Black women — and created a space for exploring the possibility of grounding Black women's experiences in Black feminist ways of knowing. I wanted to introduce the discourse of Black feminism as a theoretical framework for researching and writing about Black women's issues. I knew I could not represent all the experiences of my Black sisters, but I could draw on their personal stories, writings and theory to help shape the discussion.

As soon as I announced my proposal to teach the course I panicked because I was not sure I would find adequate materials to use. My fears were soon realized. I found many writings by or about Black-American women, but very little by or about Black-Canadian women. I did find one key text — *"We are All Rooted Here and You Cannot Pull Us Up"* — an edited collection by Peggy Bristow that includes writings by Dionne Brand, Linda Carty, Afua Cooper, Sylvia Hamilton and Adrienne Shadd. In addition I found material by Nourbese Philip and Agnes Calliste. Despite the shortage of material, I felt encouraged because many students at OISE/UT were excited to know there would be a graduate course focusing on Black women's issues.

Many of these students called me — they were curious to know what the course would offer. I made it clear that I wanted to provide a space where Black women could define their experiences, their theories, their histories and their traditions in their own voice, and that I wanted students who would like to participate in this process. I added that the course would speak very well to students from different backgrounds and would highlight the heroic work accomplished by Black women in Canada. Some students felt they would not relate to the materials if they were not Black or female, or if they were not Black but female. I told these students that it depended on what they were looking for and what their area of research was. Nonetheless, I recommended the course to them because I believed it would be a great entry point for understanding the lives of Canadian women of African descent and in participating in the development of a Black feminist theory based on their lives.

Because African women's writing is not widely published and is rarely referred to in the classroom, I designed the reading to focus on African women writers. Juliana Makuchi Nfah-Abbenyi points out that African literature is growing and including greater numbers of African women writers. Even so, African literature is often considered to be mostly made up of male writers so women writers are often overlooked: "The ignoring of African women writers on the continent has become a tradition, implicit, rather than formally stated, but a tradition nonetheless."[9] In my course I challenged this tradition by privileging African women's writing and bringing their muted words back into history and theory, just as Peggy Bristow and her co-authors did when they came together to write *"We are All Rooted Here and You Cannot Pull Us Up"*:

> As a group we came together and decided that, just as women could not wait for male historians to rewrite mainstream history to include women, we could not expect White women to include us in women's history ... We decided, therefore, to write about African Canadian women for two primary reasons. First, as women, our experiences have always differed significantly from those of men. While we are subjected to racism as are Black men, gender compounds this situation. How we have managed historically to survive both racial and gender subordination deserves special attention.[10]

The class began in September 1999 as a one-semester course. It examined, among other things, the central tenets of Black feminist thought, what informs it and how different scholars have conceptualized it; how Black feminist theory is a theory developed out of Black women's experiences and rooted in their communities; and feminisms advocated by visible minorities. It also dealt with the divergence and similarities of Black feminisms and acknowledged the heterogeneity of Black women's experiences. By the end of the semester I realized I should have proposed a full-year course as there were far too many issues to cover within one semester. Nonetheless, the students themselves created a space in which we discussed and formulated a Black feminist theory.

Connecting Theory to Practice

The emergence of Black feminist thought in North America has focused on the American experience and the production and construction of specific sites of knowledge, such as the academy, that privilege the historical and contemporary realities of Black-American women. American theorist Patricia Hill Collins has argued that Black-American women need to stop trying to fit into paradigms of resistance that do not speak to the totality of their multiple identities, paradigms such as Black nationalism or Western feminism. This applies to Black-Canadian women as well — we cannot embrace other women's feminisms, we need to define our own. We need a theory that places Black-Canadian women's experiences and ideas at the centre of analysis and that reclaims our voices and rewrites our history. Collins suggests that Black women's scholarship can contribute meaningfully to the empowerment of Black women through ideas and analytical frameworks that focus on the existing domains of power and ways to resist them.[11]

As Black-Canadian feminists, we need to create a definitive body of knowledge that privileges our experiences. It is time we took up the pen and committed to paper our own theories derived from the struggles and achievements of our foremothers, many of which are still buried within the confines of what Dorothy Smith calls "relations of ruling,"[12] in which Black-Canadian women's realities are situated. It is also important to document the legacies of slavery, colonialism and neo-colonialism and how these have shaped our realities. By writing from Black-Canadian women's perspectives, Canadian-born and immigrant women from Africa and the Caribbean can interpret these ideas, reclaim the voices of Black women who have been silenced and construct a Black-Canadian theory that places Black women in the centre.

The groundbreaking book *"We're Rooted Here and You Can't Pull Us Up"* stands as a landmark document in Black-Canadian women's historiography. It firmly locates Black women within Canadian history, identifying the contributions they have made in freeing themselves and other enslaved people in North America. The collection also provides the reader with historical insights into traditions of Black feminist thought in Canadian society. Another landmark book is Makeda Silvera's *Silenced*, which offers a critical look at the exploitation of Black Caribbean women recruited by Canadian citizens and officials to work as domestics. Her study reveals the extent to which some White Canadian women achieved gender equity on the backs of these Black women. Other Black-Canadian writers have written on such topics as sexuality, racism, mothering, community leadership, activism, the academy, work, violence, women's health, history, culture, immigration policies and the general African female diasporic experience in Canada.[13]

Using these books, the class explored the social construction of Black women and the intersecting aspects of oppression as we experience it. We examined colonial and neo-colonial identities and Black women's multiple and hybrid identities. Such exploration and discussion contribute to a Black-Canadian feminist theory, but do not succeed in harnessing the rich heterogeneity of Black-Canadian women's experiences and thus do not provide an adequate profile of Black feminist thought in Canada. Since Black-Canadian feminist theory is still carried out predominantly in piecemeal fashion, a more unified Black feminist voice needs to be formed, both on a theoretical and a practical level.

In our class we decided to take up the pen to formulate our own definition of Black-Canadian feminist thought. In our discussions, it became clear that Black women's lived experiences provided the fundamentals of their feminisms and it was critical that our definition captured these fundamental principles. After many group discussions, we agreed on the following definition:

> Black feminist thought is a theoretical tool meant to elucidate and analyze the historical, social, cultural and economic relationships of women of African descent as the basis for development of a liberatory praxis. It is a paradigm that is grounded in the historical as well as the contemporary experiences of Black women as mothers, activists, academics and community leaders. It is both an oral and a written epistemology that theorizes our experiences as mothers, activists, academics and community leaders. It can be applied to situate Black women's past and present experiences that are grounded in their multiple oppressions.[14]

For many students, an analysis of the social world using a Black-Canadian feminist epistemology can provide a voice for women who are not represented in mainstream feminism, which is based on the experiences of White, middle-class, heterosexual women whose lived experiences are analyzed without interrogation of race or colour. Theories such as Western feminism, which seek to explain the nature of women's oppression, may not speak directly to the experiences of Black women.[15] As well, Black feminist thought based in African-American theory may not speak as directly and fully to the Canadian experience. When I asked Justina,[16] a graduate student, whether she identified with Black feminist thought she said she did but to a limited extent:

> I do not identify with Black feminist thought, because it is American, but I do identify with some feminisms. Although I appreciate Patricia Hill Collins's work on Black feminisms, I have problems with how she articulates standpoint theory. I believe there is much more to standpoint theory than women's experiences of resistance or struggle. A Black women's

> intellectual discourse is not shaped only through resistance … I would like to see something more Canadian … Black Canadian … some historical material, information on psychological violence, new immigrant women's experiences, denial of jobs for qualified immigrant women, and cultural identities … I am not sure but this type of feminism might be attractive to me.

Nicky had this to say about it:

> I think it is exciting to have a feminism that I can identify with. However, sometimes I get confused because of the many strands of feminisms. In our class some women feel that Black feminism is an offshoot of mainstream feminims … but I tend to disagree with them. I think there is something unique about Black feminist thought whether it is African-American or African-Canadian. I do acknowledge that my experiences are different from yours, but I believe that as Black women we share certain things … our histories, though different, are largely shaped by colonized experiences. I think for me a feminism that speaks to my experiences is good enough … However, I cannot blindly take any theory that comes along … That is why searching for the fundamentals of Black-Canadian feminist theory is important to me.

Black-Canadian feminisms need to theorize Black women's experiences, but not by applying theories developed outside their experiential context. Justina has problems with how Collins articulates standpoint theory, stating that she believes it is more than resistance that shapes Black women's identity, a standpoint that Collins uses when she draws on the everyday acts of Black women in the United States as forms of resistance.

Yet Collins also uses standpoint theory to problematize pedagogical practices within the academy and to challenge the criteria that determine whose knowledge is valid. Her approach argues that subjugated knowledges, nurtured in communities and other non-mainstream places, are valuable in their own right. Embedded within this framework is the "outsider-within" paradigm that highlights the multiple locations of Black women in society. Collins states that "outsider-within locations are locations or border spaces marking the boundaries between groups of unequal power. Individuals acquire identities as outsider within by their placement in these social locations."[17] I am aware of the many different social locations that we occupy as Black women, the conflicts of interests, the varieties of histories of migration to Canada, and I believe that divergent locations make our feminisms unique and together will build a cohesive Black feminist thought that speaks to our experiences.

To broaden the non-academic perspective of our discussion, I invited Aileen William and Alcenya Crowley, non-academic women from the Black community, to share their personal stories and understanding of feminisms. AileenWilliam worked as an executive secretary for the government for many years and Alcenya Crowley was a teacher — they are both retired. These two women were members of the Canadian Negro Women's Association, which is no longer in existence, and held different positions within the organization for many years. They discussed their activism and their concerns about the plight of Black women in Toronto, how they believed a good education would raise the standard of living for the Black community and the many fundraising events they organized to assist families in need. Although they did not call themselves feminists, it was clear that they had engaged in feminist activism for most of their adult lives. Both Aileen and Alcenya were active members of the Negroes' Club that organized fundraising dances and dinners to assist recent immigrants in Toronto.

The class discussions that followed these presentations were deeper and more honest because of the real-life stories that broadened our definition of feminisms. As Meream remarked:

> The academy can be very isolating and unreal. Whenever these women from the community come to our class, the dynamics are different. They may not quote the current theorists,

however they know the history of Black women and organizing in Toronto quite well. What is amazing is how they articulate their feminism — they do not call it Black or White. As one of them said, they did not see the need because if the feminism they practised enabled them to change their plight in life, that was the feminism they would identify with.

African-American feminist writers, such as Patricia Hill Collins, have defined Black feminism as an activism that is grounded in women's common histories, such as colonialism and slavery, and passed on through practices that have improved the lives of their communities. While not referred to as feminist, these activities definitely shape a feminist consciousness. For many Black women, grandmothers, mothers and aunts have played a key role in shaping their activism and their feminism. When I talked to Marie, she described Black-Canadian feminism in this way:

> The feminism that I know is what my mother and my grandmothers practise. These women taught me to be strong and to speak for myself. They emphasized the need for education and independence. These women did not call themselves feminists, but I think they were. Black feminism ... (although this is a new phrase for me) ... is important if the definition given would reflect my experiences and those of my foremothers. I was not born here — I came when I was twelve years old — but I can still recall my grandmother's stately figure. But unfortunately, all through high school there was no mention of Black women except for Harriet Tubman and the Underground Railway. I guess this is a rebirth of Black- Canadian feminisms ... yes, a different feminism from Tubman's or my grandmother's or mother's, but a feminism that reflects all their heroic work, my experiences and your experiences as a woman from Africa. I am not sure how you can capture all these experiences in one single definition, but if we are

> going to have a Black Canadian feminist thought, then there is no choice but to be inclusive.

Marie recognized at an early age the exclusion of her Black Canadian experience from the educational curriculum. Peggy Bristow acknowledges that this exclusion is a common element in Black women's lives:

> We are of diverse social and political backgrounds and experiences ... [however] through our discussions we recognized that we share a common experience around racism within Canadian society. Specifically, the educational system has maintained and perpetuated the common perception that Black people were either non-existent in the development of Canada, or only arrived in Canada through recent migration from the Caribbean and Africa.[18]

If you do not see yourself reflected in society, then how do you root your identity? And if your experience is seen as Other and racialized, how do you establish a strong sense of self that is rooted in your ancestry? Lulua spoke about her own experience of difference within the community and how she struggles even today with identifying as an African woman:

> I remember when I was about eight years old I could not reconcile the fact that my ancestors were from Africa. How could I be identified with people of African heritage, people who occupied the bottom of the social hierarchy? I felt there had been a mistake. Maybe Jacy's mom did not mean to tell me that I was different from her daughter. I remember going home and standing in front of a mirror for hours. I consoled myself that I was not *thaaat* black and my hair was not *thaaat* kinky ... When I look back and reflect on my upbringing, my neighbourhood and my school experiences, I can see why Black women are so divided. For as long as I can remember, I did not want to associate with my cousins who were dark skinned or whose parents were poor. As long as I can remember, I lived a life of lies and denial. I

> denied myself, my heritage, my relatives. I am still searching for myself. It is not an easy process. These are the issues that keep us apart as Black women. We often allow our skin colour and our nationalities to come between us. I believe one day I will have the courage to call myself an African-Canadian woman. I am content to refer myself as Black-Canadian Canadian.

Riiria, a woman who grew up in Africa, also experienced this sense of difference and division within her Canadian community, which surprised her because these divisions did not exist in her African community:

> I grew up in a small village in Africa. Life looked good. I had parents, extended family members and friends who encouraged me to read and become successful. I identified myself with my mothers, grandmothers, aunts and women from my community — they were great women. I do not remember any of these women calling themselves feminists, but I believe they were some sort of feminists because of all that they did ... Living in Canada has been different. I find Black women are very divided here, unlike back home. I am not sure how we can overcome our many differences ... I do acknowledge that our histories are very different; however, I would like to highlight my colonial and neo-colonial experience. This experience made me long for the Western lifestyle and in a way it robbed me of who I was as a child. It made me aspire for something that I will never be and I would not want to be ... you know what I mean. The colonial education was used as a tool to imbue Africans with negative images of their culture — I believe a weapon to decimate the very core of our identity. Come to think of it, it was a way to perpetuate the inflated position of European culture as superior. Despite our varied historical backgrounds as Black women, I think our commonalities outweigh our differences.

Lulua's and Riiria's experiences resonate with many Black-Canadian women. Maa, a student in my course, would prefer the term African-Canadian feminism rather than Black-Canadian feminism:

> I cannot use the terminology Black because I am not Black. I am African, an African woman. Although Canadian by birth, my ancestors are African. I am proud of my origins. I do not care whether the word Black evokes the political organizing of marginalized people of colour. It has always come down to the colour of my skin and how normalized and acceptable it is. This is how the state and its institutions function. Do we have to bring this institutional mentality to our theory? Why are we not comfortable in calling our feminism African-Canadian feminist thought? We will distinguish ourselves from African women living in Africa or other parts of the world. I believe we do have an identity problem, and I feel that's what we should be tackling before we define our feminism. If on the other hand, we want to refer to our feminism by skin colour, why not use dark brown, or ebony. In any case, what is in a name?

The division between Black-Canadian women is a very challenging one. W.E.B. DuBois predicted that the problem of the colour line would be the problem of the twentieth century. Unless there are some revolutionary changes in the way we view our origins and our colour, DuBois's predictions will clearly guide Black-Canadian women through the twenty-first century. We need to see through these dividing lines in order to shape our identity and to build a visible Black feminist movement. The role of colonialism has fragmented our political activism and imposed racial divisions that separate us. It is therefore important to develop a critical consciousness that comes from feminist theory and feeds a feminist movement. As Joel explains:

> The seeds of colonialism are well entrenched in our psyche. They fragment our thinking and even our Black

> feminist discourse. Most of us concentrate on how to alienate ourselves from our own communities, our sisters and brothers because they do not measure up to certain standards. Who creates these standards? Sometimes we avoid our own for the sake of acceptability by the mainstream? Do you realize that all this is something to do with how fragmented we are, and if we do not rupture this fragmentation paradigm we perpetuate the status quo? I personally feel that there is a lot to be done to create a cohesive Black-Canadian feminist movement and theory, but I am not sure which should come first.

I believe what is crucial here is not whether the movement or theory comes first, but how we create a theoretical framework that does not fragment Black women's experiences and that overrides the divisions based on colour. The way we can do this is to develop multiple Black feminist practices that emphasize the importance of all our histories, our ways of decolonizing our minds and our ways of developing critical consciousness.[19]

Another common thread that weaves through the lives of Black-Canadian women is the legacy of emancipation and liberation. In our attempts to synthesize emancipation theories, various Black feminisms improvise integrative analyses of race, gender, sexuality and class that focus on commonalities in liberation struggles. The utility of Black feminisms in progressive movements is largely determined by our capacity to illustrate and analyze the intersections and multi-dimensionality of oppression and freedom. We have to forego a one-dimensional liberation theory that focuses on patriarchy or White supremacy or transnational capitalism or homophobia as isolated phenomena.[20] We need to contextualize the meanings of resistance and political organizing by understanding space and time in the ways that reflect the many intersecting realities of Black-Canadian women's lives.

These realities were first addressed in 1977 in *The Combahee River Collective Statement: Black Feminist Organizing in the*

Seventies and Eighties. The authors identified the importance of developing a Black feminist movement based on a political theory that recognized and analyzed the realities Black women were facing:

> We are a collective of Black feminists who have been meeting together since 1974. During that time we have been involved in the process of defining and clarifying our politics, while at the same time doing political work within our own group and in coalition with other progressive organizations and movements. The most general statement of our politics at the present time would be that we are actively committed to struggling against racial, sexual, heterosexual, and class oppression, and see as our particular task the development of integrated analysis and practice based upon the fact that the major systems of oppression are interlocking. The synthesis of these oppressions creates the conditions of our lives. As Black women we see Black feminism as the logical political movement to combat the manifold and simultaneous oppressions that all women of color face.
>
> ...
>
> Black feminists often talk about their feelings of craziness before becoming conscious of the concepts of sexual politics, patriarchal rule, and most importantly, feminism, the political analysis and practice that we women use to struggle against our oppression. The fact that racial politics and indeed racism are pervasive factors in our lives did not allow us, and still does not allow most Black women, to look more deeply into our own experiences and, from that sharing and growing consciousness, to build a politics that will change our lives and inevitably end our oppression.[21]

Black women are still engaged in political movements to combat the oppressions they face. It is therefore important to highlight the heterogeneous and multi-layered nature of Black women's experiences and to address how theorizing Black women's experience has been done in relation to their sociopolitical, economic and culturalized locations. As Black women do this, they must use the intersections of race, class, gender and sexuality as an interactive model to develop strategies of resistance that will help both women and men in society understand racism, patriarchy, sexism and other oppressive systems. In other words, meanings and paradigms situated in Black peoples' experiences can be applied to rupture and collapse the invisible and visible divides that have kept Black people in general — and Black women in particular — on the periphery.

Validating Black Feminist Theory

Black women and other marginalized groups of people have been accused of being incapable of producing the type of interpretive, objective analytical thought that is labelled theory in the West.[22] The course gave us an opportunity to dispel this myth and to prove that Black women have always been theorists. As Barbara Christian poignantly contends:

> People of color have always theorized — but in forms quite different from the Western form of abstract logic ... our theorizing (and I intentionally use the verb rather than the noun) is often in narrative forms, in the stories we create ... [in] dynamic rather than fixed ideas ... How else have we managed to survive with such spiritedness the assault on our bodies, social institutions, countries, our very humanity? And women, at least the women I grew up around, continuously speculated about the nature of life through pithy language that unmasked the power relations of their world ... My folk, in other words, have always been a race for theory — though more in the form of the hieroglyph, a written figure which is both sensual and abstract, both beautiful and communicative.[23]

Niseya's explanation that her ancestral knowledge is a direct link to her present-day theory and practices echoes Christian's argument that people of colour theorize in different ways:

> Where would I place my grandmother's teachings or drumbeats in all this? The person I am today is not from book knowledge but from stories narrated to me around the fire. The stories revealed the strength of African women and the contributions they made during the war for independence. My grandmother told us stories of healing knowledge of our ancestors. It is from my grandmothers that I learned that all of nature — earth, air, fire and water — is sacred and worthy of praise. By reflecting on these teachings, I have come to believe that our ancestors influence our life not only through personal traits but also as active beings in the spirit world.

Ancestral knowledge is not considered a valid way of knowing, nor are Black women's ways of knowing. Because they are not considered valid by the Western patriarchal structures of academia, Black feminism and its theory have been excluded. But this has not silenced Black women or stopped the production of their knowledge. One way in which Black women have attempted to redress their exclusion has been through literary theory, which has become a critical tool for exploring contextual questions about identity, patriarchy, race, gender, class, sexuality and imperialism. The conceptual focus and analytical methods derived from literary theorizing and praxis underscore the relevance of taking a critical look at Black women's history. Black women's critique of theory not only involves coming to terms with absences such as the historical but also involves examining the absence of Black faculty in the academe and the ways in which Black women have been rendered invisible, even when they have been seen.[24]

Fortunately, there has been a notable increase in representation of working-class people, gays and lesbians, visible minorities and women at all levels of the academy. This has helped to incorporate scholarships that have been traditionally excluded from academic inquiry and has enabled the slow but evident transformation in the academy through an examination and restructuring of the ways in which knowledge is organized and produced. A White, male, ruling class controls the production of knowledge and the processes of validation in our society; it also sets the terms and criteria for what will be recognized as valid social thought because it composes the community of experts which is necessary to approve such thought and which is constantly engaged in ignoring and suppressing the Other. These criteria have presented major obstacles to the advancement of knowledge for marginalized peoples.

In addition, Black feminists within the academy have advanced the most forceful, but most invalidated, critique of knowledge production. Black women critics and scholars have played a crucial role in bringing to the academy works of historically silenced intellectuals, opening up spaces for the study of Black women specifically and for the study of women of colour more generally.[25] It is therefore important to note that many marginalized groups that have been historically disempowered have been instrumental in bringing to light the ways in which theory has been applied in a hierarchical way and used to promote a type of academic elitism that embraces traditional structures of domination.[26]

It is also important to acknowledge the work done by Black feminists in academia, despite the fact that some of their work has generated a language and criticism that seems exclusionary and alienating to those who are not part of the academy. This theoretical feminism is valuable in spite of its exclusivity. Valuing the theoretical does not deny other discourses but enhances feminist theory and might be viewed as one legitimate element of a wider feminist endeavour.[27] Many scholars who have concentrated on Black women's experiences have drawn conclusions about these women, the majority of whom do not have a forum through which they can speak for themselves. Collins points out that oppressed groups are frequently placed in the situation of being listened to only if they frame their ideas in the language that is familiar to and comfortable for a dominant group. By placing Black women's ideas within the discourse of their own language, we challenge the mainstream discourses and at the same time centre the experiences of a group that has always been marginalized. We also ground the analysis in a multiplicity of voices, so as to highlight the diversity, richness and power of Black women's ideas and acknowledge the intellectual depth that resonates in our communities. As Collins asserts, "theory and intellectual creativity are not the province of a select few but instead emanate from a range of people."[28]

By the end of the semester, the students felt that it was essential for Black women to develop a theory that speaks to the plurality of their voices, their multiple standpoints and views, and the hybrid nature of their identities unique to them — while at the same time celebrating their differences. As Collins explains, there is a need for the crucially important and liberating potential of self-definition, which is key to recognizing, understanding and valuing both individual and group empowerment.[29] What did we learn from this course? Were we able to move beyond our starting point? Did we add something to the ongoing debate on Black-Canadian feminist thought through our dialogues?

Reflecting on what I have been teaching and how I have been teaching, I truly believe I have made a difference in the lives of Black women who have taken the course. It is also important to point out that these students have made a difference in my life as a Black female faculty member. Writing ourselves back into the discourse will require that we work together as Black women, and through learning about each other, we can articulate a theory that will truly speak to our varied and numerous lived experiences. We should be open to the possibility that all our experiences are unique and that they add an important dimension to Black-Canadian feminist theorizing. We should take advantage of our multiple experiences as women who have come from different historical, social and political backgrounds. Although these experiences may be painful, they create an invisible link among us. While it is important for us to learn to live and work in solidarity, the idea of common oppression should not be our only common ground because our lives are varied and complex in nature. We have to remember that solidarity strengthens our struggle for resistance in ending all forms of oppression. By having a feminism that recognizes these struggles, Black women will be empowered and will create a space where our past, present and future voices, triumphs and stories can be told, celebrated and passed down to the future generations.

Notes

1. Sylvia Hamilton, "Naming Names, Naming Ourselves: A Survey of Early Black Women in Nova Scotia," in Peggy Bristow et al., eds., *"We're Rooted Here and They Can't Pull Us Up": Essays in African Canadian Women's History* (Toronto: University of Toronto Press, 1994).
2. The term Black has been used politically to include all women of African ancestry. In this chapter, I use the term with specific reference to women of African descent; in short, this term refers to Black women of Africa and its Diaspora.
3. Juliana Makuchi Nfah-Abbenyi, "Introduction: Gender, Feminist Theory, and Post-Colonial (Women's) Writing in Gender," in *African Women's Writing: Identity, Sexuality and Difference* (Indianapolis: Indiana University Press, 1997), 7.
4. Obioma Nnaemeka, "Introduction: The Rainbow," in Obioma Nnaemeka, ed., *Sisterhood, Feminism and Power: From Africa to the Diaspora* (Trenton: Africa World Press, 1997); Nfah-Abbenyi, "Introduction: Gender, Feminist Theory, and Post-Colonial (Women's) Writing in Gender." See also, Filomina Chioma Steady, "African Feminism: A Worldwide Perspective," in Rosalyn Terborg-Penn, ed., *Women in Africa and the African Diaspora* (Boston: Harvard University Press, 1989).
5. Ata Aidoo Ama, "The African Woman Today," in Nnaemeka, ed., *Sisterhood, Feminism and Power.*

6. Molara Ogundipe-Leslie, "African Women, Culture and Another Development," in *Recreating Ourselves: African Women and Critical Transformations* (Trenton: Africa World Press, 1994).
7. See, for example, Deborah King, "Multiple Jeopardy: The Context of a Black Feminist Ideology," in A. Jaggar and P. Rothenberg, eds., *Feminist Frameworks,* 3rd ed. (New York: McGraw Hill, 1993); bell hooks, *Feminist Theory: From Margin to Centre* (Boston: South End Press, 1984); Audre Lorde, "An Open Letter to Mary Daly," in Cherrie Moraga and Gloria Anzaldúa, eds., *This Bridge Called My Back: Writings by Radical Women of Color* (New York: Kitchen Table Women of Color Press, 1983); Toni Morrison, *Beloved* (New York: Plume, 1988); Alice Walker, *In Search of our Mothers' Gardens: Womanist Prose* (Orlando: Harcourt Brace, 1983); Carole Boyce Davies, *Black Women, Writing and Identity: Migration of the Subject* (London: Routledge, 1994); Christian Smith, "Black Feminism and the Academy," in Les Back and John Solomos, eds., *Theories of Race and Racism: A Reader* (New York: Routledge, 2000); Barbara Christian, "Introduction: The Politics of Black Women's Studies," in Gloria T. Hull, Patricia Bell Scott and Barbara Smith, *All the Women Are White, All the Blacks Are Men, But Some of Us Are Brave* (New York: Feminist Press, 1982).
8. Hazel Carby, *Cultures of Babylon: Black Britain and African America* (London: Verso, 1999).
9. Nfah-Abbenyi, "Introduction: Gender, Feminist Theory, and Post-Colonial (Women's) Writing," 2.
10. Bristow et al., eds., *"We're Rooted Here and They Can't Pull Us Up,"* 3-4.
11. Patricia Hill Collins, "The Social Construction of Black Feminist Thought," in *Black Feminist Thought: Knowledge, Consciousness, and the Politics of Empowerment,* 2nd ed. (New York: Routledge, 2000).
12. Dorothy Smith, *The World as Problematic: A Feminist Sociology* (Toronto: University of Toronto Press, 1987).
13. See Makeda Silvera, *Silenced* (Toronto: Sister Vision, Black Women and Women of Colour Press, 1995); Dionne Brand, *No Burden to Carry: Narratives of Black Working Women in Ontario, 1920s to 1950s* (Toronto: Women's Press, 1991); Linda Carty and Dionne Brand, "Visible Minority Women: A Creation of the Canadian State," in Himani Bannerji, ed., *Returning the Gaze: Essays on Racism, Feminism and Politics* (Toronto: Sister Vision, Black Women and Women of Colour Press, 1993); Linda Carty, "Black Women in Academia: A Statement from the Periphery," in Himani Bannerji et al., eds., *Unsettling Relations: The University as a Site of Feminist Struggle* (Toronto: Women's Press, 1991); Wanda Bernard and Candace Bernard, "Passing the Torch: A Mother and Daughter Reflect on Experiences Across Generations," *Canadian Woman Studies/ les cahiers de la femme* 18, nos. 2/3 (Summer/Fall 1998); Annette Henry, "Missing: Black Self-Representation in Canadian Educational Research," in Suzanne de Castell and Mary Bryson, eds., *Radical Interventions: Identity, Politics and Difference in Educational Praxis* (New York: SUNY, 1997); Nourbese Philip, *A Genealogy of Resistance and Other Essays* (Toronto: The Mercury Press, 1997);

April Few, "The (Un)Making of Martyrs: Black Mothers, Daughters, and Intimate Violence," *Journal of the Association for Research on Mothering* 1 (Spring/Summer 1999).

14. This definition was developed by students in my Black feminist course between January and April 2000.
15. Valerie Amos and Pratibha Parmar, "Challenging Imperial Feminism," *Feminist Review* 17 (1997), 3–19.
16. All the excerpts quoted in this essay are taken from interviews I conducted with Black women who were either students in my Black feminist course or participants in the Black women discussion group between January 2000 and April 2001. All names are pseudonyms.
17. Collins, "The Social Construction of Black Feminist Thought."
18. Bristow et al., eds., *"We're Rooted Here and They Can't Pull Us Up,"* 3-4.
19. bell hooks, "Revolutionary Black Women: Making Ourselves Subject," in *Black Looks, Race, and Representation* (Toronto: Between the Lines, 1992), 60.
20. Collins, "The Social Construction of Black Feminist Thought."
21. The Combahee River Collective, "A Black Feminist Statement," in Gloria T. Hull, Patricia Bell- Scott and Barbara Smith, eds., *All the Women Are White, All the Blacks Are Men, But Some of Us Are Brave* (New York: The Feminist Press, 1982), 9, 11. The Combahee River Collective Satement was written in 1977 by Demita Frazier, Beverly Smith and Barbara Smith; it was copied and distributed by hand until the early 1980s when it was published in three anthologies by feminists of colour: *All the Women Are White, All the Blacks Are Men, But Some of Us Are Brave; This Bridge Called My Back: Writings by Radical Women of Color; and Home Girls: A Black Feminist Anthology.* In 1985, the Statement was published as a separate pamphlet by Kitchen Table: Women of Color Press as *The Combahee River Collective Statement: Black Feminist Organizing in the Seventies and Eighties* with a Foreword by Barbara Smith.
22. Annette Henry, "Missing: Black Self-Representation in Canadian Educational Research."
23. Barbara Christian, "The Truth That Never Hurts: Black Lesbians in Fiction in the 1980s," in Chandra Mohanty, Ann Russo and Lourdes Torres, eds., *Third World Women and the Politics of Feminism* (Indianapolis: Indiana University Press, 1990), 336.
24. Carby, *Cultures of Babylon.*
25. Carty, "Black Women in Academia," 20.
26. Anne duCille, "The Occult of True Black Womanhood: Critical Demeanor and Black Feminist Studies," *Signs: Journal of Women in Culture and Society* 19, no. 3 (1994).
27. Henry, "Missing: Black Self-Representation in Canadian Educational Research."
28. S. Kemp and J. Squires, "Introduction," in Sandra Kemp and Judith Squires, eds., *Feminisms* (Oxford: Oxford University Press, 1997), 5.
29. Collins, *Black Feminist Thought,* 34.

Chapter Two

The More Things Change ... Rethinking Mainstream Feminism

Katerina Deliovsky

NEVER HAVE I HAD so much difficulty in writing an essay. I have reasoned that maybe it is because I feel so strongly about and for feminism that I want to get it right. Maybe I am trying to find my voice and my difficulty is simply my growing pains. Or, maybe it is because many of my experiences in dealing with feminist theory and feminists themselves have not been without turmoil and, consequently, some scars have been left. In writing this chapter about the limitations of White feminism and suggesting some ways forward, I found myself remembering some of those painful moments. My relationship to feminism and academic feminists in general has never been a comfortable one. When I was introduced to feminist theory in 1992 as a second year undergraduate, I felt a strange unease with the theories that were presented. Given that feminist theory is premised on a political philosophy of consciousness-raising and liberation, I hoped it would provide me with some clarity and understanding about my life, as well as the lives of my mother and grandmother. Their lives are stories of incredible hardship — war and poverty, and gender and ethnic oppression in Canada and Europe. Carrying their wounds as well as my own, I had anticipated gaining insight about their particular suffering. I hoped to feel comforted by the empowering voices of other women and hence gain greater insight into my own experiences. Sadly, neither the comfort nor insight came.

I read the so-called classics by White feminists such as Simone de Beauvoir, Betty Friedan and Mary Wollstonecraft, and I asked myself, "What has this got to do with my life, my mother's and my grandmother's?" Initially, I thought something was wrong with me for feeling alienated by and critical of this literature. As hard as I tried, I could not correlate my experiences with any of the readings. They certainly did not speak to my experiences as a Macedonian immigrant girl-child growing up in Canada and experiencing hostility from other school children. They did not capture the feelings of total unimportance and invisibility I experienced as a girl growing up in a patriarchal, immigrant, working-class home. And certainly "classical" White feminist literature did not capture my experiences as a Macedonian woman in an interracial relationship with an African-Jamaican man. I was left with the impression that the "woman" they were theorizing was neither me nor women like me.

Just as I was ready to give up on feminism, I came across bell hooks's *Feminist Theory: From Margin to Center.* Within the first few pages of her book, my relationship to feminism changed. In one passage she wrote:

> Much feminist theory emerges from privileged women who live at the center, whose perspectives on reality rarely include knowledge and awareness of the lives of women and men who live in the margin. As a consequence, feminist theory lacks wholeness, lacks the broad analysis that could encompass a variety of human experiences. Although feminist theorists are aware of the need to develop ideas and analysis that encompass a larger number of experiences, that serve to

> unify rather than to polarize, such theory is complex and slow in formation. At its most visionary, it will emerge from individuals who have knowledge of both margin and center.[1]

Her words were inspiring and liberating and have greatly influenced my philosophy towards feminism. hooks helped to fill in some of the missing pieces that White feminism could not or was incapable of providing. As I finished her book, I came to the realization that my feelings were quite normal given that feminist theory has been largely about and for White Anglo-Saxon straight middle-class women. Eagerly, I searched for more books that helped to explain my sense of alienation. I was overjoyed by my "discovery" and wanted to share my new awareness with my fellow feminist classmates, who themselves may have felt alienated. But I was soon to realize that most White female university students and professors in these feminist courses did not share the same feelings. Himani Bannerji describes a relationship to White feminist theory:

> But very soon I began to develop a discomfort and sometimes even a feeling of antagonism towards this type of feminist writing, for reasons initially unclear to me. Of course, this was accompanied by feelings of guilt and worries that perhaps my politics were not feminist after all. Needless to say, I did not encounter feminists in the university who experienced any basic and fundamental sense of insufficiency with this feminism, which passes as *the* feminism.[2]

I, like Bannerji, did not encounter women who spoke of or experienced a sense of alienation from what was presented as feminist theory. But the incisive analysis of first hooks, and subsequently of other racialized feminists like Bannerji, helped to rescue feminist theory for me. I learned that the first-wave feminist movement, as it was/is taught in North American universities, was really a White conservative movement and its theory reflected its ethnocentrism. Despite efforts by radical and Marxist feminists to rescue feminist theory from its liberal conservative roots, the second-wave feminist movement also remained steeped in a universalistic White discourse.[3] I learned that this "woman" that White feminists were theorizing was not me, or my mother or my grandmother. She was an abstraction, "a synthetic category called woman," oppressed by a universal seamless patriarchy.[4] But this abstraction was a White Anglo-Saxon middle-class woman or sometimes a White Anglo-Saxon working-class woman, depending on whether you were reading a radical or Marxist/socialist text.

I felt angered by what I perceived to be deception on the part of White feminists yet empowered by the knowledge disseminated by racialized feminists.[5] Their words showed me that feminism does not have to be about "unhappy housewives" or about hating all men or about separatist politics. I learned from the standpoint theories of Black feminists that theory can help to firmly locate oneself in the world and not necessarily distort or mystify it.[6]

And I vowed that every chance I got, I would "set the record straight," which meant honouring the knowledge of Black feminists and other racialized feminists. It meant *not* presenting feminist theory as theories, methods and epistemologies in the name of "woman" or "women."

Unfortunately, I found much hostility towards and dismissal of works by Black feminists. Often, White students would proclaim, "All Black feminists talk about is race." Another common statement was "Oh, they are so angry!" which seemed to say that Black feminists were not justified or allowed to be angry for the exclusionary practices of White feminism. At the time I felt quite puzzled by the responses of these White women. Black feminist critiques of White feminism were erudite and timely. I did not detect anger in their works and, even if I had, I believed Black feminists were justified in their anger. As I continued reading radical books by Black feminists who challenged White feminist hegemony, I began to believe that the White women I encountered in my classes and whose works I read had an investment in maintaining the status quo in feminist theory. It was really the White students and professors who appeared angry. Their dismissal of Black feminist critiques as "too" angry or "too" narrow indicated a need to prevent further scrutiny of White women's beneficial participation in White feminist hegemony. The responses of White faculty and students disciplined individuals who were seen as rocking the boat. But the boat kept rocking.

The universalism that White feminists posited continued to be challenged by incisive critiques articulated by Black feminists, in particular, and racialized feminists more generally. By the last year of my undergraduate degree in 1996, I noticed that many of the White female students and professors were adopting what appeared to be a more radical political vocabulary, drawing on the sharpness of the Black feminists' ongoing criticisms. The buzzwords in the sociology of women classes became "race," "class" and "gender." It became "politically incorrect" to speak of gender only when addressing women's oppression. I recall feeling a sense of relief and joy as I sat in another feminist theory course and the professor lectured on issues of race, class and gender in women's lives. While the class was predominantly filled with White female students and taught by a White female professor, I thought that maybe, just maybe, feminism had taken that turn towards transforming itself. Maybe the prolific voices of women like bell hooks, Angela Davis, Himani Bannerji, Michelle Wallace and Patricia Hill Collins had been heard and incorporated into revolutionizing White middle-class feminism so that it would truly reflect the lives of all women. Unfortunately, I soon realized this was not the case.

One incident stands out in my mind. The same professor who was lecturing on issues of race, class and gender in women's lives also held tutorials that I attended. During one of these tutorials, she began discussing how women were universally oppressed "as women." Given her race, class and gender friendly lectures, I was somewhat confused and expressed my concerns around the notions of universal oppression of women. I argued that I did not think women were necessarily oppressed at all points in history and that it varied according to culture, geographic location and history, which are mediated through race, class, gender and sexuality. Before I had a chance to finish my assertion, she turned a beet red, glared at me and then continued speaking as though I were not even in the room. Although I was taken aback by her response, I continued to make my opinions known in subsequent tutorials. I made two more attempts. Each time I spoke, it was to challenge her statements or her assertions about universal notions of women's oppression, and each time her response dismissed my words, either through silence or verbal humiliation. At no point in time did any of the female students in this predominantly White tutorial step in to defend or agree with my opinions. They remained silent. I eventually stopped going.

The point of relaying this story is not necessarily to criticize this specific feminist professor's response to my challenges, but rather to illustrate what I believe is a trend in feminist academia, a trend echoed by Evelyn Brooks Higginbotham in "African-American Women's History and the Metalanguage of Race." She argues:

> The general trend has been to mention black and Third World feminists who first called attention to the glaring fallacies in essentialist analysis and to claims of a homogeneous "womanhood," "woman's culture," and "patriarchal oppression of women." Beyond this recognition, however, white feminist scholars pay hardly more than lip service to race as they continue to analyze their own experiences in ever more sophisticated forms.[7]

While Higginbotham made this statement in 1992 and the events I relayed occurred between 1992 and 1996, I would argue the state of affairs in White feminism has not changed. While there is a small coterie of White feminists who have taken race as seriously as gender and class, the recognition of race has not extended beyond superficiality in praxis and discourse in White feminism. And I write this with sadness because the hope I carried for feminism in 1992 is one that I carry in 2002. My hope is that feminism can and indeed will provide the theories to understand and consequently fight the various degrees of oppression of *all* women, not just a few specific, already privileged White women. The feeling of empowerment and clarity that comes from reading liberatory philosophy is one I hope all women can experience. The idea of developing theories that could potentially liberate women's minds is a noble enterprise but when it is infused with a spirit that embraces the challenge of transformation. The need to revolutionize and transform feminism is great.

bell hooks states that "we resist hegemonic dominance of feminist thought by insisting that it is a theory in the making, that we must necessarily criticize, question, re-examine, and explore new possibilities."[8] This is where I find myself today, wanting to meet the challenge of transformation and explore new possibilities. And this is probably why I find writing this paper so painful. My desire to contribute to a revolutionary and radical feminism is great, but so too are my feelings of insecurity, ambivalence and skepticism. Insecurity because who am I to make a difference? Ambivalence because although I am aware that my ethnicity, gender, intimate relationship with a Black man and having two mixed-race children stigmatize me, I am keenly aware that my whiteness privileges me.

Many times I have questioned how I am implicated in this White feminist hegemony, which serves neither my needs nor those of racialized women. Do I participate in the oppression of others? If so, in what way? Will my scholarly work be potentially liberatory or contribute to White feminist hegemony? I do not have all the answers nor have I resolved the tensions that have arisen from these questions. At best, I live with these doubts and insecurities and try not to let them overwhelm my efforts. But I do know that for my work to be potentially liberatory, I must be mindful of how my own discursive practices as a White feminist sociologist may potentially perpetuate and reproduce pre-existing unequal social relations. Keeping true to my principles means having a vigilant awareness of the potential for self-aggrandizement, exploitation and misrepresentation in feminist methods, research and theory. A vigilant awareness also means allowing open dialogue and ongoing criticism. Part of this open dialogue and ongoing criticism is understanding that White feminism must be radically transformed if it is to be true to feminists' claim of liberating all women.

But in order to do so, we must understand what oppresses and privileges us. That understanding includes how White feminism has colluded and participated in that oppression. And this is where my skepticism lies — I fear that most White feminists are unable and unwilling to collectively engage in *committed* self-reflection of how they participate in and reinscribe the oppression of others. To engage in a *committed* self-reflection would inevitably mean giving up White feminist hegemony. Mariana Valverde states that "white feminists as a whole are probably still not interested in giving up [their] newly acquired and still fragile institutional power (power to control women's organizations, to define feminism, to represent women vis-à-vis the state and so on)."[9] Let's face it, it is difficult to admit that one participates and benefits from a racial hierarchy. For some White feminists, by virtue of being *feminists* and positing a liberatory philosophy, it may seem inconceivable to them that they not only benefit but also participate in a racial hierarchy. And as noted, there have been individual White feminists who have engaged in committed self-reflection and their works reflect this commitment. But White feminists must do more than engage in individual self-reflection.

Kimberly Christensen, a White American feminist, admonishes White feminists for not successfully dealing with race and racism. She identifies an "inadequate individualistic definition of racism" as the primary reason for White feminist limitations on race because it misallocates attention onto individual racist attitudes. She argues that challenging and eliminating racism in society and the feminist movement must entail a concerted effort to address the wealth and power differential caused by race in North America.[10] Crucial to her argument and that of other anti-racist feminists is that to effectively deal with race and racism is to recognize that gender and race do not stand alone but are part of other "relations of ruling,"[11] or relations of oppressions. In spite of the fact that women's experiences are best comprehended through a non-monistic approach, race continues to be problematic in feminist epistemology.

As a consequence of White feminists' difficulty in examining race, racialized women have, paradoxically, had to forcefully call to attention the salience of race in women's lives. Often, as I indicated earlier, they have been wrongly accused of "focusing too much on race." In spite of this false accusation, race, because of its impact on the lives of racialized and White women, has brought to the fore contradictions and complications within feminism, which White women alone have not been able to observe. Part of this inability to grasp the complexity of race, as well as gender and class, lies in the flawed conceptualization of some of the concepts fundamental to White feminist theory. To effectively provide an epistemology that embraces a potential liberatory praxis there needs to be, at the very least, a serious reconceptualization of two fundamental concepts integral to White feminist analysis: gender and patriarchy.

My contention is that the very concepts of patriarchy and gender rest on universalizing and narrow parameters of what constitutes women's oppression. Given the exclusionary and narrow foundations of these concepts, the inclusion of a race, class, ethnicity and sexuality analysis are, at best, superficial inclusions. Without a reconceptualization and transformation of these concepts, the already exclusionary nature of White feminism will become increasingly intensified and ultimately distort or render invisible the lives of the women it is claiming to include. To demonstrate the need for the reconceptualization of gender and patriarchy, I critically examine the works of several White feminists. Though I will be critical of some aspects of their work, the use of specific passages and quotes from their work are not intended to be hostile or exhaustive critiques. In spite of what I consider the limitations of some aspects of their work, it is important to recognize that they laboured to write under conditions that discourage women to value their words and ideas. In the context of a patriarchal environment, which devalues women's intellectual (and physical) labour, it is important not to discourage women to create and own their words and ideas. However, at the same time, as intellectuals committed to emancipatory discourse, we must always have a vigilant awareness of how our work can reinscribe the dominant discourse. In light of this, my aim is to illustrate the serious shortcomings of using concepts in an exclusionary, reductionist, monistic[12] and ahistorical manner.

It is significant to note that in my critique of "White feminism," I refer to the popular tradition of intellectual discourse, which is premised on the key concepts of patriarchy and gender as put forward primarily by White feminists. Although there are schools of feminism such as French feminism and North American feminism and many kinds of feminism within these schools (liberal, radical, Marxist, socialist), these different kinds of feminism, though divergent at key points, share in common a consistent emphasis on women as an essential category encountering an essential male domination. Problematically, in fact, these concepts are derived from unique features of Western intellectualism and social development. Consequently, I am critical of the way White feminism has followed in the footsteps of Western European intellectualism. Some might respond by saying, "Not another criticism against White feminism. Haven't there been enough already?" My response is that there are many insightful critiques illustrating the universalism and essentialism in White feminism, however, these are not enough. It only becomes enough when White feminist theory has truly been reformulated and revolutionized to be an authentic emancipatory theory and praxis that includes all of us.

Gender: Women Oppressed "as Women"

It was Simone de Beauvoir who wrote, "One is not born, but rather becomes, a woman," stressing that being born a "woman" is not a "completed" reality but rather a "becoming."[13] This insight provided the starting point for distinguishing between sex and gender and for recognizing that biology is not destiny; it also validated the belief that there was indeed a universal commonality in being a "woman."[14] Thus, while de Beauvoir arrested the eternalistic and transcendental socialization perspective, which essentialized the category of women, her insight paradoxically transferred essentialism from one domain to another. No longer was "woman" biologically determined, but rather she became a creation of the social forces that brought the universal woman into being. De Beauvoir's perspective suggests that as social beings women share a common location of oppression vis-à-vis a universal patriarchy. This commonality of suffering, based on being "woman" or "women," is the premise on which feminist knowledge is produced. However, there are many more experiences, structural and personal, that inform gender identity than just being a "woman."

Over the past three decades, the concept of gender has been introduced as a central category of analysis in White feminist scholarship. Although this introduction of gender has enabled feminist scholars to theorize gender beyond the limits of sexual difference,[15] White feminism's almost exclusive focus on gender assumes that women can be solely analyzed "as women" and that women are oppressed "as women." Inherent in these assumptions is the belief that gender can be isolated from other elements of identity or sites of oppression; hence, sexism can be isolated from racism, classism and so on.[16] While Marxist and socialist feminists have been exceptions, their theorization of gender and class has been at the expense of race, ethnicity and sexuality. Due to the relentless struggle of Black women in particular, White feminists have acknowledged that dominant Western feminist thought has taken the experiences of White middle-class heterosexual women to be representative of, indeed normative for, the experiences of all women.[17] Given these incisive critiques which inveigh against the universalism of White feminism, the last twenty years have seen the development of a recognition of race as a "variable" in women's lives. However, much of the work coming out of the second-wave feminist movement exhibits a tendency for only a superficial acknowledgement of race.

For example, Julia O'Connor, in "From Women in the Welfare State to Gendering Welfare State Regimes," acknowledges that while race is central to the development and structuring of several welfare states, most notably the United States, she argues it would be more fruitful to omit race.[18] Her main argument is that when examining structural inequality, gender and class must not be analyzed in isolation. O'Connor argues it would be more advantageous to focus on the interaction of both variables. While she recognizes that class, gender and, in some countries, race is an important dimension that structures, and is structured by, welfare states, she does not engage in a race analysis of welfare states. Her use of gender and class as the primary concepts of analysis renders integral sites of racialized structural inequality unintelligible. The result is to either distort or obscure the lives, history and culture of women oppressed not only by gender and class but also by race and sexuality. At the same time, ignoring race limits our understanding of how race functions in White women's lives as well.

O'Connor makes significant points in her work, particularly that a gender-sensitive comparative analysis of welfare states will not be achieved by simply adding gender to the framework of analysis or by exclusively focusing on gender. Rather, the focus must acknowledge the gendered nature of the "universal citizen" and the interaction of class and gender in structuring inequality. In addition, she illustrates how gender, caregiving and economic dependence are inextricably linked and mutually reinforcing. These points are important in light of the androcentric approach to welfare state analysis. But she makes a troubling insistence that the incorporation of a race analysis is formidable and complex. In a manner surprisingly close to that raised for generations by male scholars, she says that "the more dimensions of difference one includes in the analysis the more complex the analysis becomes and the more difficult meaningful comparisons become."[19] A comparative focus, O'Connor believes, enhances the researcher's ability to identify not only common patterns cross-nationally but also key structuring mechanisms of welfare states. The omission of a race analysis, she argues, is necessary for the comparative analysis to be "meaningful."

To argue on one hand that race is central to the development and structuring of welfare states, yet on the other to argue that the incorporation of a race analysis is "formidable and complex" is contradictory and troubling because it obscures and distorts the lived experiences and histories of Aboriginal, African and other racialized women in the United States and Canada. This racial omission negates the existence of women who are *not* White. O'Connor's statements imply that isolating "dimensions of difference" would provide a truer picture of reality. But, according to her perspective, the more "dimensions of difference" are added the more distortion occurs. To understand structural inequality we must analyze the lives of women who are *not* suffering inequality based on race.

Separating race from gender and class also suggests that women's racial identity *can* be subtracted from their combined gendered and classed identity and assumes that White women are not raced. If we take O'Connor's argument to its logical conclusion, we would conclude that we must first analyze the lives of women whose race does not complicate the analysis — White women. In "The Occult of True Black Womanhood: Critical Demeanor and Black Feminist Studies," Ann duCille points out that unless the subject of analysis happens to be "the Other," "race is placed under erasure as something outside of immediate consideration, at once extratextual and extraterrestrial." She importantly emphasizes that despite the strident debates and information provided by feminists of colour, the "as a woman" in White feminist discourse still continues to mean "as a White woman."[20]

O'Connor's work illustrates that a sporadic reference or a superficial acknowledgement of race does not by itself erase the White middle-class privilege inherent in feminism. The assertion that race would distort a meaningful comparison of structural inequality can only be said by women who are not oppressed by race and is precisely an indication of their race privilege. And, ultimately, it is their race privilege that becomes obscured. Elizabeth Spelman asks very important questions about this kind of methodological argument. She questions whether it is possible or necessary to separate race from gender and whose interest it serves? In addition, she asks whether methodological justifications of a gender-only analysis serve specific race interests? These are important questions to ask because, as racialized feminists note, we live in a society structured by race, and since the racial identity and privilege of those subject to racism are not obscured, then separating race from a gender and class analysis really masks the racial identity of White women. Ultimately, this separation masks the bestowing of "rights" of privilege and power that come from being White. Spelman states:

> White middle-class privilege can be preserved even as one engages in "empirical investigation" into what women do and do not have in common. Depending on how they are made, comparisons among women may operate to obscure the privilege some women have over others.[21]

An example of how comparisons can obscure privilege is found in Daiva Stasiulis's "Theorising Connections: Gender, Race, Ethnicity, and Class." She argues that a reformulated political economy approach would best capture the larger yet specific and concrete historical processes that degrade, subordinate and exploit women. She insists that she does not wish to "subordinate all struggles against race/gender/class to a large class struggle,"[22] but rather wishes to underscore the inevitable intrusions of capitalist relations within the construction of intersecting forms of oppression. These intrusions of capitalist relations are something she believes Black feminist theory is not capable of extrapolating because it is hindered by a White and Black dichotomy, which links skin colour to racism rather than to structural locations of particular groups of women. According to Stasiulis this approach hinders the "capacity of Black feminism to comprehend the experiences and incorporations of different 'racial' and ethnic groups of women in Canada's economy, class structure and political and symbolic orders." To bring her point home she concludes that "one effect of structural racism in Canada is that in a multi-racial, multi-ethnic female work force, particular groups of European immigrant women have historically shared disadvantages similar to those Black working-class women and continue to do so."[23]

Stasiulis's work reflects a serious attempt to integrate race, ethnicity, class and gender in a Canadian political economy approach and, even though she warns against a superficial inclusion of race, class and gender, her assertions are problematic on several counts. To state that particular European immigrant women have historically shared similar disadvantages to Black working-class women misses the important point Black feminists have been espousing about skin colour and racism. Simply put, European women are not "cursed" by the blackness of skin. Although Black working-class women may find themselves in structurally similar positions as European immigrant women, the reality of living in "Black" skin can only be felt by women of African descent, which makes their experiences qualitatively different. Not making this distinction creates a false parallelism between women, which suggests, for example, that all women share similar disadvantages in the workplace. As Deborah King states, "[I]t is precisely those differences between Black women and White women that are crucial to understanding the nature of Black womanhood."[24]

By subsuming the experience of racialization into a political economy approach, Stasiulis renders the specificity of being Black women invisible. Once again what is created is the impression that there is a commonality of suffering "as women" but vis-à-vis class rather than patriarchy. The lack of understanding of the complex material, historical and ideological intersections of race, ethnicity, class and gender illustrate that White feminist theory needs further work to more fully develop these multiple intersections.

Patriarchy: Beyond a Universal Definition

Patriarchy is another concept integral to White feminist analysis. Although there have been debates in White feminism about the extent and the means by which patriarchy becomes an oppressive system for women, there appears to be a consensus that patriarchy privileges men over women.[25] In "The Unhappy Marriage of Marxism and Feminism: Towards a More Progressive Union," Heidi Hartmann contends:

> Only a specifically feminist analysis reveals the systemic character of relations between men and women ... We can usefully define patriarchy as a set of social relations between men, which have a material base and which, though hierarchical, establish or create interdependence and solidarity among men that enables them to dominate women. Though patriarchy is hierarchical and men of different classes, races, or ethnic groups have different places in the patriarchy they also are united in their shared relationship of dominance over their women ... In the hierarchy of patriarchy, all men, whatever their rank in the patriarchy, are bought off by being able to control at least some women ... Men are dependent on one another (despite their hierarchical ordering) to maintain their control over women.[26]

Hartmann's definition is useful here because, in her synthesis of Marxist and radical feminist theory, she attempts to provide a comprehensive definition of patriarchy. Even though Hartmann defines patriarchy within a Marxist feminist context and because of this it would be expected to differ from non-Marxist definitions, it does not. This definition, more or less, typifies how patriarchy is currently utilized in White feminism. According to Hartmann's definition, feminism is meant to reveal the systemic nature of women's oppression, which is thought to rest on a patriarchal system of social relations. These social relations, which are read as an unequal and unmediated form of power relations between men, assumes a global phallocentric, patriarchal domination of all women. Although an existence of a hierarchy among males is acknowledged, this hierarchy is imagined as internally uncontested because of the potential reward of female domination. In a sense, hierarchies of race/ethnicity, class and sexuality among men are inconsequential and unrecognized given the rewards of patriarchy.

A current example of this usage is found in Judith Lorber's *Gender Inequality: Feminist Theories and Politics.* In her introduction, Lorber provides the reader with an explanation of gender inequality. She states,

> Women are vulnerable to beatings, rape and murder — often by their husbands and boyfriends, and especially when they try to leave an abusive relationship. The bodies of girls and women are used in sex work — pornography and prostitution. They are on display in movies, television, and advertising in Western cultures. In some African and Middle Eastern cultures their genitals are mutilated and their bodies are covered from head to toe in the name of chastity. They may be forced to bear children they do not want or to have abortions or be sterilized against their will. In some countries with overpopulation, infant girls are much more often abandoned in orphanages than infant boys, in other countries, if the sex of the fetus can be determined, it is girls who are aborted.[27]

While Lorber does not explicitly use the term patriarchy in her explanation of gender inequality, she implicitly draws on the radical feminist definition of patriarchy, like the one cited by

Hartmann. Gender inequality essentially rests on universal, patriarchal relations of domination from Africa to the Middle East to North America.

This usage of patriarchy, whether implicit or explicit, raises some serious questions in a patriarchal White supremacist society. For example, does this patriarchal relationship among men "create interdependence and solidarity" when a Black man is involved with a White woman? In another example, within a gay union what "shared relationship of dominance" do gay men "enjoy" over women? Do women of different races, classes or ethnicities share in relationships of domination with "greater" men over "lesser" men (and women)? What women are blamed for overpopulation and have been forced to endure Western sponsored sterilization programs without consent? Though I attempt to address some of these questions within the limitations of this essay, I cannot provide a detailed response; however, these questions illustrate the serious contradictions and limitations that arise from the White mainstream definition of patriarchy as presented by Hartmann.

Limitations and Contradictions

There are serious limitations to using this definition of patriarchy as an analytical tool. One such limitation arises when analyzing the violence White women experience from White male relatives and strangers when these women are in intimate relationships with Black men. In a research study I conducted with six White women in interracial relationships with Black men, I found that some of the women experienced physical and psychological violence from their fathers and from White male strangers.[28] (I discuss the social implications of this further in my chapter "Transgressive Whiteness" in this volume.) My objective here is not to deny the potential or existence of abuse by Black men against their White female partners, but to point out that White men are particularly aggressive when White women are "possessed" by racialized men.

When trying to understand this phenomenon, I found the White feminist conception of patriarchy as a system of universal domination in which men strive to control women inadequate. For example, when one of my research participant's father learned of his daughter's relationship with a Black man, he exploded in a violent rage and chased the daughter out of the house wielding an axe. This violent response did not erupt when she was dating Sicilian and French men. To what extent does this White working-class father's response fit with Hartmann's definition of patriarchy, given the supposition that men depend on one another to maintain control of women? If patriarchy is a system where men "are united in their shared relationship of dominance," then why is the White father attacking his daughter for loving a Black man? Why not simply pass over control of the daughter to the Black male partner? The key point here is that the man in question is a Black man. For White men, "interdependence and solidarity among men" do not extend to their "Black brothers."

Richard Dyer, in his book entitled *White*, states that there are specific anxieties surrounding the whiteness of White women. He explains that White women, as "the literal bearers of children ... are the indispensable means by which the group — the race — is in every sense reproduced ... White Women thus carry — or, in many narratives, betray — the hopes, achievements and character of the race. They guarantee its reproduction."[29] Therefore, in the context of a raced and gendered society, a White woman's sexual involvement with a Black man signals that her womb is no longer available for the reproduction of whiteness. Ida B. Wells, a political activist, understood (over eighty yeas ago) that White womanhood is an ideology that supports and maintains White supremacy.[30] Thus, when a White woman acts in her own self-interest and dates a Black man, it is seen as an unforgivable transgression against White society generally and White men specifically. Jessie Daniels in *White Lies* identifies this point in her analysis of White supremacist discourse. She writes:

> The penultimate affront to White men's control over White women's sexuality and reproductive lives is a White woman who chooses to not only have sex with, but also bear children with, a Black man.[31]

In this context, the fathers' violence towards his daughter is a response to feeling betrayed, because his daughter has aborted the means by which she can guarantee the reproduction of whiteness and his group's particular ethnicity. Therefore, the father's violence is more than a disciplinary tactic; it is a magnified response to his daughter's intimate involvement with a man who is seen as congenitally defective and possessing undesirable traits of heightened sexuality and criminogenic tendencies.[32]

Himani Bannerji in "But Who Speaks For Us?" argues, "Decontexting 'patriarchy' or gender from history and social organization — which is structured by both cooperation and antagonistic social relations — obscures the real ways in which power works."[33] In this context, seeing patriarchy as uniform and seamless is quite problematic, given that it obscures the fact that through slavery, colonialism and imperialism White men have had monopolistic access to other men's women without the reverse being true. This power has allowed White men to enforce great sanctions against Black men and other racialized men (Aboriginal, Asian) who have tried to engage in intimate relations with White women.[34]

A universal patriarchy, or a "decontexting patriarchy," also obscures the historical reality of White men who terrorized Black men with lynching practices and threats in the U.S. and Canada[35] in order to prevent relationships with White women. In addition, a very important and overlooked point is that many White women "enjoyed" a "shared relationship of dominance" when they participated in these lynching practices against Black men and in other forms of White nationalistic expression.[36] These are important historical facts that must be understood in the context of patriarchy. To omit or obscure these facts creates a monistic conceptualization of what constitutes women's and men's oppression. As Hazel Carby writes: "[H]istorically specific forms of racism force us to modify or alter the application of the term 'patriarchy' to Black men."[37]

Another important contradiction and limitation that comes up when using the typical framing of patriarchy can be found in feminist research on wife assault. For instance, the research by Robin Neugebauer states that the law and the legal process reflect the interest of men and that the state legitimates the interest of men through coercive and authoritative measures.[38] Although Neugebauer probably did not intend to do so, she illustrates the contradictions of patriarchal unity in North America. For example, she found that the police responses to calls of wife assault were less than adequate and at times exacerbated the situation. Immigrant women had an especially difficult time because the police response was at times accompanied by racist and ethnocentric attitudes. During situations when White police officers were dispatched to the homes of racialized women, the police officers frequently used offensive racial slurs. In addition, women of African and Aboriginal descent faced the particular fear that their partners might be beaten to death. As one woman put it, "We would like police officers to arrest our husbands, not necessarily kill them."[39]

Access to institutional patriarchal power, then, is often determined by the "race" of the victimizer. In light of this, conceptualizing patriarchy as a universal expression of masculine co-operation is incorrect. Neugebauer's argument that the "state coercively and authoritatively sustains the existing social order in the interest of men"[40] must be problematized; a more nuanced definition of patriarchy could expand feminist theory beyond an "us vs. them" approach.

The examples given here illustrate the limitations and contradictions that arise from using the typical concept of patriarchy developed and used primarily by White feminists. There is a need for the mutual recognition of race and history, among other factors, in order to articulate the complexity of social relationships among all men and women. The omission of a race and history analysis creates three specific problems within White feminist theory. First, it creates blinders to alternative and valid explanations of violence against women. What results is a concept very narrow in its application. Second, it cannot mobilize and empower women based on narrow concepts that could potentially result in an increase in the victimization of women. Third, it obscures historical and current relationships among men and women rendering the conceptualization of patriarchy reductionist and monistic.

Where Do We Go From Here?

Thus far, I have argued that there are serious shortcomings to the continued use of gender and patriarchy as tools for feminist epistemology. To continue to do so, could result in the development of "white solipsism." As early as 1979, Adrienne Rich warned against this tendency:

> To think, imagine, and speak as if whiteness described the world ... a tunnel vision which simply does not see non-white experience or existence as precious or significant, unless in spasmodic, impotent guilt-reflexes, which have little or no long-term, continuing momentum or political usefulness.[41]

However, I also believe the continued use of gender and patriarchy in an ahistorical, monistic and reductionist fashion demonstrates a reluctance to give up the power and privilege of White feminist hegemony. Marilyn Frye, in "On Being White: Toward A Feminist Understanding of Race and Race Supremacy," suggests that White women have solely analyzed their connection to men in terms of gender, sexism and male dominance because they have been secure in their White supremacy. White women have not been motivated to recognize and question their whiteness. If White feminists speak of racism and classism as something that *happens* to women who are African or poor rather than something that White women *do*, then they can avoid implicating themselves. Therefore, White middle-class women often rally around gender oppression based on systems of patriarchy to avoid recognizing their participation in the politics of domination.[42]

bell hooks argues that the conscious mystification of social divisions between women in feminism was no accident. It has been informed by a bourgeois ideology which advocates a competitive, atomistic, liberal individualism that permeates feminist thought and undermines the potential radicalism of a feminist struggle. The rallying cry of a common oppression, or sisterhood, is "less a strategy for politicization than an appropriation by conservative and liberal women of a radical political *vocabulary* that masked the extent to which they shaped the movement so that it addressed and promoted their class interest."[43] White feminists have something to gain by structuring gender oppression solely in terms of male domination. In constructing all men as the enemy and women as victims, White middle-class feminists get "a piece of the pie" without radically altering or transforming a society based on hierarchies of sex, class, ethnicity and race.

This is where I believe we find ourselves today. We have a feminism that has adopted a language of inclusion but in reality is exclusionary. We have a feminism that has developed concepts that emphasize the lives of primarily White women. Where do we go from here? Short of starting all over again there needs to be a serious reconceptualization of these two main feminist concepts: gender and patriarchy. Gender does not have to be a euphemism for White (middle-class) women. Patriarchy does not have to mean by definition that all men are equally "the enemy." bell hooks advocates that feminists develop theoretical and pedagogical tools that examine interlocking systems of domination.[44] Himani Bannerji advocates that feminism develop a sociohistorical and cultural framework that critically deconstructs cultural, common-sense and everyday practices in order to forge liberatory connections between how we think and how we live.[45] Both offer promising and complementary approaches to feminist theory. Regardless of which path is taken, we can no longer use concepts that reinscribe the dominant discourse because they ultimately imposes a form of "spirit-murder" on those women they render invisible.[46]

A serious reconceptualization also means more than just changing words. White feminists must not only acknowledge that a radical transformation is needed in the first place, they must also recognize how they wilfully or unintentionally participate in the creation of a White feminist hegemony. However, this recognition does not mean that White feminists get to "analyze their own experiences in ever more sophisticated forms."[47] A liberatory feminism cannot be an abstract endeavour. It must be connected to everyday practices of all women. Barbara Smith explains:

> Feminism is the political theory and practice that struggle to free all women: women of color, working-class women, poor women, disabled women, lesbians, old women — as well as White, economically privileged, heterosexual women. Anything less than this vision of total freedom is not feminism, but merely female self-aggrandizement.[48]

In a passionate discussion with a "comrade in the struggle," it was suggested to me that a new language for the equitable articulation of women's lives needs to be infused into White feminist discourse. We need a new language that gives all women a vocabulary to articulate, interpret, reflect and theorize their lives, realities and histories. Maria Lugones and Elizabeth Spelman, in "Have We Got A Theory for You! Feminist Theory, Cultural Imperialism and the Demand for 'The Woman's Voice,'" speak to this issue when they address the language of exclusion in White/Anglo feminism:

> We and you do not talk the same language. When we talk to you we use your language: the language of your experience and your theories. We try to use it to communicate our world of experience. But since your language and your

> theories are inadequate in expressing our experiences, we only succeed in communicating our experience of exclusion.[49]

This quote suggests that the answer to "Where do we go from here?" is "Back to the drawing board."

But how do we develop a new language that embraces the struggles of all women? Part of the development of this new language lies in a reconceptualization of concepts integral to feminism. For example, Kate Davy, in "Outing Whiteness," suggests that in order to understand the complex historical constructions of White and Black women, it would be helpful to understand the concept of saturation. Davy quotes Robyn Wiegman from *The Lesbian Postmodern* to illustrate her point: "[C]ategories don't simply overlap but so thoroughly saturate one another that gender ... rarely refers to the same constellation. Differences in racial position must therefore be understood to produce quite different (feminine) genders."[50] The idea that there are different genders when gender is saturated with race is very useful because it allows for the conceptualization of women's multiple oppressions (and privilege). Thus, to follow Davy's and Wiegman's lead we need to *saturate* the concepts of gender and patriarchy with race, class, gender and sexuality. Kate Davy provides a wonderful example of how to use saturation. She states that when an unmarked category such as White is saturated with bourgeois middle-classness, it produces

> an ideal of whiteness or an epitome of whiteness, the dynamics of which bestow privilege on all white people and justify white supremacy. Played out in the politics of respectability, whiteness becomes the dynamic that underpins a process of racialization that feeds privilege to all white, so to speak, without letting all white people sit at the table.[51]

Saturating race (whiteness) with class (bourgeois middle-classness) allows for an analysis that makes visible complex relations of power that produce social stratification. What this means, then, is that concepts integral to feminist theory cannot be used in isolation of the "relations of ruling" that inform women's (and men's) experiences and positions in the world. We must attend to how race, class, gender and sexuality saturate one another to produce specific forms of oppression and privilege. While I argue for a more specific and nuanced analysis of women's oppression and privilege I am not advancing a postmodern politic. Rather, it is crucial that these specific forms are clearly linked to the larger organizing principles that structure systems of domination.

Having said this, the development of a new language does not necessarily mean that an inclusive liberatory feminism will follow. Despite Black feminists calling attention to the complex and varied dimensions of women's oppression, White feminists have continued to conceptualize and practise feminism in ways that reinscribe whiteness. In light of this, I believe defining an equitable articulation cannot come from White feminists, although they will play a role. White feminists must remember that they have had the power to inject their ideas into academic and political discourse and to construct feminist theory largely as a consequence of a hierarchy of race which positions them on top and unfairly distributes advantages and disadvantages to those in the hierarchy.[52] Kate Davy recognizes this fact and asks,

> When we as white women let an investment in institutional credibility take precedence over the action agenda needed to change the power structures and process that produce elitist and exclusionary conditions, aren't we as white women making an(other) investment in whiteness, renewing, as it were, our allegiance to the race? Instead of viewing the institutionalization of women's programs as a recent phenomenon born of white women's newly found position of legitimacy in the academy, we might understand it as the function of a current-day politics of respectability grounded in our very real historical investment in whiteness.[53]

If White feminists have had an investment in whiteness then it must be racialized women who define what an equitable articulation would look like. *Back to the Drawing Board* attempts to speak to this articulation. I also believe a part of this radical feminist transformation entails rendering visible that which has been obscured in White feminist theory — White women's privilege and collusion in oppressive and dominant discourses, as Ruth Frankenberg writes:

> Attention to the construction of White "experience" is important, both to transforming the meaning of Whiteness and to transforming the relations of race in general. This is crucial in a social context in which the racial order is normalized and rationalized rather than upheld by coercion alone. Analyzing the connections between White daily lives and discursive orders may help make visible the processes by which the stability of Whiteness — as location of privilege, as culturally normative space, and as standpoint — is secured and reproduced. In this context, reconceptualizing histories and refiguring racialized landscapes are political acts in themselves.[54]

Thus, drawing attention to the racial construction of White women's bodies is a critical step towards understanding how the racial order is normalized and rationalized and how this is connected to White feminist hegemony. In addition, revealing the racial identity of White women will expand the assumption in White feminist scholarship that race is only associated with "women of colour."

It is important that White feminist scholarship acknowledge that the historical construction of white womanhood has been a process of racialization that has benefited white women and white feminist scholarship. Most importantly, only in making whiteness visible can it be decentred. As long as the whiteness of White women goes undefined and undemarcated then their position of privilege and power goes obscured. An undefined and undemarcated whiteness is one of the primary ways that privilege and power is secured in feminism. And if that privilege and power come at the expense of others, then feminist theory cannot claim to be a liberatory praxis, because that liberation comes at the expense of many.

Notes

1. bell hooks, *Feminist Theory: From Margin to Center* (Boston: South End Press, 1984), ix.
2. Himani Bannerji, *Thinking Through: Essays on Feminism, Marxism, and Anti-Racism* (Toronto: Women's Press, 1995), 42.
3. Allison Jaggar, *Feminist Politics and Human Nature* (Totawa: Rowman and Allanheld, 1983), 5. Jaggar explains that political activists of the New Left in the second wave of the women's liberation movement tried to shift the focus from "rights and equality" to "oppression and liberation." It was an attempt to radicalize feminist politics.
4. Bannerji, *Thinking Through*, 68.
5. See Tamari Kitossa, "Criticism, Reconstruction and African-Centred Feminist Historiography," chapter 3 in this volume. Kitossa argues that the term racialized better captures the assignment of racial differentiation. In light of the explosion of "critical White studies," it is clear that White people have a colour as well. As a result of the visibility of whiteness, Kitossa argues that a new terminology is needed to better capture the social construction of race and the process of racialization, which is experienced by groups who are neither politically nor phenotypically White.
6. Patricia Hill Collins, "The Social Construction of Black Feminist Thought," in N. Tuana and R. Tong, eds., *Feminism and Philosophy: Essential Readings in Theory, Reinterpretation, and Application* (Boulder: Westview Press, 1995), 526–47.
7. Evelyn Brooks Higginbotham, "African American Women's History and the Metalanguage of Race," *Signs: Journal of Women in Culture and Society* 17, no. 2 (1996), 252.
8. hooks, *Feminist Theory*, 11.
9. Mariana Valverde, "Racism and Anti-Racism in Feminist Teaching and Research," in C. Backhouse and D. Flaherty, eds., *Challenging Times: The Women's Movement in Canada and the United States* (Montreal: McGill-Queen's University Press, 1994), 160.

10. Kimberly Christensen, "'With Whom Do You Believe Your Lot is Cast?' White Feminists and Racism," *Signs: Journal of Women in Culture and Society* 22, no. 3 (1997), 618.

11. Dorothy Smith, *The Everyday World as Problematic: A Feminist Sociology* (Toronto: University of Toronto Press, 1987).

12. Deborah King, "Multiple Jeopardy, Multiple Consciousness: The Context of a Black Feminist Ideology," *Signs: Journal of Women in Culture and Society* 19, no. 3 (1994), 51. King describes monism as the attempt to reduce or explain social relations to one principle or factor such as the economy, state or gender.

13. Simone de Beauvoir, *The Second Sex* (New York: Vintage Books, 1983), 267.

14. Elizabeth Spelman, *Inessential Woman: Problems of Exclusion in Feminist Thought* (Boston: Beacon Press, 1988), 66.

15. Juliana Makuchi Nfah-Abbenyi, *Gender in African Women's Writing: Identity, Sexuality, and Difference* (Bloomington: Indiana University Press, 1997), 16.

16. Spelman, *Inessential Woman*, 165.

17. Patricia Hill Collins, *Black Feminist Thought: Knowledge, Consciousness and the Politics of Empowerment* (New York: Routledge, 2000).

18. Julia O'Connor, "From Women in the Welfare State to Gendering Welfare State Regimes," *Current Sociology* 44, no. 2 (Summer 1996), 10.

19. Ibid., 10.

20. Ann duCille, "The Occult of True Black Womanhood: Critical Demeanor and Black Feminist Studies," *Signs: Journal of Women in Culture and Society* 19, no. 3 (1994), 607.

21. Spelman, *Inessential Woman*, 164.

22. Daiva Stasiulis, "Theorising Connections: Gender, Race, Ethnicity, and Class," in Peter Li, ed., *Race and Ethnic Relations in Canada* (Toronto: Oxford University Press, 1999), 290, 294.

23. Ibid., 290.

24. King, "Multiple Jeopardy, Multiple Consciousness," 46.

25. Although there have been debates in White feminism around patriarchy, they have mainly been around the relationship between capitalist class structure and patriarchy. The fundamental premise of patriarchy, that men dominate all women, has largely been untouched in White feminism.

26. Heidi Hartmann, "The Unhappy Marriage of Marxism and Feminism: Towards a More Progressive Union," in Lydia Sargent, ed., *Women and Revolution* (Boston: South End Press, 1981), 15.

27. Judith Lorber, *Gender Inequality: Feminist Theories and Politics* (Los Angeles: Roxbury Publishing Company, 2001), 78.

28. Katerina Deliovsky, "Jungle Fever: The Social Construction of Six White Women in Interracial Relationship with Black Men" (MA thesis, McMaster

University, 1999).

29. Richard Dyer, *White* (London: Routledge, 1997), 29.

30. Ida B. Wells, *Selected Works of Ida B. Wells-Barnett,* Compiled and with an Introduction by Trudier Harris (New York: Oxford University Press, 1991).

31. Jessie Daniels, *White Lies: Race, Class, Gender and Sexuality in White Supremacist Discourse* (New York: Routledge, 1997), 81.

32. Paul Hoch, *White Hero Black Beast: Racism, Sexism and the Mask of Masculinity* (London: Pluto Press, 1979).

33. Bannerji, *Thinking Through,* 69.

34. See, for example, Hoch, *White Hero Black Beast;* Martha Hodes, *White Women, Black Men: Illicit Sex in the Nineteenth-Century South* (New Haven: Yale University Press, 1997); Sarah Carter, *Capturing Women: The Manipulation of Cultural Imagery in Canada's Prairie West* (Montreal: McGill-Queen's University Press, 1997).

35. There is a popular misconception that negative responses towards White women's unions with Black men are specific to the American South, however Canada has its own historical experience with the construction of interracial unions as threatening to the social order. See Colin Thomson, *Blacks in Deep Snow: Black Pioneers in Canada* (Don Mills: J.M. Dent and Sons Ltd., 1997), for further discussion.

36. David Baker, "Race, Racism and the Death Penalty in the United States An Historical, Theoretical and Empirical Analysis" (PhD diss., U.M.I., 1987), 103. Baker discusses how lynchings were experienced as a communal affair. White men, women and children would participate in lynching practices that were characterized by public fanfare and circus-like jubilee.

37. Hazel Carby, "White Women Listen!" in Les Back and John Solomos, eds., *Theories of Race and Racism: A Reader* (London: Routledge, 2000).

38. Robin Neugebauer, "Misogyny, Law and The Police: Policing Violence Against Women," in K. McCormick and L. Visano, eds., *Understanding Policing* (Toronto: Canadian Scholars Press, 1992), 2.

39. Ibid., 5.

40. Ibid., 2

41. Adrienne Rich, "Disloyal to Civilization: Feminism, Racism, Gynephobia," in *On Lies, Secrets, and Silence* (New York: Norton, 1979), 299.

42. Marilyn Frye, *The Politics of Reality: Essays in Feminist Theory* (Freedom, CA: The Crossing Press, 1983).

43. hooks, *Feminist Theory,* 6. Emphasis added.

44. Ibid.

45. Bannerji, *Thinking Through.*

46. Patricia J. Williams, "Spirit-Murdering the Messenger: The Discourse of Fingerpointing as the Law's Response to Racism," in A. K. Wing, ed., *Critical Race Feminism: A Reader* (New York: New York University Press, 1997). Reprinted in this volume as chapter 9.
47. Higginbotham, "African American Women's History and the Metalanguage of Race," 252.
48. Barbara Smith, "Toward A Black Feminist Criticism," in *The Truth That Never Hurts: Writings on Race, Gender and Freedom* (New Brunswick, NJ: Rutgers University Press, 1999), 50.
49. Maria C. Lugones and Elizabeth Spelman, "Have We Got a Theory for You! Feminist Theory, Cultural Imperialism and the Demand for 'The Woman's Voice,'" in Tuana and Tong, eds., *Feminism and Philosophy*, 498.
50. Cited in Kate Davy, "Outing Whiteness: A Feminist/Lesbian Project," *Theater Journal* 47, no. 2 (1995), 189–205; Laura Doan, ed., *The Lesbian Postmodern* (New York: Columbia University Press, 1994), 18.
51. Davy, "Outing Whiteness," 202.
52. Marlee Kline, "Women's Oppression and Racism: Critique of the 'Feminist Standpoint,'" in Jesse Vorst et al., eds., *Race, Class, Gender: Bonds and Barriers* (Toronto: Garamond Press; Winnipeg: Society for Socialist Studies, 1991), 52.
53. Davy, "Outing Whiteness," 203.
54. Ruth Frankenberg, *White Women, Race Matters: The Social Construction of Whiteness* (Minneapolis: University of Minnesota Press, 1993), 242.

Chapter Three

Criticism, Reconstruction and African-Centred Feminist Historiography

Tamari Kitossa

Feminist historiography — women writing women into history — is a political struggle that takes place at the levels of methodology and in the experiences of insurgency against patriarchal social and intellectual domination. Feminist historiography and feminism are two halves of a whole, both can be isolated, but to speak of feminist historiography is to speak of women's politics that has engendered it. For existentially, to see oneself positively referenced in the world is to see oneself as a subject of history. And, recognizing that the denial of women's history is a consequence of patriarchal exclusion, women recognize that the reconstruction of history shapes reality. This reconstruction, ultimately, is radically political; for feminist historiography is but one enabling arm of political consciousness through which women can analyze and act on social conditions as agents with sound political judgement.

Inasmuch as feminist historiography is a successful insurgent struggle to write women into the drama of human experience, this struggle runs counter to traditional (male) historiography. And, *a lut continua.*[1] The context in which feminist historiography is generated reflects the very political conditions which feminist historiography explicitly criticizes. In the economic crisis of academe and the begrudging recognition in which studies of women are held in the White male-centred academy, the history of women stands precariously outside the domains of valued intellectual exercise.[2] By putting women's historiography in its legitimate space in the academy, insurgent feminist scholars continue to develop creative methods and practices for recovering women from male-imposed obscurity.

Feminist historiography emphasizes women as both author and subject in the narrative of history — the story however does not end there. As I note above, that telling of women's stories is suffused with politics, because, individually and collectively, women must articulate discourses that legitimate their social and historical experiences. However, the struggle of feminist historiography is not political merely because women are the subject matter. It is rather the case that *all* historiography is political, because who is represented and how and who is doing the representing inevitably reflect and fold into the social tensions about being, representation and materiality. Himani Bannerji reminds us that historiography "is not a transparent affair ... [T]he writing of history entails issues of representation, which in their own turn entail issues of epistemology and ideology."[3] Epistemology and ideology, inasmuch as they are sites of feminist insurgency against patriarchal historiography, are themselves gravitational sites of struggle about which there is struggle over issues of representation among women.

To epistemology and ideology, then, we must add materiality and culture because both the latter give shape and are shaped by the former. And, it is on materiality and culture that attention must be focused in order to understand the form and content of feminism and feminist historiography. Who then are the women authorized to represent the history of "women"? What are their guiding epistemologies and ideological belief systems? And, to what worldview are they committed? Which women are their subject matter? And how are these women represented? Do these feminist historiographers derive their epistemologies, ideologies and materiality from a culture that is oppressive to other women and people? In taking these questions seriously, we see that "women" are not represented but that certain types of women are represented and by certain types of historiographers. Feminist historiography faces the criticism that it is White middle-class and heterosexual women, authorized by their whiteness, who have constructed the tradition of feminist historiography with White middle-class women as the universal archetype of "woman." This has caused considerable debate about racial representation and the sociopolitical implications of a feminist historiography that universalizes the experiences of White women and negates the role of race in feminism, history and social relations. In short, the criticism runs that the tradition of feminist historiography reflects the tradition and condition of White domination in society.

In 1993, Lorraine Code credited feminists of African descent for being especially "articulate in pointing out how consistently feminist discourse, articulated out of white middle-class experience, has arrogated to itself the right to speak for all women, black or white, rich or poor, heterosexual or lesbian."[4] To be sure, this criticism has produced some soul searching and has encouraged some White women to commit themselves to cross-racial sisterhood in an anti-racist feminist struggle. A small but significant body of work has emerged from White British and American feminists who examine racism, whiteness and imperialism in the political philosophy and praxis of early White feminists. To these are added the anti-racist feminist works of White women who have taken up the challenge of anti-racism in feminism seriously.[5] Without dismissing these notable works, Evelyn Brooks Higginbotham voices a concern echoed by many racialized[6] feminists:

> Notwithstanding a few notable exceptions, this new wave of feminist theorists finds little to say about race. The general trend has been to mention black and Third World feminists who first called attention to the glaring fallacies in essentialist analysis and to claims of a homogeneous "womanhood," "woman's culture," and "patriarchal oppression of women." Beyond this recognition, however, white feminist scholars pay hardly more than lip service to race as they continue to analyze their own experience in ever more sophisticated forms.[7]

If few feminists of European descent in Britain and America question the role of race in feminism and feminist historiography, even fewer in Canada do so. Arun Mukherjee has argued that although the impact of the challenges raised by racialized feminists are now being felt among White feminists, where race is concerned, she suggests that it is lip service at best.[8] It seems the failure of White-Canadian feminism and feminist historiography is the failure to be aware of the crisis of legitimacy that results from mis/representation. Associated with this is the failure to comprehend the dynamics which leads racialized feminists to pursue approaches to feminism that validate their unique experiences as raced, classed, sexed and gendered bodies.[9]

As in the U.S. and Britain, racialized feminists in Canada are pushing the margins in criticizing the limitations and contradictions of White feminism and feminist historiography. Racialized feminists do not criticize White feminist historiography because of its subject matter; they contend, rather, that in the wider social environment of White domination, White feminist historiographers, in general, have not eschewed the privilege of whiteness or the universality of White femininity. Racialized feminists have argued that White middle-class Canadian feminism has built for itself a gilded cage, based on the assumption of a stable feminine category rooted in the bodies of White women, from which it has difficulty escaping. There is some corrective work that is being done through the examination of White working-class women's lives. In the main, however, White feminist historiography continues its archaeology of Anglo-Celtic-Christian-Canadian middle-class women in ever expanding nuance and detail. The criticisms advanced by racialized feminists have challenged the White-dominated feminist movement to address issues of racism and to question the monistic assumption that gender is the single site of oppression for women.[10]

Notably, some feminists and feminist historiographers in Canada have undertaken the serious integration of race as a tool of analysis in the history and praxis of feminism in Canada.[11] The work of Mariana Valverde appears unique because it systematically interrogates racism and nationalism as both connected with and foundational to White feminism's nineteenth-century origins. Valverde reveals that the politics of historical representation intimately links today's White Canadian feminists with the taken-for-granted racial epistemologies of their predecessors: "The racism of white feminism is neither externally caused nor accidental: it is integral to what the mainstream Anglo-Saxon tradition has called 'feminism.'"[12] I believe this point closely expresses the concerns raised by African-Canadian feminists who argue that because of racism, feminism and feminist history in Canada have not meaningfully represented the interests of African-Canadian women.[13] As a consequence, African-Canadian women have developed methodologies derived from their experiences as raced bodies, which allow them to engage the history of their existence. Could it be otherwise? It seems that because whiteness authorizes particular understandings of the social and historical universe that validates White women at the expense of others, unless and until this fact is addressed by the White feminist establishment, feminism and feminist historiography will be ghosts of their promise.

There are efforts to fulfill this promise. In fact this essay emerges from my taking feminist history courses at OISE/UT, some of which attempted to productively calibrate the tension that results from feminism's weakness in integrating race. In fact, as an African-Canadian man seeking to challenge my own patriarchal endowments, I took these courses to learn more about women in history, and African women in particular. As with other feminist courses I had taken, I found myself raising familiar criticisms around race and representation. The effort to address the role of race in history and historiography was attempted with some faculty and courses, and totally ignored in others. In one particular course, which I dropped, I found myself frustrated with readings, students and faculty because my discussions of race were silenced with silence. And, even where discussions about race were encouraged, it seemed they were unconsciously contained within parameters of comfort that did not shake the ideological and epistemological foundations of feminism and feminist inquiry.

An open and honest discussion about race, a polluted idea, is polluted further by conditions of social and cultural inequality that generate different perspectives on a shared reality. I use "polluted" here to signal that the heavy tensions inherent in discussions about race rarely, if ever, use this tension productively to arrive at a point beyond which White people shut down and racialized people are screaming to be heard. Be that as it may, the difficulties of "race-talk" must not prevent open discussion. For inasmuch as African and White Canadian feminists share a common social reality, that they encounter this reality from culturally opposite poles means that their struggles are as different as they are similar. The differences of history and social position between African and European women are crucial to understanding why African-centred feminism emerged and why it is growing. Because it is grounded in more than gender, African-centred feminism presents a critical interpretive frame through which to reconstruct the presence of African women in history as much as it offers a conceptual framework through which to criticize White hegemonic feminism.

This essay takes a slice of both polarities to offer an explanation for White feminist historiography's exclusivism and gender centrality. In the first instance, I offer the basic methodological outline of what constitutes African-centred feminist historiography. Then I sketch the application of this methodology to the role of African-Canadian women in suffrage, temperance and community-building. Second, I address the problems in White feminist historiography as I see them in terms of methodology and sociology. In relation to this, I apply an African-centred criticism of White feminist historiography through how it represents the Women's Christian Temperance Union in the context of race to demonstrate how a non-inclusive White feminist historiography reinforces its own existence.

African-Centred Feminist Historiography

At the precise moment where race, class and gender intersect, Sojourner Truth's oft-quoted impromptu "ain't I a woman?" takes on political significance for the development of an African-centred feminist historiography. The example of Sojourner Truth illustrates how class, gender and race operate as multiple sites of oppression from which women of African descent must engage the politics of liberation in North America. The tradition of African-women liberators, such as Harriet Tubman, Sojourner Truth, Nani the Maroon, Mary Ann Shadd Cary and other African women of the continent and Diaspora who often struggled in obscurity, demands a methodology that constructs historiography from multiple sites of agency and resistance to oppression. An African-centred feminist approach begins with recognizing the historical and social forces that call the agency of African women into being. And, like Sojourner Truth who dared to name her experience, an African-centred feminist historiography dares to engage the political process of naming and reclaiming African women's humanity and woman-ness even though African women are considered not human enough to be the subjects of history.[14]

The development of an African-centred feminist approach to historiography begins with two distinct orientations. The first begins with women as historical actors prior to the transatlantic enslavement. The objective of this focus is to take African women outside the White feminist ideological belief in women's transhistorical and transcultural oppression. Naturally, the effort to recover the stories of African women prior to transatlantic slavery challenges the essential idea of "woman." This historicizing examines African women in their various cultures as agents embedded in societies — either matrilineal, matrifocal and even patriarchal — that created spaces for women in which to exercise independence and even influence over their societies.[15] The other orientation centres on the state of being that emerged from the transatlantic slave trade — that monumental break in traditional African social and cultural continuity. The Western European enslavement of African peoples, the courage of African women to resist and forge survival techniques under the adversity of slavery's sexual racism,[16] and again to spearhead human rights struggles from the 1960s onward, must profoundly shape any construction of African women's history in the Diaspora.

The unique experience of African women during enslavement to Western Europeans demonstrates from the outset that African and European women shared so entirely different worlds that it is racist ahistoricism to argue the opposite. Yet, in spite of obvious differences, the ideology and epistemology of mainstream feminism that centres exclusively on gender, seeks to continually reaffirm gender while excluding racialized women. For example, in her essay "Pioneers and Suffragists," Jane Errington contends, following the work of Veronica Strong-Boag and Anita Fellman, that "[i]n some ways women's lives resemble each other's as much or more than they resemble those of the men they are closely associated with."[17] The implication of this assumption occludes basic differences in how women are constituted in a "saturated field of racial visibility."[18] In many respects, such problems can be resolved if the White female is not presumed as the universal female subject. For where African-Canadian women are concerned, the assumption of an essential woman denies the historical experiences of slavery, exploitation, struggle and community-building in Canada.[19]

From the inception of their experiences on the African Diaspora, the struggle of African women went beyond the boundaries of gender to which White feminism has largely confined itself. Any serious study of what constitutes African-centred feminist historiography must concern itself with a "feminist, pro-woman perspective that acknowledges the reality of sexual oppression in the lives of Black women, as well as the oppression of race … class"[20] and sexuality. And like Sojourner Truth, a part of that perspective is daring to name both self and oppression alike:

> Merely to use the term "Black women's studies" is an act charged with political significance. At the very least the combining of these words to name a discipline means taking the stance that Black women exist — and exist positively — a stance that is in direct opposition to most of what passes for culture and thought on the North American continent. To use the term and to act on it in a white-male world is an act of political courage ... Like any politically disenfranchised group, Black women could not exist consciously until we began to name ourselves.[21]

Naming their experiences is crucial for African women because their historical agency is negated by White male chauvinism and often appropriated by White middle-class feminists insofar as African women's experiences are used to bolster the primacy of gender. In the limited spaces which patriarchy permits women's agency, White middle-class heterosexual feminists have agitated effectively to define the struggle for emancipation in terms consistent with their desires and lived experiences as non-racialized women. This means that gender, rather than a combined analysis of gender, class, sexuality, race and even regional integration into capitalist structures, becomes the principal defining element of the feminist movement for White women.

The reasons for White mainstream feminists' focus on gender are not hard to see: being White and contending for power-sharing with White men, some White women by and large deny race and articulate their struggle through gender (and class to a lesser degree).[22] Problematically, inasmuch as White women contend for power-sharing with White men, the obverse also prevails: "[T]he maintenance of racial privilege by one group implicitly establishes a bond between males and females of the privileged group."[23] By virtue of enjoying the power and privilege of White skin, not least of which is the power to deny non-White people access to be heard, White mainstream feminism and historiography reproduce the ideological and epistemological conditions which make gender a monistic category.

In the configuration of nineteenth-century feminism, race and class were obscured to promote the claims and desires for access that middle-class White American feminists were advancing. The primary feminists of the day — from Susan B. Anthony, Elizabeth Cady Stanton, Frances Willard to Charlotte Perkins Gilman — were perfectly clear that the feminist struggle must be consistent with the advancement of European middle-class civilization.[24] To demonstrate the longevity of this ethnic chauvinism, bell hooks asserts the implications of nineteenth-century White American middle-class feminist racism and classism still remains with us today, in large measure because race as a "relation of ruling"[25] still remains outside "White-stream" feminist analysis:

> Racism abounds in the writings of white feminists, reinforcing white supremacy and negating the possibility that women will bond politically across ethnic and racial boundaries. Past feminist refusal to draw attention to and attack racial hierarchies suppressed the link between race and class. Yet class structure in American society has been shaped by the racial politic of white supremacy; it is only by analyzing racism and its function in capitalist society

> that a thorough understanding of class relationships can emerge.[26]

Given that African women during slavery articulated their struggle for their human rights in myriad acts of insubordination, insurrection and suicide, and afterwards in acts of political agitation, the struggles of African women, while related to that of White women, should in no way be seen as synonymous. In their collection on African-Canadian women, Peggy Bristow and her colleagues argue that the inclusion of African-Canadian women in mainstream history is a recent phenomenon. Further, they note, "just as women could not wait for male historians to rewrite mainstream history to include women, we [African-Canadian women] could not expect white women to include us in women's history."[27] But, there is another source of exclusion, as Afua Cooper reminds us: "[H]istorians have been content to permit the men of the race to represent the women in almost every category."[28]

The image emerging from Canadian African-centred historiography is that African-Canadian women were vibrant and active agents for social change in the mid-nineteenth century. The influx of African-Americans fleeing enslavement and persecution during this period was a political stimulus to existing populations of Black Empire Loyalists in Ontario. For while a sizable portion of African-Canadian women were, by the 1850s, refugees from American slavery, an educated vocal minority were political advocates for racial integration and equal rights for women.[29] As early as 1854, African-Canadian women had formed at least two "literary societies" dedicated to women's enlightenment and political activism. The importance of such "societies" for feminist history becomes clearer when we understand that they existed twenty-two years before Dr. Emily Stowe's politically and historically significant literary society was formed in Toronto. Peggy Bristow informs us:

> A literary Ladies Society, formed in Chatham by Amelia Freeman Shadd, was similar to one organized in Windsor

> and presided over by Mary Bibb, with members meeting to "hear speeches and improve their minds." But despite their titles, these organizations did more than pursue cultural activities. The Windsor Ladies Club, form[ed] in 1854 by Mary Bibb, probably heard more than speeches .... Mary Bibb started a school for Black children in her house, and no doubt members of the Ladies Club organized around the education of Black children. The Ladies Literary Society organized by Amelia Freeman Shadd was involved in a variety of activities ranging from giving financial aid to *The Provincial Freeman* to helping needy women and men ... In its 6 October 1855 issue, *The Provincial Freeman* appealed to its female readers for support. It declared: "Let our sisters throughout the country go to work on behalf of the defender of their rights ... *The Provincial Freeman.*"[30]

In fact, *The Provincial Freeman*, an activist newspaper dedicated to racial equality, abolitionism and women's rights, was the labour of Mary Ann Shadd Cary, the first woman in North America to publish and edit a newspaper.

There is evidence that even before the establishment of the Women's Christian Temperance Union (WCTU) formed in 1874, escaped and free African women in Canada were active in establishing a climate of temperance in their communities. Prior to the 1850 Fugitive Slave Bill in the United States that forced the African-American exodus to parts of what is now Ontario, temperance had a long tradition among African-Americans in northern free states. Indeed, after 1835, abolition and temperance were twinned in the struggle for African-American freedom. One African-American abolitionist leader, Henry Highland Garnet, called on the sacred memory of their African forbears as proof against using alcohol: "Men and women, descendants of Africa: our ancestors were distinguished for their wisdom in the arts and sciences. If you would imitate their good example ... you must be strangers to the intoxicating cup."[31] It is therefore not accidental that this tradition found early expression in the new settlements of African-Canadians in southern Ontario. And, although early African-Canadian immigrants worked exclusively among themselves in temperance efforts, it is not that they wanted to do so in a segregated climate, but the racial hostility of Anglo-Canadians made this segregated approach to temperance organizing inevitable. Interestingly, churches, schools and temperance halls were heavily dependent upon the contributions of African-Canadian women who helped to build, staff and sustain these institutions.

So strong was the sentiment towards temperance that Mary Ann Shadd Cary often devoted lengthy columns of *The Provincial Freeman* to the cause of temperance education. On April 15, 1854, in a column titled "Intemperance — What it Costs and What it Causes," Shadd wrote passionately, no doubt fearing White stigmatization of her community, about the association between intemperance and public lawlessness: "The facts are striking and conclusive against the liquor traffic, as productive of a very large proportion of the offenses that are tried before the police and criminal courts."[32] Despite the largesse of American, British and Canadian Christian and philanthropic organizations, Shadd and other leaders were rightly concerned that the harshness of resettlement conditions in a context of enforced racial segregation tended towards despair and substance abuse among some of the refugees. Their concern was that intemperance diverted attention and meager resources away from community-development efforts.

Although there were some successful settlements that legislated heavily against alcohol, African-Canadian women's self-help organizations had "zero tolerance" policies for moral and alcohol intemperance. For the African-Canadian women who formed the Victoria Reform Benevolent Society for Social Relief, conventional morality and alcohol temperance were pre-conditions for those African-women refugees in need. The society was strictly for women "between the ages of sixteen and forty-five years old who were not 'addicted to intoxication or have a plurality of living husbands.'"[33] This was more than a commitment to nineteenth-century moral and ethical codes, it was also a manifestation of the effort to escape being labelled racially and sexually degenerate.

The concern over alcohol was equally matched with the concern over sexual temperance for the African-Canadian communities in Ontario. Women leaders were themselves committed to the belief that women bore the burden of shoring up their race, thus they felt African-Canadian communities could little afford to have their women imagined as less than "true" mothers and "true" women.[34] Peggy Bristow shows that according to *The Voice of the Fugitive*,

> the most powerful and beneficial of the influences ordinarily at work in the formation of human character is that of woman ... Man in life is what he is, to a great extent, by the power of woman. His infancy being committed to her charge, and his childhood spent in her society.[35]

Ironically, and because of pressure from the normalizing gaze and judgements of the host culture, African-Canadian women's liberation objectives were consistent with an internalized regulation and policing of their sexuality.[36] *The Provincial Freeman* advocated heavily in favour of moral temperance and monogamy:

> [The recipe] for Matrimonial Happiness — Preserve the privacies of your house, marriage state, heart, from father, mother, sister, brother, aunt and the world. You two, with God's help, build your own quiet world; every third or fourth one whom you draw into it with you will form a party and stand between you two. That should never be. Promise this to each other. Renew the vow at each temptation.[37]

Certainly African-Canadian women were subject to the same moral codes that regulated the lives of all women in Anglo-Saxon dominated Upper Canada, however the pattern of patriarchal domination within their community was not so thorough as to preclude their equitable participation in the building of African-Canadian communities. The participation of African women in building and maintaining churches, schools and political movements such as abolition and suffrage were indispensable. In Upper Canada, "Black women were the backbone of the church. They planned and ran church fairs and picnics, and bazaars at harvest time. And while they did not deliver sermons from the pulpit, Black women's spirituality embodied values necessary to an endangered group."[38]

Those with education and training, such as Mary Ann Shadd Cary, Mary Bibb, Sarah Grant and Elizabeth Shadd Shreve, engaged in charity work and opened schools from their homes or wherever they could find suitable surroundings. African-Canadian women effectively exerted themselves in community building and "elevating the race from the subordinate position forced on it."[39]

By the examples presented here, it is clear that African-Canadian women were active agents in their communities who structured their politics through a broad understanding of the implications of class, gender and race.

Motherhood, Nation and Race in White Feminist History and Historiography

When I began researching this essay in 1998, my quest took me to York University's Scott Library. At the entrance of the library was a large and prominently placed quilted mural celebrating the "founders" of Canadian feminism: Emily Ferguson Murphy, Dr. Emily Jennings Stowe, Dr. Augusta Stowe Gullen, Adelaide Hoodless and Agnes MacPhail. The mural suggested to me that the challenge of inclusion and the challenge to reconceptualize feminism had yet to transform itself into praxis in White feminist approaches to history, and it visually conveyed what White feminist historiography proclaims — that feminism in Canada resulted from Anglo-Saxon women's agency.

Jane Errington, for example, locates the beginning of women's history in Canada with the bodies and experiences of White women: "Canadian women's history is but one part of the larger story of the history of European and North American women." Further to this she notes that "European women first made their appearance in what would become Canada in the mid-seventeenth century."[40] It is significant that Indigenous women are ignored and that racialized women are not mentioned as pioneers and suffragists. When Errington identifies women's history with White women and their experiences she negates the ways that race, class and gender defined the orientation of nineteenth-century White feminists and how they re/produced meanings that policed the borders of the constitutionality of womanhood as synonymous with middle-class Anglo-Saxon womanhood.

The recording of feminist history has depended on the ways in which White Canadian feminist historiographers have chosen to interpret defining historical moments. For example, writing about the important dates and figures of Canadian suffrage, Deborah Gorham tells us that Dr. Emily Stowe's Toronto Women's Literary Club of 1876 is of primary historical significance. Following the work of Catherine Cleverdon's *The Woman Suffrage Movement in Canada*, Gorham states that "the beginnings of organized Canadian feminism [dates] from the founding of this club, and it is becoming commonplace to use this date as a signpost." She qualifies this by saying, "Like the Seneca Falls Convention of 1848, which is usually taken to mark the beginning of an organized movement in the United States, the date of the founding of the Literary Club should be seen as a convenient land-mark but should in no way be taken as a rigid or definitive starting point for the whole feminist movement." In spite of this qualification, Gorham concludes, however, that "it is likely that [Stowe's Literary Club] mark[s] the first attempt to publicize the equal rights issue."[41]

Jane Errington also supports this ideological dating by arguing that "[t]he first suffrage organization, the Toronto Women's

Literary Club, founded in 1876, was a small group of middle-class, educated, professional women."[42] It is important for my argument to note the absence of racial qualifiers in Errington's supposition. While I am not controverting the historical evidence that this society was indeed formed in 1876 for its avowed purpose, I cannot ignore how race and class asserted themselves to confer legitimacy on Dr. Stowe and her colleagues in their well-intentioned goals. Nor can I ignore the role of historiographers who sustain the ideological and epistemological assumptions that universalize the political activities of White women as the only women who engaged in politics for women's rights. For this reason it is imperative to recognize that when Dr. Stowe "and a small energetic group of Toronto Women"[43] launched their literary society in Toronto they did so exclusive of Indigenous, working-class and racialized women.

Since there were African-Canadian women involved in an organized struggle for suffrage and temperance before Emily Stowe's group, the question is, Why is it not ideologically and epistemologically possible to contend that the beginning of Canadian feminism began with Mary Ann Shadd's group? What is at stake? How would the ideological and epistemological foundations of feminism change as a result? And could this result in a feminism that articulates unity without sacrificing the historical fact that women are differently located in history and society and have all made valuable contributions to the history of women?

As we have seen, African-Canadian women were politically active in movements for temperance and suffrage, yet they did not have the luxury of whiteness that would ensure that gender would become the principle site of struggle. By conspicuously omitting race as a central factor in Canadian women's experiences, White feminist historiography in general magnifies gender (and class to a lesser degree) as the principal category to which feminism owes its origins. The negation of race and whiteness led classical feminist historiographic texts to claim that "from what we know of it at present, the Ontario women's rights movement would appear to have been largely middle-class in origin."[44] As long as this fact is not qualified by race as well, we are presented with a universality of whiteness and with the White woman as the universal woman. While gender is made synonymous with whiteness and whiteness synonymous with being middle-class, feminist historiography creates the justification for its myopic emphasis on gender through the correlates of marriage and family.[45]

Mainstream White feminist historiography sustains the priority of gender over multiple dimensions of women's being through the fascination with exceptional personalities and the exceptionalizing of certain White feminist organizations — a discursive strategy for sealing the borders of re/presentation of the feminist struggle in Canada.[46] I suppose there is little wrong with focusing on exceptional personalities and organizations to the extent that these personalities and organizations are examined in the ideological, social and material context of their time and are shown to be relevant to ours. However, there are two risks involved in doing so. First, given our prevailing socio-cultural order, which prefers to recognize White agency as universal agency, the exclusive attention of White feminist historiography on exceptional personalities and organizations naturalizes whiteness at the same time that whiteness is hidden. Second, the image typically presented of White feminist founders focuses attention on their progressive political action around gender, but pays scant attention, if any, to their questionable commitments to eugenics, imperialism, nativism and racism.

Images such as the murals that hung at York University's Scott Library deepen the association between whiteness and the exceptional — middle-class — personalities who are constructed as the "founders" of Canadian feminism. For example, in the introduction to the 1972 edition of Nellie McClung's *In Times Like These*, Veronica Strong-Boag suggests that exceptional personalities such as McClung "personified Canadian feminism for the first quarter of the twentieth century." McClung obtained this personification by becoming "the foremost practitioner of the politics of sexual confrontation."[47] There is no doubt that McClung is as important as Strong-Boag suggests, for, after all, in an inclusive feminist historiography White women can have their heroes too; they cannot however presume their heroes are for everyone else.

What, however, is problematic with Strong-Boag's remarks on McClung's activism is that it sacrifices criticality for bland statements of facts that disguise negative elements of McClung's politics as merely "liberal naivete."[48] For inasmuch as McClung was the "foremost practitioner of the politics of sexual confrontation," she problematically, as the first woman MLA in Alberta, suggested that eugenics could aid the "nation's health."[49] In the context of the then-current perspective about a "great Canadian race," McClung suggested that *women* (i.e., White women) of the Prairies should exercise their "talents to save and serve the race."[50] While Strong-Boag breezily points out that McClung was a "nativist" (the Anglo-Saxon belief that the productive Aboriginal lands should be vacated of their Indigenous people and settled by Europeans only), McClung herself articulates a cosmopolitan nativism that proclaimed the Western provinces open to European colonization:

> It would seem reasonable, too, that such a condition might be brought about in a new country, and in a country as big as *ours, where there is room for everyone and to spare.* Look upon our rolling prairies, carpeted with wild flowers ... [I]t does not seem too ideal or visionary that these broad sunlit spaces may be the homes of countless thousands of happy and contented people.[51]

In the context of a strong nation-building movement, then still drawing force from Confederation, McClung's status as a feminist leader and elected political official cannot be hived-off from her commitments to race, nationalism, eugenics and colonialism.[52]

By way of polemics, let me propose the absurd for a moment: How would Nellie McClung's sexual politics have fared if she existed in the raced body of an African woman? Would her sexual politics of confrontation be imagined by latter-day feminists as liberatory when the African woman's body was constructed in the nineteenth-century imaginary as congenitally prone to immorality and "unlady-like" sexual aggression?[53] While surely McClung's politics may have been liberating for Anglo-Canadian women in general, and the middle-classes in particular, such an imagination of feminist personification had little meaning for African-Canadian women who were still fighting to be recognized as women and as human. It is important, therefore, to recognize that Strong-Boag's error was not to recognize that McClung's whiteness permitted her to have voice and autonomy in a nineteenth-century social and political landscape that was committed to racist visions of empire and colonization.

When the insurgent politic of rewriting history encounters the established politic of history, to charge nineteenth-century feminists with nationalism and racism may be regarded as an unfair projection of our present "values" of anti-racism or other moralities onto the past. Given that history is inherently political, and gives meaning and reflection to our present social condition, the version of history that is given legitimacy is one which, *a priori*, legitimates taken-for-granted assumptions and social practices. In this context, a fact that bedevils White Canada is not so much the practice of racism, but, more dangerously, the practice of denying that racism has ever existed or ever exerted its corrosive effects on social relations in this country. It is therefore important to observe that in as much as McClung articulated a persuasive argument for White middle-class women's emancipation, we must not ignore her cosmopolitan nativism and flirtation with eugenics cavalierly. If any such separation is made, we are left with the ideological conclusion that "in all [her] assumptions she was a creature of her time and place."[54]

Another scholar of the "women's" movement offers the intriguing proposition that while some nineteenth-century White feminists were racists, at least by modern standards, because they "did not live in our age or hold to our notions of equity ... it seems unfair to judge them by criteria which they would have found decontextualized and lacking in pride."[55] The problem with the "racism is past" and alternatively that the "past was not racist" theses is that they are ideological fields of containment which do not admit the continuity of the past into the present. For, regardless of the definitions we may use, Lewis Mumford reminds us that we are creatures of the past for whom "long-forgotten traumas in history may have a disastrous effect upon millions who remain unaware of them."[56]

Echoing Mumford, Valverde suggests that just because White feminists have brought patriarchy into the forefront of social consciousness, this "does not mean that racism is either non-existent, or ... [that] the racism of x or y feminist is an unfortunate external blot due to the 'racism of the time.'"[57] In point of fact, she continues, thus affirming Mumford's dictum on the ideology of history, "the racism of white feminism is neither externally caused nor accidental: it is integral to what the mainstream Anglo-Saxon tradition has called 'feminism.'" The uncomfortable truth is that inasmuch as other aspects of the past imperceptibly insinuate themselves in the unconscious living of life, the "racism of the time" is ever in our time, even if its presence is imperceptible to those who are its beneficiaries. In the final analysis, the denial of racism implicates both past and present dialectically and continually in feminist historiography as elsewhere in Canadian society. The assumption that racism is a "thing of the past" unfairly burdens racialized women with the responsibility of silence.

We have seen that some "founders" of the feminist position in Anglo-Saxon Canada were committed to the "deeply ethnocentric belief that European women are the paradigm (and paragon) of womanhood in general, and that the specifically European women's movement is the vanguard of civilization."[58] Leading feminist organizations, too, explicitly articulated the quest for suffrage through a feminized racialist discourse hinging on patriarchal ideals about women's role. For example, in arguing for Anglo-Saxon women's suffrage, the WCTU asserted, "Governments rise and fall by votes, and until women have electoral value, their reforms, their labours, their dreams of an uplifted race, a purified country with 'protected' homes, will lack fulfillment."[59] If, then, the quest for Anglo-Saxon women's suffrage rested upon the dynamic interaction of these contradictory discourses, how did organizations such as the Women's Christian Temperance Union imagine African women and their role in both temperance and suffrage? How does mainstream White feminist historiography represent the actions of the WCTU? And how can an African-centred feminist approach help us to interpret the experiences of African-Canadian women in regards to temperance and suffrage differently from representations of passivity or invisibility offered by White feminist historiography?

Vron Ware contends that the Ida B. Wells's anti-lynching campaign in America and Britain "demonstrated the possibility of an alliance between black and white women in which white women went beyond sisterly support for black women."[60] What does feminist historiography reveal about the relationship between Black and White women in feminist organizations in the late nineteenth and early twentieth centuries? Mariana Valverde maintains that when African-Canadian and Anglo-Canadian women came into contact for the feminist cause, it was principally through organizations such as the WCTU. In this important feminist organization, Valverde observes, the relationship between these group of women mirrored nineteenth-century patterns of White domination and African-Canadian subordination. In this context, the ideals of White feminists converged ethnocentrism with nationalism, and motherhood with race puritanism as the operative frameworks that defined the aims and actions of the WCTU towards African-Canadian women and their communities.

To be sure, nineteenth-century feminist principles challenged the supremacy of men to dominate both public and private spheres of life. Additionally, feminists challenged the social

Darwinian claim that relegated women to an inferior socio-biological position. Problematically, turn of the century White feminists, because they accepted the ideals of race regeneration and race supremacy, located the public role of women within the familial sphere. In this formulation, Anglo-Canadian women imagined themselves as the moral superiors to Anglo-Canadian men in the context of the family — the presumed foundation of racial and social preservation. For the WCTU, whether in Britain, America or Canada, motherhood was "the pinnacle of every woman's life and her supreme task was thought by the WCTU to be mothering: 'If a mother failed in the task of raising healthy, seriously minded and well trained children, she sent forth 'damaged material.'"[61] Noting, however, that this ideal took place in a social context committed to empire whose every visibility is saturated by race, Vron Ware argues that the fusion of motherhood, racial advancement and imperialism became central to what it meant to be a woman (i.e., an Anglo-Saxon woman):

> It was not just as mothers that British women performed a central role in maintaining the Empire: the ideology of white womanhood, structured by class and race, embraced women in all their familiar roles. Whether as Mothers of the Empire or Britannia's Daughters, [White] women were able to symbolize the idea of moral strength that bound the great imperial family together.[62]

In this sense, conceptions of motherhood in the expanding colonial state had grave implications for the political stability and advancement of the "Anglo-Saxon race" in Canada.

In Canada, as it was elsewhere in America and Britain, the WCTU enacted visions of White womanhood, which were juxtaposed to racialized women in general and African women in particular. Deborah Gorham reminds us that the WCTU was avidly "nativist" and therefore "hostile or at least suspicious of immigrant groups that were not Anglo-Saxon."[63] Anglo-Saxon feminists, having lost much-publicized efforts to win suffrage, rather than confront Anglo-Saxon men who had the power to deny them the vote, instead turned their frustrations into the scapegoating of men from "weaker races" who had voting rights. The WCTU lashed out by asking, "Why should the ballot be given to these aliens who own not a tithe of the property owned by Canadian women who are without the ballot?"[64] The refusal of the suffrage movement was seen by the WCTU as a betrayal. By racializing their quest, WCTU members drew themselves deeper into a narrow gender politics articulated through discourses of racial fidelity and purity.

It is evident the WCTU was committed to a racialist vision of its work. In spite of this troubling history, the problem of a non-inclusive feminist historiography continues to limit a holistic examination of the WCTU's contribution to the feminist movement in Canada. For, while clearly the mainstream historiography of the WCTU accurately presents it as an activist organization, this history is a complicated admixture of the romanticization of White feminist organizations and a parenthetical engagement with race criticism and the experiences of racialized women. As an example, and contrasting sharply with Mariana Valverde's critical analysis of the WCTU's attitude towards African-Canadian women, Sharon Cook asserts that "the [WCTU] made a concerted attempt to empower black women as temperance advocates in their homes and communities."[65] Further, she suggests that the WCTU demonstrated a charitable attitude towards African-Canadian women by creating a separate "department of work among coloured people."[66] Although such departments were created, there is no evidence that the WCTU officially sanctioned segregation.[67] Despite its practice of segregation, these *positive* representations of the WCTU in the domain of race assume that African-Canadian women *needed* to be empowered by White women.

Cook notes that in spite of this separate department, "[s]urviving reports about black departments and unions around the province suggest that the local unions did not sufficiently tap the leadership potential of black women."[68] We can surmise that the failure of these departments was a function of a pre-existing tradition of temperance among African-Canadian women, and that "the scant mentions of women of colour in the WCTU press are condescending and maternalistic."[69] Valverde asserts further that the WCTU's attitude towards the superiority of Anglo-Saxon motherhood

> automatically precluded black women or children from being "pure," [and] the fact that purity was equated with whiteness, and hence indirectly with European culture, made it difficult if not impossible for Canada's women of colour to identify with the brand of feminism elaborated by the WCTU.[70]

This perspective stands in stark contrast to Cook's account of the WCTU:

> The women of the Ontario WCTU were a product and deeply reflective of their age. They had no pretensions about seeing the problematic issue of "race" any more than other members of society. But the full record suggests that the organization was more tolerant than many of the contributions to Canada made by other races and ethnic groups, and was sometimes reliant on women in those communities to develop temperate and civic virtues amongst their menfolk. To do justice to the question of racism, and also to the women of the WCTU, it is necessary to consider both the intentions of the WCTU policies and the means by which these women attempted to implement those intentions ...[71]

What are we to make of these contradictory accounts of the WCTU and how can they help us understand White feminist historiography's difficult engagement with race? Put together, these contradictions reveal the dynamism of early feminism, its problems and, as well, the prospects and limitations of feminist historiography itself. For between the divergent accounts we see that the challenges advanced by African-Canadian and racialized women are differentially operationalized by two categories of White feminists. On one hand, Valverde's account knows *how* to integrate a deeply reflective inclusive feminist historiography that admits the experience of race without appropriating the voices of African-Canadian women. Valverde's perspective may in part reflect her own engagement with race and ethnic exclusion as a woman of Latin American heritage. Sharon Cook's work as well reveals the echoes of the challenge that African-Canadian and racialized women have raised. But between Valverde's and Cook's analyses, it is not any longer the problem of lip service that confronts us, but the more thorny issue of *how* the analysis of race and racism are integrated into White feminist historiography. The problem here is not that race and racism have not been acknowledged, but that too often it is integrated without disturbing the centrality of gender in White feminism and feminist historiography. An inclusive feminist historiography demands such a disturbance.[72]

♦

The omission of African-Canadian women in Canadian historiography is being addressed by African-Canadian feminist scholars such as Peggy Bristow, Afua Cooper, Adrienne Shadd and Dionne Brand, and while these scholars will continue their insurgent knowledge production, which values the historical presence of African-Canadian women, this is not enough. The academy must be compelled to open spaces for the hiring of African-Canadian faculty and the encouragement of African-Canadian women graduate students. This will, of course, necessitate a struggle against institutional racism: a test of the willingness of White feminists to stand in solidarity with African-Canadian feminists in the struggle for employment equity. The question is, What has prevented this solidarity thus far? What have White mainstream feminists to lose in the process? And can they gain more than they lose?

These questions suggest that the challenge to White mainstream feminism and feminist historiography is a difficult but not insurmountable task. It requires that more White and racialized women create spaces to articulate a revitalized feminist discourse that strives for solidarity and recognizes difference. In the process it is critical that White feminist historiographers critique their earlier work and pay heed to the criticisms raised by African-Canadian and other racialized feminists. Inasmuch as White feminists are expected to take race seriously, a caveat is in order: care must be taken not to move from lip service to an inclusion that authorizes White women to be exclusive experts in the history of African women. "The road to hell is paved with good intentions," and even in taking race seriously, White feminists must be mindful to check the appropriative impulses of whiteness. For as long as White feminists do not question their racial privilege and that of their predecessors, the history of women in Canada will continue to be incomplete, competitive, fractious and acrimonious. I am not arguing for synchronicity, but suggesting a productive utilization of historical tensions towards an inclusive women's history.

Certainly, "rewriting" history is a task reluctantly undertaken by any historian, and it is equally difficult to change personal value systems that shaped our culture's perception of the world. Yet the challenge before us in feminist historiography is the same as in "many other areas of feminist inquiry — we have to start over again from the beginning."[73] The stakes are too high not to.

Notes

While this essay is radically transformed from its earliest incarnation, the first draft is indebted to Professor Sara Z. Burke for her encouragement, course readings and helpful comments, and Dr. Afua Cooper for graciously providing comments, references and photocopies of *The Provincial Freeman.* I am also grateful to Whitney Sanford who patiently read and commented on each line of this essay. I would like to thank Dr. Njoki Wane, Kathy Deliovsky and Erica Lawson for inviting my contribution to this book. Finally, my gratitude to Beth McAuley for enduring a long and difficult editorial process. In spite of my debts to others, all responsibilities are mine.

1. I would like to thank Dr. Charles Simon-Aaron for introducing me to the phrase "the struggle continues," which has been translated from the Portuguese. It is the slogan popularized in the late 1950s by Eduardo Mondlane, a founding figure of FRELIMO, Mozambique's revolutionary independence party.
2. Mariana Valverde, "Racism and Anti-Racism in Feminist Research," in Constance Backhouse and David H. Flaherty, eds., *Challenging Times: The Women's Movement in Canada and the United States* (Montreal: McGill-Queen's Press, 1992), 160; Gisella Bock, "Women's History and Gender History: Aspects of an International Debate," *Gender and History* 1, no. 1 (Spring 1989), 7.
3. Himani Bannerji, "Politics and the Writing of History," in Ruth Roach Pierson and Nupur Chaudhuri, eds., With the Assistance of Beth McAuley, *Nation, Empire, Colony: Historicizing Gender and Race* (Bloomington: Indiana University Press, 1998), 287.
4. Lorraine Code, "Feminist Theory," in Sandra Burt, Lorraine Code and Lindsay Dorney, eds., *Changing Patterns: Women in Canada* (Toronto: McClelland and Stewart Inc., 1993), 47.
5. Bettina Aptheker, *Woman's Legacy: Essays on Race, Sex, and Class in American History* (Amherst: The University of Massachusetts Press, 1982); Susan S. Lanser, "Feminist Criticism, 'The Yellow Wallpaper' and the Politics of Color in America," *Feminist Studies* 15, no. 3 (Fall 1989), 415–41; Vron Ware, *Beyond the Pale: White Women, Racism and History* (London: Verso, 1992); Gail Bederman, *Manliness and Civilization: A Cultural History of Gender and Race in the United States, 1880-1917* (Chicago: The University of Chicago Press, 1995); Judith Butler, "Endangered/Endangering: Schematic Racism and White Paranoia," in Robert Gooding-Williams, ed., *Reading Rodney King, Reading Urban Uprising* (London: Routledge, 1993), 15–22; Marilyn Frye, "On Being White: Toward A Feminist Understanding of Race and Race Supremacy," in *The Politics of Reality: Essays in Feminist Theory* (Freedom, CA: The Crossing Press, 1983), 110–27.

6. I have opted for racialized instead of "women of colour" and "minority women" for practical and political reasons. "Women of colour" is a definitional category which, though widely used, no longer holds meaningful value for the differentiation between White women and non-White women. With the explosion of White people studying whiteness, it is clear that White people have a colour as well. As a result of the visibility of whiteness new terminology is needed to capture the social construction of race and the assignation of racial differentiation upon women and people who are not either politically or phenotypically White. As a result, the idea of the "minority" is and has been offensive for racialized people who have neither created nor benefited from the confusion associated with numerical misinformation. Since many racialized people in the West tend to view their associations in global rather than national terms, it is really White people who are the minority. By looking at racial membership and definitions in this way, it is possible to capture the reality that a minority of the world's population have disguised the true nature of the inverse correlation between their numbers and the gross sums of global resources that they have arrogated unto themselves.

7. Evelyn Brooks Higginbotham, "African-American Women's History and the Metalanguage of Race," *Signs: Journal of Women in Culture and Society,* 17, no. 2 (1992), 251.

8. Arun Mukherjee, "A House Divided: Women of Colour and American Feminist Theory," in Backhouse and Flaherty, eds., *Challenging Times,* 165.

9. Afua Cooper, "Putting Flesh on Bone" (2002), 2–3. Unpublished paper in author's possession and cited with permission.

10. For universality of White femininity, see Gloria T. Hull, Patricia Bell Scott and Barbara Smith, "Introduction: The Politics of Black Women's Studies," in Gloria T. Hull, Patricia Bell Scott and Barbara Smith, eds., *All the Women Are White, All the Blacks Are Men, But Some of Us Are Brave: Black Women's Studies* (New York: The Feminist Press, 1982), xx-xxi. On the gilded cage argument, see Cooper, "Putting Flesh on Bone," 2; Code, "Feminist Theory," 47; Judith Butler, *Gender Trouble: Feminism and the Subversion of Identity* (New York: Routledge,1990). For examples of working-class women's history, see Sherry Edmunds-Flett, "'Abundant Faith': Nineteenth-Century African Canadian Women on Vancouver Island" (unpublished paper in author's possession), 2. For challenges to racism in White feminism, see Deborah King, "Multiple Jeopardy, Multiple Consciousness: The Context of A Black Feminist Ideology," *Signs: Journal of Women in Culture and Society* 14, no. 1 (1988), 51.

11. Sarah Carter, *Capturing Women: The Manipulation of Cultural Imagery in Canada's Prairie West* (Kingston: McGill-Queen's University Press, 1997); Marianna Valverde, "'When the Mother of the Race is Free': Race, Reproduction, and Sexuality in First-Wave Feminism," in Franca Iacovetta and Mariana Valverde, eds., *Gender Conflicts: New Essays in Women's History* (Toronto: University of Toronto Press, 1992), 3–26.

12. Valverde, "Racism and Anti-Racism in Feminist Research," 162.

13. Peggy Bristow, Dionne Brand, Linda Carty, Afua Cooper, Sylvia Hamilton and Adrienne Shadd, "Introduction," in Peggy Bristow et al., eds., *"We're Rooted Here and They Can't Pull Us Up": Essays in African-Canadian Women's History* (Toronto: University of Toronto Press, 1994), 4.

14. bell hooks, "Black Women Intellectuals," in bell hooks and Cornel West, *Breaking Bread: Insurgent Black Intellectual Life* (Toronto: Between the Lines 1991), 153.

15. Philomena Chioma Steady, "The Black Woman Cross-Culturally: An Overview," in Philomena Chioma Steady, ed., *The Black Woman Cross-Culturally* (Rochester: Schenkman Books, Inc., 1992).

16. Simms, "Beyond the White Veil," 178.

17. Jane Errington, "Pioneers and Suffragists," in Sandra Burt, Lorraine Code and Lindsay Dorney eds., *Changing Patterns: Women in Canada* (Toronto: McClelland and Stewart Inc., 1993), 60; Veronica Strong-Boag and Anita Clair Fellman, *Rethinking Canada: The Promise of Women's History* (Toronto: Copp Clark Pitman, 1986), 2.

18. Butler, "Endangered/Endangering," 15.

19. Cooper, "Putting Flesh on Bone," 3.

20. Hull, Scott and Smith, "Introduction," xxi.

21. Ibid., xvii.

22. Kimberly Christensen, "'With Whom Do You Believe Your Lot is Cast?': White Feminists and Racism," *Signs: Journal of Women in Culture and Society* 22, no. 3 (1997), 617–48.

23. Steady, "The Black Woman Cross-Culturally: An Overview," 27.

24. Bederman, *Manliness and Civilization*, 38; Mukherjee, "A House Divided," 169.

25. Dorothy E. Smith, *Texts, Facts, and Femininity: Exploring the Relations of Ruling* (New York: Routledge, 1990), 6. Dorothy Smith does not actually argue that race is a relation of ruling. I have, however, borrowed the concept to demonstrate that race, along with class and gender, must be considered as such.

26. bell hooks, *Feminist Theory: From Margin to Center* (Boston: South End Press,1984), 3.

27. Bristow et al., "Introduction," 4.

28. Afua Cooper, "The Search for Mary Bibb, Black Woman Teacher in Nineteenth-Century Canada West," *Ontario History* 83, no. 1 (March 1991), 40. Reprinted in this volume as chapter 4.

29. Peggy Bristow "'Whatever You Raise in the Ground You Can Sell It in Chatham': Black Women in Buxton and Chatham, 1850–65," in Bristow et al., eds., *"We're Rooted Here and They Can't Pull Us Up,"* 97.

30. Bristow, "'Whatever You Raise in the Ground," 122.

31. Earl Ofari Hutchinson, *"Let Your Motto Be Resistance": The Life and Thought of Henry Highland Garnet* (Boston: Beacon Press, 1972), 28.

32. *The Provincial Freeman,* 15 July 1854.

33. Bristow, "'Whatever You Raise in the Ground,'" 120.

34. Shirley J. Yee, "Gender Ideology and Black Women as Community-Builders in Ontario, 1850–70," *The Canadian Historical Review* 75, no. 1 (March 1994), 59.

35. Bristow, "'Whatever You Raise in the Ground,'" 84.

36. Ibid., 94.

37. Mary Ann Shadd Cary, *The Provincial Freeman,* 25 April 1857.

38. Ibid., 92.

39. Ibid., 87; Edmunds-Flett, "'Abundant Faith,'" 22; Yee, "Gender Ideology and Black Women as Community-Builders in Ontario," 68.

40. Errington, "Pioneers and Suffragists," 60.

41. Deborah Gorham, "The Canadian Suffragists," in Gwen Matheson, ed., *Women in the Canadian Mosaic* (Toronto: Peter Martin Associates Limited, 1976), 31.

42. Jane Errington, "Pioneers and Suffragists," 78.

43. Catherine Cleverdon, *The Woman Suffrage Movement in Canada* (Toronto: University of Toronto Press,1978), 20.

44. Gorham, "The Canadian Suffragists," 35.

45. Higginbotham, "African-American Women's History and the Metalanguage of Race," 273; Bonnie Thornton Dill, "Race, Class, and Gender: Prospects for an All-Inclusive Sisterhood," *Feminist Studies* 9, no. 1 (Spring 1983), 133.

46. Dill, "Race, Class, and Gender," 133.

47. Strong-Boag, "An Introduction," vii.

48. Ibid., xx.

49. Strong-Boag writes that while McClung served in the Alberta Legislative Assembly (1917–1922), she "favoured birth control and supported Alberta's act for the sterilization of the mentally unfit as a means of improving the nation's health" (xiv).

50. Ibid., viii.

51. McClung, *In Times Like These,* 97. Emphasis added.

52. Nellie McClung was clearly not alone in her views of race and nationalism. Other feminist "founders" such as Emily Murphy for example, a self-proclaimed "Nordic" supremacist, also gave full expression to racist views in her famous anti-immigrant/anti-narcotic broadside, *The Black Candle* (Toronto: Thomas Allen Publisher, 1922). See Mariana Valverde's "'When the Mother of the Race is Free'" for critical analysis of Murphy's text.

53. Kate Davy, "Outing Whiteness: A Feminist/Lesbian Project," *Theater Journal* 47, no. 2 (May 1995), 195.

54. Strong-Boag, "Introduction," xx.

55. Sharon Anne Cook, *"Through Sunshine and Shadow": The Women's Christian Temperance Union, Evangelicalism, and Reform in Ontario, 1874–1930* (Montreal: McGill-Queen's University Press, 1995), 193.

56. Lewis Mumford, *The Condition of Man* (London: Martin Secker and Warburg Ltd.,1944), 14.

57. Valverde, "Racism and Anti-Racism," 162.

58. Ibid., 10.

59. Valverde, "'When the Mother of the Race Is Free,'" 16–17.

60. Vron Ware, *Beyond the Pale*, chap. 4, "'To Make the Facts Known': Racial Terror and the Construction of White Femininity," 220.

61. Cook, *"Through Sunshine and Shadow,"* 80.

62. Ware, *Beyond the Pale*, chap. 3, "Britannia's Other Daughters: Feminism in the Age of Imperialism," 162.

63. Gorham, "The Canadian Suffragists," 40.

64. Valverde, "'When the Mother of the Race is Free,'" 19.

65. Cook, *"Through Sunshine and Shadow,"* 103. Emphasis added.

66. Ibid., 104.

67. Valverde, "'When the Mother of the Race Is Free,'" 15.

68. Cook, *"Through Sunshine and Shadow,"* 105.

69. Ibid., 15.

70. Ibid., 20.

71. Ibid., 103.

72. Dorothy Smith has argued from a political economy perspective, which speaks equally well to historiography, that "[i]ssues of racism confront ... a barrier confining thinking and analyses to the racist tracks of the ruling of contemporary racism. The problem isn't to make women of colour a topic within a feminist political economy, nor yet to invite women of colour to speak in this zone of discourse. The problem I am explicating is of a different kind; it is a problem of the concealed standpoint, the position in the ruling relations that is taken for granted in how we speak and that bounds and constrains how a political economy of women can speak to women, let alone Third World women ... The centre still remains; the standpoint within ruling is stably if invisibly present. Nothing will serve but the dissolution of objectified discourse, the decentring of standpoint and the discovery of another consciousness of society and systematically developed from the standpoint of women of colour and exploring the relations of political economy and sociology from a ground in that experience." *Writing the Social: Critique, Theory, and Investigations* (Toronto: University of Toronto Press, 1999), 43.

73. Ibid., 164.

Chapter Four

Black Women and Work in Nineteenth-Century Canada West: Black Woman Teacher Mary Bibb

Afua P. Cooper

My decision to do a paper on Mary Bibb came out of my study of the history of women and education in nineteenth-century North America. A study of Black female teachers who taught in Canada West during this period presented itself as a useful task. After discovering several names — including Matilda Nichols, Mary Shadd, Sarah and Mary Anne Titre, and Mary Bibb — I realized that to do a study on all these women would be too great a task at the moment. Therefore, I decided to be less ambitious and study only Mary Bibb. Although she was "well known," not much material could be found in traditional sources. My quest for her set me on a course for alternative sources, where I discovered compelling and valuable information on her life and on Black education in Canada in general and Canada West in particular.[1]

In the fall of 1850, Mary Bibb, her husband Henry Bibb, and her mother-in-law Mildred Jackson migrated from Boston to Sandwich, Canada West.[2] They had been forced out of the United States by the passage of the Fugitive Slave Law.[3] The Bibbs, as soon as they arrived in Canada, initiated projects to serve the needs of the growing Black community in Sandwich and its environs. (Sandwich was the name of a township in southwestern Ontario – Canada West – that included the villages of Windsor and Sandwich within its borders.) One of these projects was a school set up by Mary Bibb for Black children in the Sandwich area. It was the beginning of a series of schools she would operate to serve the needs of Black children in the areas where she lived.[4] ...

In the middle decades of the nineteenth century, the tensions inherent in slavery in the United States were clearly manifesting themselves. Numerous slaves had escaped to the northern states and elsewhere. The slaveholding states were pressuring the federal government to act on their behalf. In 1850, a "compromise" was reached and in September of that year, the dreaded Fugitive Slave Law was passed by the U.S. Congress. Its immediate result was the exodus of thousands of Blacks, both escaped slaves and free, from the United States to Canada and other places. The law granted slave-owners the right to pursue and capture their slaves who had sought refuge in the North. Free Blacks were not safe either; they too could be kidnapped and sold into slavery. The safety of every Black individual was threatened.[5]

In this atmosphere of terror and fear, thousands of Blacks left home, family, possessions, and secure jobs to flee oppression.[6] For Henry Bibb, a known fugitive [from slavery], the United States was definitely an unsafe place. The Bibbs had no choice but to leave, and they chose to come to Canada. On arriving in Sandwich, Canada West, they initially sought to "uplift" the growing Black community in two ways.[7] Henry Bibb was responsible, with the help of his wife, for establishing a newspaper, and Mary, a school.[8] In a letter to white abolitionist and philanthropist Gerritt Smith, with whom the Bibbs had a close relationship, Mary Bibb wrote:

> My dear Friend,
>
> Will you aid us by sending as many subscribers as convenience will permit. There are hundreds of slaves coming here daily. My husband & self consider this the field at present. We are about to engage in this. I expect to take a school next week, any aid from the friend will be acceptable. Please let me know what you think of the movement.
>
> In haste,
M. E. Bibb
Sandwich, C. west
Nov. 8th 1850[9]

The newspaper in question was *The Voice of the Fugitive,* edited and published by Mr. Bibb. The first issue appeared on 1 January 1851.[10]

The school Mary Bibb mentions in her letter to Smith began in her home in November or December 1850. It was vital to a community that was denied equal access to public schooling. The same year the Bibbs came to Canada West, the provincial legislature passed an act legalizing separate schooling. The law gave Blacks the option to open their own schools. The relevant section of the act reads: "… on the application, in writing, of twelve, or more, resident heads of families, to authorize the establishment of one, or more, Separate Schools for Protestants, Roman Catholics or Coloured People."[11]

White school supporters interpreted the act to mean that Blacks could and should be denied entry to the local common schools and be required to set up their own. Acting on their interpretation, white school supporters barred many Black children from the common schools, and those Black children who did not have access to a separate school received no schooling at all.[12] Alexander Murray stated: "Of all manifestations of Negrophobia the attempt to deny Negroes the equal use of public schools was the most successful. In communities where problems of land sales, voting rights, or jury service never arose, a large number of white inhabitants agreed with efforts to keep Negro children from the schools."[13]

Separate schooling for Black children in Canada West was a reality well before 1850. As early as the 1830s, white prejudice forced Blacks in several districts in the province to establish their own schools.[14] The act of 1850 gave legitimacy to what was already a common practice. An immediate reaction to the school act by whites was that more and more Black children were driven from the common schools because whites felt they could legally do so. Black parents had no alternative but to set up their own schools.[15] But not enough schools were established, and many of those that were often lacked the necessary support needed to sustain the growing Black school population.

When Mrs. Bibb arrived in Sandwich, there was no schooling for Black children in the township. As shown in her letter to Smith, she took action, which was not only influenced by her desire to uplift her community, but was also a loud political statement. Recognizing the racism within the school system and society, she set out with very meagre resources to challenge them.

The Voice, in its first issue of 1 January 1851, announced the opening of her school. "In Sandwich township we have great need of a school.

Mrs. M. E. Bibb has commenced with 25 pupils at her residence, with the hope that some suitable place will be provided, and means for carrying out the school properly." The school had apparently started with fewer than twenty-five scholars, but by the time *The Voice* printed the above quote the number had increased. Later the school grew even larger. ...

Obviously, by this time, Mrs. Bibb had moved the school from her house to a larger place. Teaching for Mary Bibb involved mental stress and physical labour. She was not only the teacher of the school, but the caretaker as well. Daniel Hill notes that she had to carry the firewood used for heating the school herself.[16] She encountered these hardships not only because her school was Black; this was the nature of many schools, especially in rural areas, as the educational enterprise began to expand. However, the problems of the Black schools were compounded, as they received little or no financial support from the educational state.[17]

Mary Bibb's school was purely a self-help effort, as were the schools founded by several of her Black sisters in Canada West.[18] Placed in the broader context of the development of education in Canada West, her action was typical of the pioneering teachers, both Black and white, who started schools. Susan Houston and Alison Prentice, commenting on the drive behind many of the province's early schools, conclude: "One way or another teachers were at the centre of the Upper Canadian quest for schooling. Theirs was an entrepreneurial spirit. Young and old, married and single, female and male, they were often the creative forces behind their schools."[19]

Mary Bibb's school suffered from the lack of financial and material resources. She charged each pupil six cents a week, but only a "very few of those attending the school could afford to pay."[20] In April 1851, two months after her article in *The Voice,* she wrote to the *Anti-Slavery Bugle,* an American newspaper, informing its readers about the state of her school. The demoralizing effect of not having the means to enable the school to function smoothly was taking its toll. "My school is not as large as it has been during winter. Many have hired out to farmers for the season, yet it is now quite large — too large for the room we occupy. I have not yet received a dollar for my labor. I hardly know what is [my] duty in regard to continuing it. I cannot afford to give all my time. A small compensation would satisfy me, but even this has not yet been given."[21]

By October of that year, the *Bugle* reported that Mrs. Bibb "has received no compensation for all her labors, or not more than ten dollars."[22] This was after eleven months of teaching. ...

The difficulty in teaching and managing the school forced Mrs. Bibb to resign as teacher. The school did not simply "collapse." It was taken over by two other teachers, Misters Jackson and Russell. *The Voice* confirms the appointment of Mr. Jackson and that the school had become a 'government' one (Mrs. Bibb's emphasis). In an article titled "Colored Settlements and Schools," *The Voice* notes: "There is a government school in operation at Sandwich, with from twenty to thirty scholars. It is taught by Mr. Jackson, a man of color."[23] But the meagre support the school received from the government and the parents was not enough to keep it going. It had foundered by April 1852, after a life span of about one year and four months.[24] Its closure meant that Black children in the area were again without formal education.

I would argue that the school was closed for two reasons: the poverty of the pupils' parents and the reluctance of the government to finance its long-term functioning. The parents' inability to pay the fees brings into focus the financial situation of Blacks in Essex County. Many were needy recent arrivals. We must remember that many families and individuals left possessions and properties in their flight from the United States owing to the Fugitive Slave Law. Families also moved away from border towns like Sandwich and settled inland as soon as they became acquainted with the region. This movement led occasionally to the instability of some schools, as their support was sporadic.[25] ...

After giving up her first effort, Mary Bibb launched a second school in September 1852. We learn of this endeavour from her letter to Mann. This new school began during the latter part of 1852, after the Bibbs moved to Windsor from Sandwich. However, by the time she wrote to Mann, the new school was thriving. She wanted the school to be open to all "irrespective of color." Did she receive some white scholars also?[26] She intended for both Blacks and whites to come to this school and was determined to make it work. ...

Mary Bibb's involvement in education extended to the religious sphere where, along with her husband, she was active in the Sunday school movement. The Sunday school with which they were involved not only held Bible classes but also taught reading and writing. According to Daniel Hill, the Sunday school conducted by the Bibbs was the only schooling available to many youths and adults in the Black community of Essex.[27]

Her efforts to assist members of her race extended beyond teaching.

An ardent abolitionist, upon her arrival in Canada, she helped to established the Windsor Anti-Slavery Society. The society greatly helped many refugees who had fled to Canada from the United States. Her home was sometimes used as a shelter for many of these refugees who had fled to Canada from the United States. Mary and her husband were the Canadian directors of the Refugee Home Society, a colonization scheme established to help Blacks acquire land in the province. Not only did she assist in the establishment of *The Voice,* she also influenced its editorial direction, and during part of 1851, when her husband was on the lecture circuit in Wisconsin and Illinois, she oversaw its production. In addition, she was also involved in the emigrationist movement.[28] She was engaged in several of these undertakings with her husband.[29]

Emancipation day, 1 August 1854, was a turning-point in Mary Bibb's life.[30] Her husband died that day, after an illness. The Black community and the abolitionist movement had lost one of their most dynamic spokespersons and leaders. Mary Bibb lost a husband, companion friend, colleague, and "help-meet." When Henry Bibb died, he was thirty-nine years old and she was almost thirty-four. They were childless.[31]

Now on her own, Mary Bibb knew she had to draw on whatever resources she had in order to maintain herself. She continued teaching. Boston abolitionist and journalist Benjamin Drew toured Canada West in 1855 to assess the condition of life of the Blacks living there. He found Mrs. Bibb teaching: "Mrs. Mary E. Bibb, widow of the late lamented Henry Bibb, Esq., has devoted herself to teaching a private school in Windsor, and with good success. During the last spring term, she had an attendance of forty-six pupils, seven of whom were white children."[32] ...

Mary Bibb's last school was her most successful. Again, because it was a private school, the government had no hand in its affairs. From the time Mary Bibb arrived in Canada, she intended to open a private school supported by the parents of her pupils. Her first school did not last. Her experience with the Sandwich government school certainly may have reinforced her desire to have as little as possible to do with the government. The success of her last school suggests her determination to be free and independent from the government.

For the many years that Mary Bibb taught in Canada she was acutely aware that the powers-that-be meant for Blacks to be placed firmly at the bottom of society's ladder. Inferior education was one way to ensure this outcome. Her continued efforts to provide schooling for Black children were battles against racist practices. Maybe one reason that Bibb gave up teaching was because she was tired, physically and mentally. Tired to be constantly fighting a racist society that kept shutting the doors of opportunities in the face of Black people. ...

Mary Bibb was committed in her efforts to bring about the destruction of American slavery and the eradication of the racism faced by the Black community in Canada. She taught school because her skills as a teacher were indispensable to a community that was victimized by racism, a community that was poor and needful of such skills. She taught not only because she was trained to but because she considered it her duty. She believed that with education her race would be "strengthened and elevated."[33]

Notes

Excerpted from Afua P. Cooper, "Black Women and Work in Nineteenth-Century Canada West: Black Woman Teacher Mary Bibb," in *"We're Rooted Here and They Can't Pull Us Up": Essays in African Women's History* (Toronto: University of Toronto Press, 1994), by Peggy Bristow, Co-ordinator, Dionne Brand, Linda Carty, Afua Cooper et al. Reprinted with permission of the author.

1. I have discussed my research for Mary Bibb and the methodological problems encountered in the construction of the story of marginalized peoples in Afua Cooper, "The Search for Mary Bibb, Black Woman Teacher in Nineteenth-Century Canada West," *Ontario History* 83, no. 1 (March 1991), 39–54.
2. Henry Bibb's mother, Mildred Jackson, was an ex-slave from Kentucky. Bibb arranged for her to be taken from the south after she obtained her freedom. She came to live with him in Boston and then later in Canada West. C. Peter Ripley, ed., *The Black Abolitionist Papers*, vol. 2 (Chapel Hill: University of North Carolina Press, 1986), 110, 221 (hereafter *BAP).*
3. The Fugitive Slave Law was a "compromise" bill, passed in the American Congress to appease its slaveholding members and supporters, which granted slaveholders the right to hunt down and capture their escaped slaves. But before 1850, factors other than the FSL were pushing free Blacks out of both the North and South. Discriminatory racial practices made life for free Blacks very difficult. For a discussion of this slave code and its effects on Black people in the United States, see Herbert Aptheker, *A Documentary History of the Negro People in the United States, From Colonial Time to the Founding of the NAACP in 1910* (New York: Citadel Press, 1951), 220. For conditions of free Blacks by 1850, see Leon F. Litwack's *North of Slavery: The Negro in the Free States, 1790–1860* (Chicago: University of Chicago Press, 1961); and Ira Berlin, *Slaves Without Masters: The Free Negro in the Antebellum South* (New York: Pantheon Books, 1974).
4. *BAP*, 110–16.

5. Well before the Fugitive Slave Law, discriminatory laws had pushed many free Blacks from the American republic. However, the FSL exacerbated the already tenuous position of many free Blacks. Thousands chose to leave. Thousands came to Canada.
6. "Two weeks after President Fillmore signed the Fugitive Slave Bill, a Pittsburgh dispatch to the *Liberator* stated that 'nearly all the [Black] waiters in the hotels have fled to Canada … They went in large bodies, armed with pistols and bowie knives, determined to die rather than being captured.'" "The members of a Negro community near Sandy Lake in northwestern Pennsylvania, many of whom had farms partly paid for, sold out or gave away their property and went in a body to Canada." For these and other quotes, see Fred Landon, "The Negro Migration to Canada after the Passing of the Fugitive Slave Act," *Journal of Negro History* (1920), 24–5.
7. The "uplifting" of the race was a nineteenth-century philosophy espoused by the Black middle class. It was felt by members of this class that those Blacks, female and male, who had some money and education, and most assuredly those who were freeborn, should help their less privileged sisters and brothers. Mary Bibb belonged to this Black middle class and she too subscribed to "race uplift"; therefore, given her beliefs and her relatively privileged origin and position, she was a ready and willing candidate to start a school. For a discussion on "race uplift," see Linda Perkins, "Black Women and Race Uplift Prior to Emancipation," in F.C. Steady, ed., *The Black Woman Cross-Culturally* (Cambridge, MA: Schenkman Books, 1981), 317–34.
8. Mary Bibb had much more formal education than her husband, and so it can be safely concluded that she was involved in the production of the paper. *BAP,* 110–1.
9. Ibid., 108.
10. *The Voice of the Fugitive* is available on microfilm at the Robarts Library of the University of Toronto, Toronto's Metro Reference Library, the Archives of Ontario (Toronto), and in other locations in the province.
11. J. George Hodgins, *Documentary History of Education in Upper Canada,* vol. 9 (Toronto: L.K. Cameron, n.d.), 38.
12. Alexander Muray, "Canada and the Anglo-American Anti-Slavery Movement" (PhD diss., University of Pennsylvania, 1960), 329.
13. Ibid., 328.
14. *The Voice,* 9 April 1851; Daniel Hill, *The Freedom-Seekers, Blacks in Early Canada* (Agincourt, ON: Book Society of Canada, 1981), 149; Jason H. Silverman, *Unwelcome Guests* (New York: Faculty Press, 1985), 130.
15. See "Petition to the Coloured Inhabitants of Simcoe," December 1850, to Egerton Ryerson, RG2 C6C, Archives of Ontario; Murray, "Canada and the Anglo-American …," 238–333.
16. Hill, *Freedom-Seekers,* 156.
17. Conditions were wretched in many of the province's fledgling schools, but there was hope of improvement as the state began to take education more seriously and to allot more money for the education of its young. However, race was a crucial factor in this process; over time, in many of the Black separate schools, conditions worsened. Lack of government financial support was one of the factors responsible. *BAP,* 97–8.
18. Amelia Freeman and Mary Ann Shadd were two other Black women who founded schools for Black children in Canada West. *BAP,* 185–6, 489–90.
19. Susan Houston and Alison Prentice, *Schooling and Scholars in Nineteenth-Century Ontario* (Toronto: University of Toronto Press, 1988), 61.
20. Mary Bibb writing to Horace Mann, 20 January 1853, Horace Mann Papers, Massachusetts Historical Society, Boston.

21. *The Anti-Slavery Bugle,* 12 April 1851. The issue of unpaid labour was one that plagued several Black teachers during their tenure. Teachers Julia Turner and Amelia Freeman sometimes taught for little or no wages during many of their teaching years. This question of unpaid labour should be fitted into the broader subject of women, work, class, and ethnicity in the nineteenth century.
22. *Bugle,* 4 October 1851.
23. *The Voice,* 29 January 1852.
24. Bibb to Mann.
25. "The scattering of Negro families in many cases made it more difficult for them to organize and keep a school of their own." Donald G. Simpson, "Negroes in Ontario from Early Times to 1870" (PhD diss., University of Western Ontario, 1971), 377; Mary Ann Shadd, writing to George Whipple about her Windsor school, stated: "This being very near to the U.S., the fugitive population has been of a transient character, many remaining so long as they can make further arrangements for the interiors so that the school has been somewhat affected by it." Mary Ann Shadd to George Whipple, 3 April 1852, American Missionary Association Papers, Amistad Research Center (AMA-ARC), Tulane University, New Orleans.
26. See Benjamin Drew, *Narratives of the Fugitive Slaves in Canada* (Boston: Jewett and Company, 1856), 321–2.
27. Hill, *Freedom-Seekers,* 210; *The Voice,* 13 August 1851.
28. Many Blacks in Canada West, given the hostile racial environment they lived in, soon became attracted to Black emigration beyond the North American continent. West Africa and the Caribbean were two favoured places for emigration. Two influential advocates of the emigrationist cause were Martin Delaney and James Theodore Holly. Mary Bibb was an officer at the National Emigration Convention held in 1854 in Cleveland, Ohio. *BAP,* 34–5, 437.
29. For some details on the work that Mary Bibb did with her husband, see Floyd Miller, *The Search for a Black Nationality* (Urbana: University of Illinois Press, 1975), 145; William and Jane H. Pease, *Black Utopia* (Madison: Madison State Historical Society of Wisconsin, 1963), 109–22; *BAP,* 111; Hill, *Freedom-Seekers,* 179, 210; and Peter Carlesimo, "The Refugee Home Society: Its Origin, Operations, and Results, 1851–1876" (MA thesis, University of Windsor, 1973).
30. Blacks in Canada celebrated 1 August to commemorate the *Emancipation Act of 1833.* By this Act, slavery was abolished throughout the British Empire. *BAP,* 95.
31. Henry Bibb had a daughter, Frances, from his first marriage with Malinda Bibb.
32. Drew, *Narratives,* 321–2. The question of the precise location of Mary Bibb's second school is ticklish. In her letter to Horace Mann, she informs him that the school is in Sandwich (she does not say if she means the village or the general township). Her assistant, Matilda Nichols, in a letter to her sister, revealed that she had to walk four miles from Windsor where she boarded with the Bibbs to Sandwich (the village) where the school was. Yet both Benjamin Drew (1855) and William Wells Brown (1861) in their eyewitness accounts informed us that Mary Bibb's school was in Windsor. Perhaps this vexing issue can be resolved as follows. We can give primacy to Bibb's and Nichols's letters, as they are more authoritative, and infer from them that the school was started and kept for a while in Sandwich; and speculate that, after Nichols's departure in July 1853, Bibb moved the school to Windsor, where her home was. This would match Drew's and Wells Brown's description of the school's location. See also Nichols to Fuller, 15 July 1853, AMA-ARC; and William Wells Brown in *BAP,* 478.
33. From an editorial in *The Voice,* 15 January 1851.

Part II

Education and Activism

Chapter Five

Black Women in Graduate Studies:

Transforming the Socialization Experience

Dolana Mogadime

The institutional climate at the departmental level in higher education poses particular challenges to Black women and other women of Colour[1] who are graduate students and faculty. Canadian Black feminists and other racial minority women scholars have produced a body of critical literature that highlights these challenges despite the fact that mainstream Canadian higher educational literature hasn't engaged these experiences in serious or substantive ways.[2] The work of Black feminists and other feminists of Colour in Canada, which carefully documents their "outsider-within" locations at the margins of academia, has done much to fill this gap.[3] Dionne Brand, Linda Carty, Himani Bannerji and Patricia Monture-Angus have all reflected on their experiences of academia as both graduate students and faculty in Canada.[4] These critical reflections demonstrate how autobiographical narrative is important because they document how social relations in academia have constituted Black women and women of Colour as Other. These authors stress how their experiences of the social world in academia is different than their White colleagues' because of their racial and gender locations, and they contextualize how these positions "cast a different angle"[5] on the problem of the White masculinist middle-class hegemony of the university environment.

The unacceptable low level of racial inclusion of Black women and other women of Colour as faculty in higher educational institutions has been a pressing subject of discussion raised by these scholars. For example, Linda Carty describes her work as a Black woman teaching at the university level as "extremely rare" and questions the view of White women who see her presence as evidence of "the strides feminism and 'non-white' women are making."[6] Elaborating on the problem of being the only non-White faculty in her department, Himani Bannerji delineates the alienation, frustration and limits it poses. In an account of her experience fighting for greater self-representation of women of Colour in institutions, Bannerji asserts, "We, non-white women, have to be there in large numbers to make our point."[7] Similarly, Sherene Razack urges a more critical examination of the problem "that an overwhelming majority of professions are white."[8]

In this chapter, I provide a critique of the institutional constraints and limitations that contribute to the oppressive reproduction of Black women who are located at the margins of academia. A study I undertook with students in an MA/MEd and PhD program at two universities points to the role that the professional social environment and socialization process play in the development of academic careers. Questions about why there are such low numbers of Black women and other women of Colour faculty appointed in Canadian institutions need to connect to the issues that arise from this socialization process. The research shows how this socialization process both supports and discourages the ambitions of Black women and students who want to pursue and establish academic careers. Further, it points out possible ways to increase the participation of Black women and other women of Colour as graduate students and faculty members.

At the same time, it is important to acknowledge that Black women and other women of Colour are not a homogenized group and that barriers to both a successful graduate career and faculty participation are experienced differently. For example, in the history of the two institutions where my study was conducted, a Black women had not yet been hired into the tenure stream at the time when I undertook the research in 1998, whereas women of Asian and South Asian cultural backgrounds had been hired, even though this was a smaller number in comparison with White women faculty. I initiated my research to study these discrepancies and better understand the experiences of Black women and other women of Colour in higher education. Ten Black women and other women of Colour[9] participated in the in-depth conversational interviews; however, as the research proceeded, it became apparent that Black women students faced a different set of constraints which required a more-focused scrutiny. The lack of Black female faculty in these two Ontario universities signalled the possibility that there are particular constraints that Black women as graduate students might undergo in the academic socialization process as well as in the faculty hiring process upon completion of their degrees.[10]

In order to understand the particular socialization process Black women experience during their graduate studies from the standpoint of the students themselves, I analyzed the everyday experiences of five Black women in graduate school. I integrate the standpoint of these students as a methodological approach to better understand how their experiences are structured within power relations or "relations of ruling,"[11] which have eventually contributed to their erasure as participating faculty.

As Vijay Agnew points out, feminists have argued for quite some time now that "all analyses stem from specific identities and locations." In other words, "who one is and what one's relationship to the subject under investigation are issues that determine both one's questions and, to some extent, one's answers about the subject."[12]

My desire to study the experiences of other women like myself who are Black, grew out of my own struggles to "thrive in and survive" graduate school. The questions that I asked of the participants were the same questions that I had asked myself: What inspired you to study at the graduate level? (Or, why are you here?) Why did you choose the particular discipline you are enrolled in? What have your experiences been like in this discipline? Have you been able to fully explore your interests within the confines of the discipline? Has the discipline shaped your current research interests or have you asserted your own? How does your gender, race, class or cultural background influence the choices you make in relation to your interests? (Or who are you here for — yourself or your community?) What kind of support from professors have you received in relation to your interests? Do you envision an academic career after you successfully defend your thesis or dissertation? If not, then what do you perceive your professional ambitions to be after graduate school? Do you feel you are receiving adequate preparation for that now? Do you have a mentor or someone that supports your academic career? As Canadian mainstream research literature on higher education is silent on the issue of Black women aspirants and academics alike, I consider my work to be a contribution that extends this largely U.S.-based literature into the Canadian context.

Perspectives of Black Women Students

In my political activist work as a graduate student serving on tenure-stream hiring committees and pushing for the hiring of Black faculty and faculty of Colour, I became cognizant of the subtle process that calls into question the implementation of equity in employment along racial lines. When three tenure-stream positions were filled by White women, I became the lone student voice, insisting on the need to change what I openly named and critiqued as "the homogenous White face of the faculty." In a committee of seven, mine became the decisive vote (withstanding the resistance of faculty who contested student involvement) in favour of hiring the Black candidate.

I also objected to the ways in which White graduate students in my program were actively supported and primed for academic positions while Black graduate students were not, although I only made these objections to my fellow Black graduate colleagues (both high school and elementary teachers) who recognized these practices of exclusion. We were critical among ourselves about the allocation of course directorships along racial lines that favoured White students. It was a common practice at the university I was attending for MA/MEd students to be awarded a teaching assistantship in their first term followed by a course directorship, teaching the same course in the second term. However, Black graduate students were never awarded the directorship positions. We remained as teaching assistants throughout our graduate studies. One Black student (who was an experienced high school teacher) protested but was never awarded a directorship.

These events took place between 1994 and 1996. At the time, I was not aware of higher education literature that critiqued the racial differences in the socialization process that supports graduate students in their pursuit of an academic career. Experience told me, however, that White students were being given course directorship opportunities or experience which would enhance their applications as viable and experienced faculty hires, whereas Black graduate students were being shut out. I have now come to understand opportunities like course directorships as "opportunities for professional socialization." Caroline Sotello Viernes Turner and Judith Rann Tompson's study of graduate women students contrasts the racial differential access to opportunities for professional socialization between students of Colour and White students.[13]

In addition to witnessing these racial differential preferences first hand, my experience on the hiring committee, where I observed the reproduction of Whiteness in the hiring process, eroded my own belief that Canadian universities (and graduate faculty of education departments in particular) really want the racial inclusion that they purport in their advertisements (which uniformly "encourage minority" candidates to apply). In fact, these inequitable situations made me seriously call into question my own academic aspirations when I initially began my PhD studies in 1997. This, coupled with the lack of a single tenure-stream Black woman faculty hire at the educational institution I was attending, made me question my very presence in the program.

When I began the research project with Black women graduate students, neither junior nor senior Black women faculty (tenured stream or tenured) existed in our institution. The fact that not one Black woman before me had as yet surmounted the barrier of inclusion caused me to question the viability of Black women's aspirations and endeavours to pursue academic careers to begin with. In the spring of 1999, Njoki Nathani Wane and Rose Folson made history at the OISE/UT by becoming the first and second tenure-stream Black women hired. It is both remarkable and astounding that Black women have only recently been permitted entry into the academy as faculty at one of Canada's leading graduate schools of education. Though my research is placed before the advent of this transformative moment in OISE/UT's institutional history, it is important to mark the struggles that have specifically arisen out of the lack of our own representation as "the knower," "the academic" and "the professor." My experience provides a particular view about the implications of this new "historical" position for the consciousness, aspirations, hope and wholeness of the Black woman student. In breaking historical barriers, these two Black women academics embody a new entry point where Black women students can begin to imagine what recently seemed unimaginable.

Professional Socialization: Adding Black Women to the Equation

Traditionally, the professional socialization of graduate students has been conceptualized as one that "ensur[es] that entering students undergo a transformation of identity, so that they leave the program ready to fill the role and status of academic professionals."[14] Turner and Thompson further suggest that "socialization is the process by which a person learns the ways of a group in order to become a functioning participant." In their discussion about higher education literature, which focuses on analyzing the socialization of graduate students, they describe it as a process that "typically involves a lengthy period of adult socialization in cognitive skills, appropriate attitudes toward research and scholarship and field-specific values." While Turner and Thompson acknowledge that both "minorities and women" come to graduate programs with backgrounds that might actually conflict with the traditional dominant White male culture of the university, they argue that "opportunities for successful socialization" are critical for both "a successful graduate career" and for "a successful academic career."[15]

In support of their argument, the authors identify the following three stages as being crucial to the socialization of doctoral women:

(1) anticipatory socialization, recruitment, and choice of field,

(2) occupational entry and induction focusing on extensive formal training in graduate school including attendance in classes, advising, preparation for exams and dissertation, internships, mentoring, publishing, presenting, and getting a job, and

(3) faculty role continuance or retention.[16]

Using these stages as a theoretical basis, Turner and Thompson's study compares the access to "socialization opportunities" between "minority" and "majority" women doctoral students. Their findings from interviews with thirty-seven "minority" women doctoral students and twenty-five "majority" doctoral women students report that "minority" women in general had fewer opportunities for professional socialization experiences than majority women, that "the social environment for majority women was generally much richer," that "more majority women had apprenticeship and mentoring experience," and that "more frequently they (majority students) reported the presence of support networks inside their departments."[17]

Similarly, the questions I asked the five participants (Janine, Tricia, Patricia, Alexis and Elaine)[18] about their professional socialization were designed to explore their interactions with the conditions of their social environment. While the questions I asked singled out faculty student relations, such as opportunities for mentoring as important influences in the socialization process, I also invited the participants to narrate or provide descriptive accounts of classroom relations with professors and relations with other students that centred on the choice of a discipline. The method I chose to use was informed by Eric Margolis and Mary Romero's and Mary Romero and Debbie Storrs's studies of how graduate women of Colour experience professional socialization in graduate sociology programs, the purpose being to "uncover elements of the curriculum and professionalization process that have long remained hidden." That is, "(t)he students of Color [they] interviewed for [their] study reveal in particular how the graduate school curriculum in sociology not only produces professional sociologists, but also simultaneously (re)produces gender, race and other forms of inequality."[19]

The Hidden Curriculum

The significance of Morgolis and Romero's study (as the authors themselves point out) is that the ways in which women of Colour experience the hidden curriculum in sociology also "suggest patterns of interaction with intended and unintended consequences that make it particularly difficult for students of Color, women and students from working-class backgrounds to survive and thrive in graduate school."[20] The authors argue that the subjective position of the women of Colour in their study help to distinguish two aspects that are central to the operation of the hidden curriculum in graduate school: the "weak form" and the "strong form." The weak form refers to the "professional process" that is essential to becoming a sociologist, this includes becoming astute in a theoretical knowledge of sociology and the internalization of a professional self-image (this idea reflects Turner and Thompson's ideas on "successful graduate socialization" discussed earlier).

Margolis and Romero as well as Egan are more critical than Turner and Thompson in terms of highlighting how this process of professional socialization holds possibilities for eroding or lowering students' self-esteem. For example, the two former studies suggest that graduate students have to undergo "status degradation" as they are "stripped of their past identities"[21] and have to acquire a "new identity and intellectual perspective (that) suggests that old identities, beliefs and values must be unlearned and abandoned."[22] Egan describes this process as "resocialization."[23] While Turner and Thompson briefly touch on the problem of how women of Colour bring experiences that contrast with this socialization process, Margolis and Romero pay greater attention to how graduate women of Colour interact, negotiate and form strategies "for creating alternative professional identities and skills ... by which resistance becomes an alternative socialization process."[24] My analysis of Black women in Women's Studies also indicates this same process and thus attempts to continue "a dialogue on graduate school socialization practices that go far beyond sociology departments," as Margolis and Romero suggest.[25]

Margolis and Romero's description of the second aspect of the hidden curriculum again highlights the racially differential ways in which women of Colour interact with university learning. They describe the "strong form" of the hidden curriculum as "reproducing(ing) inequality through the exclusion of racial/ethnic issues from the curriculum." In my study of Black women in Women's Studies, I explore the ways that White feminists can control the Women's Studies university curriculum and feminist theory in general. This control can sometimes (unintentionally or intentionally) reproduce a hidden curriculum that marginalizes the research interests Black women bring to their academic work. The critiques by Black women and other women of Colour, writing as both professors and students, in this study and elsewhere,[26] demonstrates how "non-White" women's interests become positioned on the periphery of a liberal White feminist intellectual project.[27]

At the same time, it is important to note that the interviews I conducted with Black women students demonstrated that these processes of marginalization varied not only between women who attended different institutions but even between students who were located in the same department. That is, as the students' stages of progress changed (from initial entry to attending classes, to writing qualifying exams and fulfilling dissertation requirements) so did their decrease or increase of marginality within the program. For instance, working at the advanced stage of the program with a supervisor who was willing to engage with both issues of race theory and gender theory, changed the experience of students significantly. This suggests that while there are White feminist professors who were/are politically wedded to a racially exclusive feminist project and are not willing to undergo the kind of transformation that is necessary in order to accommodate the interests of Black women,[28] there are also White feminist professors who were/are critical of the ways in which a White liberal feminist project reproduces the marginality of Black women and other women of Colour.[29]

Feminist professors who have exerted agency in questioning the socially constructed power/knowledge basis within feminist theorizing, which holds up White women's experiences as representative of the universal woman in Women's Studies,[30] have also negotiated with the curriculum. Interactions with these professors has not only inspired Black women to study feminism but has supported their academic work in the field of Women's Studies.

Socialization in Women's Studies

The literature on graduate women students identifies choice of discipline as a significant socialization factor. Keeping this in mind, I approached women students in an integrated Women's Studies program. Some of the Black women students I interviewed chose this specialization (or concentration) in their graduate studies because of a general feeling of self-empowerment, which they experienced at the undergraduate level.[31] Janine explains:

> I borrowed a book from a friend who was in a Women's Studies course on post-colonial women's literature. After reading the book, I loved it so much that I decided to take a Women's Studies course, and taking that Women's Studies course changed my life forever. Here was this discipline that I had intuitively wanted to do. I wanted to question knowledge production [in a major field of study], I wanted to challenge things that I knew I couldn't accept but I didn't really have the language to talk about it or to articulate exactly why it didn't wash with me. And this course, the Women's Studies course, and the whole perspective gave me a language through which I could be critical of things that I always knew experientially in my everyday experiences as a Black woman but couldn't really name or explain. So ... I decided to go to graduate school because I wanted to develop the language of critique.

Similarly, Alexis expresses her interest in pursuing Women's Studies as a means to claiming agency in knowledge production, which clearly features the subjectivity of the Black woman at the centre of feminist analysis:

> The support and encouragement that I got in my undergraduate degree [in Women's Studies] had a lot to do with considering graduate school. I ended up doing an independent study that was focused on the construction of Black women's sexuality. And feeling very passionate about Women's Studies had a lot to do with the interdisciplinary choice.

Students' race, class, gender and social locations influenced the kind of knowledge production they were pursuing and the expectations they had when they entered into a graduate Women's Studies program, as Alexis explains:

> Women's Studies is a particular area where I can try and work or make a contribution to work that is attempting to synthesize class, race, gender, sexuality, colonialism and power ... It's an environment where I think that I can find the tools to do some good work.

However, as these students changed university settings and programs, they were exposed to different Women's Studies departments, and the graduate climate proved to be remarkably contradictory to their undergraduate experience. The students were decidedly more critical of what they viewed as "liberalism" in their departments, which, as Janine points out, has been "moving towards bringing in Black students [and other] students of Colour into the program and Women's Studies [especially at the master's level], but not doing the necessary work to prepare for the students." That is, the students came across the limitation of a liberalized agenda that purports inclusivity by counting the numbers of Black students and students of Colour as evidence of change. This approach left intact both the need for the reworking of the curriculum to reflect the growing diversity in their department as well as the problem of a homogenous White female faculty whose own research agenda didn't seriously consider how issues of race and class intersect with gender.

Marginality in the Feminist Classroom

For these students, the feminist classroom became a site where conflicts in feminism were played out in ways that left them seriously disillusioned with feminism. As they challenged Black women's marginalization in the discipline of Women's Studies and questioned the construction of feminism as White, they experienced the classroom as a site of contestation. As Janine explains of her classroom experience:

> There was no room for the kind of knowledge and experience that I wanted to bring. Because somehow, I don't know why, but White liberal feminists [in my department] wanted to legitimate their own project ... they didn't really want to deal with us and what we would bring. I don't know if they just expected us to come and shut up or if we were supposed to be so grateful to be there that we were not going to say anything that spoke to who we were and where we came from.

Alexis reported that when she insisted on a theoretical analysis that integrates race with gender issues, she was shut down:

> Sometimes I think I might talk too much in class and there are limitations in doing that ... for instance you get boxed in. So that when you speak [about race], you're thought of as speaking from a particular position. In this way what you say gets boxed into representing a way of thinking and it's easy to shut you off.

Alexis acknowledges that her racial location informs the interpretive lenses she brings to classroom discussions, and she clearly sees that when she speaks from this perspective it is easily dismissed in the classroom by the feminist professor. Black feminists and other women of Colour have argued for some time that their position as "outsider-within," as marginal intellectuals whose social locations provide them with a particular perspective on self and society, has influenced their insistence that race should be taken seriously within feminist analysis.[32] In fact, Maxine Baca Zinn and Bonnie Thornton Dill argue that "multiracial feminism encompasses several emergent perspectives developed primarily by women of Colour: African Americans, Latinas, Asian Americans, and Native Americans." Although they represent very different histories and cultures, Baca and Dill support the view that "our feminisms cohere in their treatment of race as a basic social division, a structure of power, a focus of political struggle and hence a fundamental force in shaping women's and men's lives."[33]

Yet inherent in Alexis's account of being "boxed in" or "shut down" in class is a description of the discomfort and isolation that results from not only speaking from her racial location but also from being the only Black in the classroom. Here she is left with the very difficult job of performing what she calls a "painful" task. She explains: "There is pain involved in having to explain racism and White supremacy in countries where originating stories stem from White settler colonies." In fact, Alexis explains the severity of the "pain" as causing enough impetus for her to consider dropping out of the graduate Women's Studies interdisciplinary degree all together. Hers is the experience of being on the receiving end of "the dominant group's exclusion from their inability to hear the voice of the marginalized." Alison Jones describes this as "silence in the ears of the powerful," and argues that this leads to the dominant group members' inability "to understand the speaker because they do not have the ears to hear."[34]

Tricia's narration of relations with White students in feminist classrooms reflects these relations of silence when the dominant group refuses to hear the marginalized's perspective:

> I had problems with this course, it was called "Women and Culture" ... they should have just labelled it "White Women and Culture" and it would have been just fine ... And there were times when I was actually butting heads with White

> women in the course who would swear that they had knowledge about blackness and Black history, so they would to some extent try to disempower me each time I opened my mouth. And this one White woman stopped talking to me because we disagreed in the class about *The Color Purple.*
>
> And her opinion was that the Black community was upset because Alice Walker had shown Shug and Celie as lesbian ... And I said I think that is, in fact, incorrect. I think most of the backlash had come from Black nationalism and Black men who had fundamental problems seeing themselves portrayed in such a negative manner, because I had done a paper about the negative portrayal of the abusive Black male. It wasn't about the perceived lesbian scene that took place between Shug and Celie, but she just couldn't or didn't want to see any other point of view, she just stopped talking to me ...

In some cases, Black students refuse in any way to participate in the dominant relations of power. For example in Carmen Luke's feminist classroom, indigenous students refused to speak and considered their silence as a "political strategic move to assert their identity by not giving 'the Black point of view' for the benefit of White students or the White teachers."[35] But Tricia and Alexis wanted to create a legitimate space for themselves in their feminist classrooms. They wanted to be the authors of a Black perspective that was heard and brought into the discussion. Yet their attempts were questioned by both the White feminist professor and the White students. By doing so, the teachers and students reinforced the relations of silence.

Classroom Dialogue and Pedagogical Practices

The Black women students were also highly critical of the dialogue in the classroom because it was taken up in ways that minimized intellectual exchange. Alexis elaborates:

> Those students who are aspiring towards an academic career are very obvious in class ... they seem to want to please the

> professor. Whatever she says, there isn't a sense of scholarly debate or a willingness to challenge ideas raised which might be contradictory.

Patricia also commented on the desire for greater intellectual engagement in the classroom:

> I've noticed the type of student she favours and they tend to be willing to listen and to be shaped by what she tells them. Whereas in my previous degree, I was with professors were up for the challenge of intellectual debates and disagreements.

The competitive nature of the classroom worked in subtle ways to encourage what the students described as "teacher pleasing." This is important to mention because it highlights how taking a contradictory position to that of the feminist professor played out in ways that became isolating for Black women. It puts into context Janine's comment that the "classroom was a battle zone," where she became "badgered" by the professor for expressing an oppositional position.

Instances like these might also reflect the professor's style of teaching and learning where students are expected to be the passive learners or "teacher pleasers" who reflect back the professor's positions. This "banking model"[36] of teaching was challenged by students who assumed an oppositional position not only to the pedagogical practices of the teacher but also to the curriculum material they used. This material was described as "racist" (Janine), "racially exclusive" (Tricia), "placing Black women and (other) women of Colour on the periphery" (Elaine), and "making gestures of inclusion with one or two articles by women of Colour" (Alexis).

These women wanted to construct new meaning from the course texts they had read and had critically interpreted. In a sense, they demanded an anti-racist approach to feminism that has gained favour in larger international curriculum transformation initiatives of Women's Studies curriculum.[37] However, the gap between the theory and rhetoric of an inclusive Women's Studies curriculum and the realities of their departments left these Black women students with serious doubts about their location in Women's Studies. The more they experienced the classroom as an unsafe place to pursue their critical enquiries, the more they started to question just who the feminist classroom was constructed for. In Janine's own words:

> I was so unhappy, I started to really question why I was there, because White students seemed content. But when I looked around, I saw that us Black women in the program were not very happy.

As a result, Janine and other students became highly dissatisfied with the White feminist critique of the androcentric knowledge base in academia, which expects equality with men while it is uncritical of the ways in which White women are complacent with the oppression of Black women and other women of Colour.[38] Rather than abandoning Women's Studies for this reason, as many Black women and other women of Colour have,[39] they chose instead to resist being socialized into a White liberal feminist agenda through counter-hegemonic strategies. For instance, Alexis pointed out that her research on Black women in aesthetic genres such as poetry and creative writing became a way that she could resist a hidden curriculum. In this way she fulfilled her aim to "not do something that is on line with the course content on [White] women and culture," which Tricia critiqued.

Alexis also mentioned that Black women students need to cultivate strategies to help them resist the reproduction of the hidden curriculum in order to pursue their interests:

> I can't say of Women's Studies students or even professors that they have read a large body of work by women of Colour or on Black feminism, so you just have to find a way to work within the system to be credited for the work that you have done and to forward it as much as you can into the agenda.

In order to direct their own research agenda during their course work and their dissertations so that it featured Black women at the centre of their projects, the students had to negotiate theoretical limitations that didn't include Black women's realities and at the same time "be politically and intellectually mature." However, this process required a level of confidence that not all the women had when they started their program. Along with a loss of self-esteem during the period of professional socialization, these graduate students also had to create their own voice through expressing dissidence with the theories of a White liberal feminist agenda.[40] Questioning one's relationship to the discipline where one is located can be an equally disempowering or empowering process.

Graduate Supervisors and Student Relations

The role of the graduate supervisor was central in supporting the students through their process of finding and maintaining a critical voice as a way to overcome marginalization within Women's Studies departments. Tricia explains the important role her supervisor played in her studies:

> They [liberal White feminists] don't want to be challenged, and if you challenge them, then all of a sudden you get labelled this or that. But I have to say in terms of my supervisor, and I know that I am very blessed compared with other Black women in my program ... I know that for whatever reasons, I mean I'm sure that there are vested reasons for me to do well where she is concerned, but she cares about me, you know what I mean? I don't know what would have happened if she wasn't around ... And she helps me to shape my work and in terms of [her] thinking and disrupting very essential notions of race, she tries to familiarize herself with what is current so that she can assist me.

Tricia recognizes and appreciates the professional development that her supervisor was willing to undertake in order to supervise her dissertation. However, not all the students could access feminist professors who could or would support them in their enquiries. For example, Janine narrated her struggles to find and keep a supervisor. Keeping control of her project so that it evolved in the way she wanted it to meant changing supervisors and extending the time for completing her degree. For Janine, the delays which resulted from making supervisory switches raised doubts as to whether or not she should complete her degree:

> I couldn't find a feminist who was also a critical race theorist ... They don't seem committed to changing the face of the faculty ... and a lot of women of Colour who are appointed to other departments, because the faculty is cross-appointed and they could be appointed to Women's Studies if they wanted to, [but] I know of women of Colour faculty, personally, who don't want anything to do with Women's Studies.

Inadequate support, which could quite possibly be a result of insufficient faculty development or even resistance (around issues of race and race relations), might contribute to (some) Black students abandoning their graduate degrees. Here, Black women students' disillusionment and disengagement with racially exclusive feminist practices in some Women's Studies departments mirrors the disillusionment of women of Colour who are faculty, as Janine has explained. The reproduction of a hidden curriculum has had the effect of making participation in this interdisciplinary specialization particularly unattractive to both Black women students and women faculty of Colour alike. As Tricia points out:

> I don't see anybody in my department having any power but White folks. What I see in my department is that power is centralized and it is in the hands of White women. I'm not making myself out to be a victim, but the real decision-making power is in their hands.

Participating in Change and Transformation

Despite the barrier of racial exclusivity within the structure of Women's Studies interdisciplinary degree programs, Black students persisted in their specialization because they had cultivated a critical stance which sought out productive transformations within Women's Studies. Instead of internalizing disengagement and disillusionment as an individual problem, they believed that they could contribute to changing the power relations by taking on initiatives through opportunities in course directorships (in Elaine's case), in their roles as tutorial leaders within a teaching assistantship capacity and in holding on to their own research agenda (with or without adequate support). In this way, the commonly identified academic "opportunities for socialization" that they were presented with, in order to become "inducted" into their disciplinary degree, were in fact reconceptualized to incorporate their resistance to and transformation of the racially exclusive practices in Women's Studies. For instance, while working as a course director in Women's Studies, Elaine restructured the curriculum for "The History of Colonialism in the Caribbean" course, which had been handed down to her. She did so by placing literature that was written by Black women and produced in the Caribbean on the reading list. In Elaine's own words, "That's how I fight, that's my resistance."

Tricia reflected on her role as a teaching assistant and a change agent:

> In terms of my role in the classroom and what I bring to the classroom around anti-racist work, I can see myself being useful in academia. As a political endeavour, I can see making changes in that arena and I have seen students benefiting from my presence there. And I have also seen that to a certain extent there can be resistance, I mean, I have seen White students resisting, clearly what they don't want to know and what they don't want to hear but I think we need more people that are really, really committed to that kind of teaching.

In her work as a teaching assistant in a classroom (outside the Women's Studies department) run by a woman professor of Colour, Tricia felt a sense of liberation and had the freedom to conceptualize the importance of anti-racist work in relation to the study of women's issues.

Lastly, attempts at transforming the privileging of a White feminist perspective were achieved by "writing" the experiences and histories of Black women into feminist knowledge production through their own dissertation research. Their research on Black women in the African Diaspora, Black women and immigration, and Black women, work and the professions (whether it be in the healthcare profession, the profession of teaching[41] or other labour sectors), took on a commitment to investigate the lived realities of Black women and the ways in which interlocking systems of oppression structure their lives. Their work contributes to a greater knowledge of African-Canadian communities and Black women's individual and collective struggles for equity and social justice.

Once they graduated, would the next stage of the academic career path of seeking a tenure-stream position seem obtainable to these women?[42] They responded to my query about the possibility of them carving out an academic career with a degree of ambivalence, even though they affirmed that they would, in fact, like to secure an academic appointment. For instance, Janine, who had "aspired to an academic career all her life," was left "shaken after graduate school" and really was "not so sure anymore." However, she did admit she would accept an academic position if it was offered to her. The women also identified conditions within the academic climate that rendered an academic life unattractive. For instance, they grappled with the gap between their communities and academia. Though they viewed their possible participation as a site for political work in redressing these divisions, they were also concerned about the possibility of working in an academic department as the sole representative *for* having the burden of assuming *the* Black woman's voice in the wilderness.

Himani Bannerji discusses the absence of collegial support among women of Colour faculty as an outcome of being the only woman of Colour in her department.[43] Graduate Black women academic aspirants have similar concerns. For example, they see how important it is for "institutions to develop anti-racist initiatives," such as the hiring of colleagues with similar interests in social justice and equity. Without these initiatives, as Tricia pointed out, "it would be difficult" for them "to envision working in academia on a daily basis."

Inclusion and Accountability

The socialization process that these Black women graduate students have gone through in Women's Studies points to the need for these departments in Canada to engage in rigorous self-critique. Transformations of Women's Studies departments have come from a growing willingness of women in positions of power as heads of departments and professors to reinterpret a curriculum that reflects the standpoint of White liberal middle-class women. It is widely accepted among feminists internationally that "the exclusion of women of Colour from feminist theory renders it incomplete and incorrect and perpetuates unacceptable applications of theory." However, the narratives of Black women in Women's Studies make it known that gaps remain between "knowing and acting upon our knowledge." Building bridges between knowing and acting or theory and practice involves ethics of personal accountability. Going beyond the acknowledgment of other voices, then, means "making a conscious commitment to choose change" and "to be accountable."[44]

Part of that accountability involves research. For instance, Margolis and Romero's study on women of Colour in sociology came out of "the Social Issues Committee of Sociologists for Women in Society (SWS), which had expressed concern that women of Colour graduate students and faculty were under-represented in sociological associations, including SWS itself." As

Margolis and Romero point out, their study "uncover[s] elements of the curriculum and professionalization process that have long remained hidden."[45] These aspects clearly function to reproduce forms of inequity in the socialization of the Black women students who participated in my study.

Here in Canada, the proceedings from the 1990 Canadian Women's Studies Association Conference reflect the "belief that diversity is an important characteristic of research in Women's Studies,"[46] yet there still remains a problematic gap between the recognition of the need for diversifying Women's Studies and the realities of programs. Further, there is a real deficit in relation to the development of a knowledge base that reflects accountability in relation to Black women and other women of Colour who are in these programs. For instance, there are many articles that document the actual process Women's Studies departments in the United States have undergone in order to transform the curriculum towards a more inclusive, multiracial representation.[47] Critiques on the need for change are not in shortage, yet Canadian literature, other than the criticism from Black women and women of Colour themselves, is silent on these issues.[48]

My research on Black women with consideration of other women of Colour in higher education grew out of the desire to question the issues and experiences surrounding racially different located groups in Canadian higher education. Knowledge about the socialization of women students who enter Women's Studies departments (and other broader departments, for that matter) needs to be interrogated in order to further understand the under-representation of Black faculty and other faculty of Colour in the larger university setting. This understanding should be raised within the context of equitable hiring policies in higher education and the movement towards policy change and accountability in academia.

Notes

1. It is well known that Black women in Canada represent heterogeneous cultural backgrounds spanning from Africa to the Carribean. While the common perception of Blacks in Canada is one of recent immigration, African-Canadian women historians inform us that Blacks have had a presence in Canada for over four hundred years. See Peggy Bristow, "Introduction," Peggy Bristow et al., *"We're Rooted Here and They Can't Pull Us Up": Essays in African Canadian Women's History* (Toronto: University of Toronto 1994), 3–12.

   I use the phrase "Black and other women of Colour" or "Black and other racial minority women" in order to acknowledge the ways in which the politics of racism in Canada simultaneously impacts on women who are racially marked in ways that both intersect and are very different. While I would affirm Chandra Talpade Mohanty's politics of alliance across racial differences in her assertion that "what seems to constitute women of Colour or third world women as a viable oppositional alliance is a common context of struggle rather than colour or racial identifications," I am also cognizant of the problem that Black women's particular experiences of racism run the possibility of becoming obscured behind use of the term "women of Colour." For an extended discussion of the term "women of Colour," see Chandra Talpade Mohanty, "Cartographies of Struggle," in Chandra Talpade Mohanty et al., eds., *Third World Women and the Politics of Feminism* (Bloomington: Indiana University Press, 1991), 7. For a discussion on the problem of finding a single term in naming a "suitable collective reference for a nonwhite female person," see Gwendolyn Etter-Lewis, "Introduction," in Gwendolyn Etter-Lewis and Michele Foster, eds., *Unrelated Kin: Race and Gender in Women's Personal Narratives* (Routledge: New York, 1995), 1–12.

2. See Himani Bannerji, "Racism, Sexism, Knowledge and the Academy," *Resources for Feminist Research* 20, no. 3/4 (1991), 5–11; Himani Bannerji, "But Who Speaks for Us? Experience and Agency in Conventional Feminist Paradigms," in Himani Bannerji et al., eds., *Settling Relations: The University as a Site of Feminist Struggles* (Toronto: Women's Press, 1991), 67–107; Himani Bannerji, *Thinking Through: Essays on Feminism, Marxism, and Anti-Racism* (Toronto: Women's Press, 1995); Dionne Brand, *Bread Out of Stone* (Toronto: Vintage, 1994); Linda Carty, "Women's Studies in Canada: A Discourse and Praxis of Exclusion," *Resources for Feminist Research* 20, no. 3/4 (1991), 12–18; Linda Carty, "Black Women in Academia: A Statement from the Periphery," in Bannerji et al., eds., *Settling Relations,* 13–44; Patricia Monture-Angus, *Thunder in My Soul: A Mohawk Woman Speaks* (Halifax: Fernwood, 1995). More recently, see Candace Bernard, Wanda Thomas Bernard, Chioma Ekpo, Josephine Enang, Bertyln Joseph and Njoki Wane, "She Who Learns Teaches Othermothering in the Academy: A Dialogue Among African Canadian and African Caribbean Students and Faculty," *Journal of the Association for Research on Mothering* 2, no. 2 (2000), 66–84.

For examples of American academics in the field of higher education, see Caroline Sotello Viernes Turner and Judith Rann Thompson, "Socializing Women Doctoral Students: Minority and Majority Experiences," *The Review of Higher Education* 16, no. 3 (1993), 355–70; Caroline Sotello Viernes Turner and Samuel L. Myers, Jr., *Faculty of Color in Academe: Bittersweet Success* (Boston: Allyn and Bacon, 2000). For American academics in sociology, see Eric Margolis and Mary Romero, "'The Department Is Very Male, Very White, Very Old, and Very Conservative': The Functioning of the Hidden Curriculum in Graduate Sociology Departments," *Harvard Educational Review* 68, no. 1 (1998), 1–32; Mary Romero and Debbie Storrs, "'Is That Sociology?': The Accounts of Women of Color Graduate Students in Ph.D. Programs," in D. M. Dulap and P. A. Schumck, eds., *Women Leading in Education* (Albany: State University of New York Press, 1995), 71–85.

3. Patricia Hill Collins uses the concept "outsider-within" status to theorize about the knowledge academics bring to their work who have traditionally been the outsiders to the discipline of sociology. Collins develops sociologist George Simmel's idea about the significance of the "stranger" who, among other things, "has the ability to see patterns that may be more difficult for those immersed in the situation to see." Collins argues that "Black intellectuals, especially those in touch with their marginality in academic settings, tap this standpoint in producing distinctive analysis of race, class and gender." See Patricia Hill Collins, "Learning from the Outsider Within: The Sociological Significance of Black Feminist Thought," *Social Problems* 33, no. 6 (1986), 514–34. Multiracial feminists have applied Collins's use of "outsider-within" to dialogue about themselves as "marginal intellectuals." See Maxine Baca Zinn and Bonnie Thornton Dill, "Theorizing Differences from Multiracial Feminism," *Feminist Studies* 22, no. 2 (1996), 324. Similarly the intellectual work of Black women and women of Colour in Canada is informed by "outsider-within" locations.

4. See Brand, *Bread Out of Stone,* 165–78; Carty, "Women's Studies in Canada," 12–18; Carty, "Black Women in Academia," 13–44; Bannerji, "Racism, Sexism, Knowledge," 5–11; Bannerji, "But Who Speaks for Us?" 67–107; Bannerji, *Thinking Through,* 97-118; Monture-Angus, *Thunder in My Soul,* 53–73.

5. Patricia Hill Collins, *Black Feminist Thought: Knowledge Consciousness and the Politics of Empowerment* (New York: Routledge, 1991).

6. Carty, "Black Women in Academia," 40–1.

7. Bannerji, *Thinking Through,* 116.

8. Sherene Razack, *Looking White People in the Eye: Gender, Race and Culture in Courtrooms and Classrooms* (Toronto: University of Toronto Press, 1998), 161.

9. Originally, when I began the study, I was interested in knowing the commonalities and differences between the experiences of graduate women of Colour as racialized and gendered subjects. With this intent in mind, I sought out representation from multiple racial and cultural locations. Hence six

students out of the ten were of African descent. Of these six, three were from the Caribbean, two were Carribean/African Canadians, and one was from East Africa. Of the remaining four women students, three were from South America (Chile, Guatemala and Brazil) and the last student was from a small Mediterranean island. However, for the reasons which I explain, I have chosen to focus on the experiences of the five Black women students in order to more fully understand the particular nuances of our lived realities in university settings. The narrative of Chris, the sixth Black woman student, is given in-depth analysis in Dolana Mogadime, "Contradictions in Feminist Pedagogy: Black Students' Perspectives," *Resources for Feminist Research,* forthcoming.

10. For a focus on Black women and the academy, see Bernard et al., "She Who Learns Teaches," 66–84; Ruth Farmer, "Place But Not Importance: The Race for Inclusion in Academe," in Ruth Farmer and Joy James, eds., *Spirit, Space and Survival: African American Women in (White) Academe* (New York: Routedge, 1993), 196–217; Dionne Brewer, "Giving Name and Voice: Black Women Scholars, Research and Knowledge Transformation," in Louis Benjamin, ed., *Black Women in the Academy: Promises and Perils* (Tampa: University of Florida, 1997), 68–80; Yolanda T. Moses, "Black Women in Academe: Issues and Strategies," in Benjamin, ed., *Black Women in the Academy,* 23–37.

11. Dorothy E. Smith, *The Everyday World as Problematic: A Feminist Sociology* (Boston: Northeastern University Press, 1987).

12. Vijay Agnew, *Resisting Discrimination: Women from Africa and the Caribbean and the Women's Movement in Canada* (Toronto: University of Toronto Press, 1996), 5.

13. Turner and Thompson, "Socializing Women Doctoral Students," 359.

14. Later in the chapter I discuss Janet Malenchek Egan's criticism of the internal process graduate students are required to undergo while participating in the "well-intended (professional) socialization process" in graduate school. See Janet Malenchek Egan, "Graduate School and the Self: A Theoretical View of Some Negative Effects of Professional Socialization," *Teaching Sociology* 17, no. 2 (1989), 200–17.

15. Turner and Thompson, "Socializing Women Doctoral Students," 356, 357.

16. Ibid., 357.

17. Ibid., 359.

18. The participants are referred to by pseudonyms.

19. Margolis and Romero, "The Department is Very Male," 2.

20. Ibid.

21. Ibid., 7.

22. Egan, "Graduate School and the Self," 201.

23. Ibid.

24. Margolis and Romero, "The Department is Very Male," 6.

25. Ibid., 2.

26. See Agnew, *Resisting Discrimination,* 5; Bannerji, *Thinking Through,* 64; Linda Carty, "Combining Our Efforts: Making Feminism Relevant to the Changing Sociality," in Linda Carty, ed., *And Still We Rise: Feminist Political Mobilizing in Contemporary Canada* (Toronto: Women's Press, 1993), 7-21; Juliana Nfah-Abbenyi, "Why (What) Am I (Doing) Here: A Cameroonian Woman?" in Margaret Gillett and Ann Beer, eds., *Our Own Agenda: Autobiographical Essays by Women Associated with McGill University* (Montreal: McGill-Queen's University Press, 1995), 250–61.

27. Multiracial feminists have described a White (liberal) feminist project as one that pays attention only to women's struggle to win equality with men and is not cognizant of the ways in which "'gender' is implicated in both creating and maintaining class and racist domination." See Bannerji, *Thinking Through,* 69; bell hooks, *Killing Rage: Ending Racism* (New York: Henry Holt, 1995), 99. In holding up the universal inequality of women in comparison to men, contradictions or differences among women become pushed to the margins. The criticism with this agenda then, is that it "becomes a cloak for smuggling in the interests of privileged (White middle-class) women" while silencing the representation of women of social difference from feminist theory. See Bannerji, *Thinking Through,* 70; hooks, *Killing Rage,*100. This has been widely termed as "exclusionary feminism" by multiracial feminists and has been the cause for conflicts and debates in feminism for quite some time now. See Mary Maynard and June Purvis, eds., *New Frontiers in Women's Studies: Knowledge, Identity and Nationalism* (Portsmouth, UK: Taylor and Francis, 1996). It is important to note here, as I attempt to do elsewhere, that my position in this chapter acknowledges the ways in which anti-racist feminist theory and pedagogy has worked towards redressing these conflicts. See Blanche Curry Radford, "On the Social Construction of a Women's Gender Studies Major," in Sara Muson Deats and Lauretta Tallent Lenker, eds., *Gender and Academe: Feminist Pedagogy and Politics* (Maryland: Rowman and Littlefield, 1994), 3–16; Frances Maher and Mary Kay Tetreault Thompson, *The Feminist Classroom: An Inside Look at How Professors and Students are Transforming Higher Education for a Diverse Society* (New York: Basic Books, 1994). However I maintain a critical stance in relation to practices that have not moved towards change, particularly as they affect Black women and other women of Colour in Women's Studies.

28. Nancy L. Aston, "Involving Faculty in Curriculum Transformation: Overcoming Resistance at Richard Stockton College," in Ellen G. Friedman et al., eds., *Creating an Inclusive College Curriculum: A Teaching Sourcebook From the New Jersey Project* (New York: Teachers College Press, 1996), 52.

29. Radford, "On the Social Construction," 9.

30. Mary Maynard, "Challenging the Boundaries: Towards an Anti-Racist Women's Studies," in Maynard and Purvis, eds., *New Frontiers in Women's Studies,* 12.

31. The experience of Women's Studies as a means to "self-empowerment" confirms the first goal Daphane Patai and Noretta Koertge, rate as uppermost, or number one, in a list of nine objectives considered essential for Women's Studies programs to provide for their students. See Daphane Patai and Noretta Koertge, *Professing Feminism: Cautionary Tales from the Strange World of Feminist Studies* (New York: Basic Books, 1994), 168.

32. Zinn and Dill, "Theorizing Differences from Multiracial Feminism," 324.

33. Ibid.

34. Alison Jones, "Pedagogy Desires and the Border: Absolution and Difference in the University Classroom," paper presented at Winds of Change: Women and the Culture of Universities Conference, University of Technology, Sydney, Australia, 1998, 13-14.

35. Carmen Luke, "Women in the Academy: The Politics of Speech and Silence," *British Journal of Sociology of Education* 15, no. 2 (1994), 222.

36. A "banking concept" of education as described by Freire, regards students as passive, manageable beings who work at storing the deposits of knowledge entrusted to them by their teacher. This positions the professor as the authorial knower or the subject of the learning process and students as the objects. Gaining favour with the professor, then, involves being willing to capitulate to or mimic the professor's ideas. Instead, students preferred or expected graduate studies to support them in developing a "critical consciousness" that allowed "their intervention in the world as transformers of the world." See Paulo Freire, *Pedagogy of the Oppressed* (New York: Continuum, 1993), 54. Towards the end of this chapter, in the section entitled "Participating in Change and Transformation," I discuss the critical consciousness students cultivated in order to reinterpret a Women's Studies education.

37. See Radford, "On the Social Construction"; Maher and Tetreault Thompson, *The Feminist Classroom;* Maynard, "Challenging the Boundaries."

38. hooks, *Killing Rage,* 99.

39. Collins, *Fighting Words,* 66; hooks, *Killing Rage,* 100.

40. Egan suggests that graduate students generally experience this loss of self-esteem during the professional socialization process. However I argue that Black women had the additional challenge of developing counter voices in their discipline of study. See Egan, "Graduate School and the Self," 202.

41. For a discussion of Black women in the profession of teaching, see Dolana Mogadime, "Black Girls/ Black Women-Centred Texts and Black Teachers as Othermothers," *Journal of the Association for Research on Mothering* 2, no. 2 (2000), 222–33.

42. Turner and Thompson, "Socializing Women Doctoral Students," 357.

43. Bannerji, *Thinking Through,* 116.
44. Radford, "On the Social Construction," 9, 10.
45. Margolis and Romero, "The Department Is Very Male," 2–4.
46. Sandra Kirby, "Introduction," in Sandra Kirby et al., eds., *Women Changing Academe: The Proceedings of the 1990 Canadian Women's Studies Association Conference* (1999), i–iv; see especially page ii.
47. Barbatra F. Luebke and Mary Ellen Reilly, *Women Studies: The First Generation* (New York: Routledge, 1995); Maher and Tetrault Thompson, *The Feminist Classroom.*
48. Bannerji, *Thinking Through,* 116; Bernard et al., "She Who Learns Teaches," 66–84; Carty, "Women's Studies in Canada," 12–17; Carty, "Combining Our Efforts," 7–18; Razack, *Looking White People in the Eye,* 161.

Chapter Six

Reconceptualizing Our Classroom Practice:

Notes from an Anti-racist Educator

Grace Mathieson

Our challenge, and it must be a collective challenge, is to transform educational systems as we know them today. One reason that the challenge must be a collective one between Aboriginal Peoples and Canadians, is that it is only in this way that we can break the patronizing, parochial and colonial nature of our educational relations. We must expose and denounce the racism.

— Patricia Monture-Angus, *Thunder in My Soul*

All of us educated in the mainstream, no matter whether we grew up in the Caribbean, North America, Britain, or Africa, have been educated from a colonialist perspective which has taught us to either disregard or disrespect the majority of non-White peoples on earth ... it is axiomatic that we reconceptualize what we teach and how we teach.

— ANNETTE HENRY,
Taking Back Control

THIS CHAPTER DISCUSSES how Black feminist perspectives can be used to transform Eurocentric curriculum and pedagogical practices. I write this as a White woman, an educator and an anti-racist activist. I also write as a single mother of two teenage children who are students in the educational system. I cannot separate these two parts of myself as I write, for they give me my voice and are the driving force that determine who I am and what I do. And as I write, I draw on the knowledge of Black feminists and other anti-racist activists to create a space of social transformation. They point out that this space can only be created by the resistance of systems of domination, the decolonization of people's minds and the creation of a transformation pedagogy. Like Patricia Monture-Angus and Annette Henry, I encourage educators to resist systems of domination by transforming the classroom into a space of social and racial justice.

This transformation cannot happen unless we are able to ask ourselves, as Nora Allingham does, "How can an education which teaches, implicitly and explicitly, that one culture, one religion and one colour deserve the most and the best, be good for anyone?"[1] All children need opportunities to learn about the knowledges, histories and perspectives of diverse cultures and peoples and to develop an awareness of the historical racism that exists in Canada and in the world. We can no longer deny, dismiss and ignore how an oppressive educational system affects students of colour.

Being connected to White histories of colonialism and imperialism and having been schooled, both formally and informally, within a Eurocentric worldview, I agree with Becky Thompson, a White anti-racist educator, that there is a feeling of living a double life — of being white and benefiting from privilege on the one hand, and opposing the ideology of whiteness in education on the other.[2] Yet I recognize that it would be less than honest to think that Whites who are doing anti-racist work are any less affected by our White privilege. Our positionality requires us to recognize that our privilege is based on our racial location and that as a racial group we are accorded an inequitable distribution of resources and power. As James Scheurich stresses, it is necessary to remind ourselves that "it does not matter whether we are a 'good' or a 'bad' White; all Whites are socially positioned as Whites and receive social advantages because of this positionality. No individual White gets to be an exception because of his or her antiracism."[3]

As bell hooks points out, "There must exist a paradigm, a practical model for social change that includes an understanding of ways to transform consciousness that are linked to efforts to transform structures."[4] As members of the dominant group we carry the legacy of racism with us, and although we may be conscious that we are not responsible for our historical racist roots and that racist thought and ideology are not something we invented, we need to critically self-reflect on the ways we are affected by and possibly invested in the very ideology of whiteness we oppose. At the same time, we need to understand how whiteness operates as a hegemonic force in our schools to oppress, exclude and silence the knowledges, experiences and histories of Aboriginal peoples and people of colour.

When we engage in a dialectical process of deconstructing Eurocentric hegemony and decolonizing our own minds, we are rethinking schooling and finding ways to transform our classrooms. We know that we cannot change the overall structure through our everyday teaching practices, and, as one of my professors frequently mentioned, the anti-racism work that one teacher does in one classroom can be undone by another teacher in another classroom. Yet in spite of this, anti-racist educators recognize the power we have in the classroom to make a difference in our students' lives. As Paulo Freire states, "We have to believe that if men and women created the ugly world that we are denouncing, then men and women can create a world that is less discriminatory and more humane."[5]

Black Feminist Theory

Black feminist educators and critical theorists understand the importance of promoting an alternative, more humane worldview to bring about change in society and in education. As bell hooks describes it:

> How do we create an oppositional worldview, a consciousness, an identity, a standpoint that exists not only as that struggle which also opposes dehumanization but as that movement which enables creative, expansive self-actualization?[6]

Black feminists have constructed an alternative body of knowledge, grounded both in their collective history of oppression and their struggle to envision and create an Afrocentrism that reflects their political commitment to constructing positive African-centred worldviews. Black feminists have long advocated the need to articulate a Black feminist standpoint that speaks to their own particular history and experiences, while simultaneously acknowledging the rich diversity and difference among themselves.

When bell hooks wrote *Ain't I A Woman* in 1981, she found that not only was there very little written about Black women's experiences but also that racism and sexism were so entrenched that their experiences were dismissed as insignificant and unworthy of scholarly attention.[7] The literary works in existence at that time, written by Black males or White females, distorted Black women's stories and experiences through racist or sexist assumptions. Placing Black women's experiences within a feminist context, then, addresses the issue of authentic voice and power — Black feminists want to tell their own stories and unravel the negative effects that both race and gender have had on their past and present lives.

In Canada, Black history has not yet been established as a legitimate field of historical inquiry as it has in the United States.[8] That slavery and segregated schools existed in Canada is still not widely known among Canadians, and although Black communities date back several hundred years, their historical presence has been largely omitted from Canadian history. This leaves the erroneous impression that Blacks are relative newcomers to our country. Further, because Canada has been seen as a haven for runaway fugitives from the United States, an aura that Canadians are morally superior to their southern neighbours has been constructed. The myth is that we are not a racist society like the United States. The national image we have of ourselves as a multicultural society hides the deep racism that has run through this country since its conception.

Black feminists know that their histories and experiences have been and often continue to be silenced and undervalued in the educational curriculum. Incorporating an African-centred pedagogy is one approach to breaking down the narrow and hegemonic position that White and male constitute the normative in schools. An African-centred pedagogy promotes the development of a critical consciousness, so that history and structural power are analyzed within intersecting social locations, while at the same time promoting the development of an African worldview and legitimizing African knowledge. It is important, however, to keep in mind how easy it is to fall into privileging the male perspective over the female experience, even within the context of an African worldview. When we do this, we are continuing to oppress on the basis of gender.

If we want to strengthen our anti-racism educational practice, then we must pay attention to the ways that both race and gender shape our lives. Beverly Tatum states that although we all have multiple identities, "some dimensions of our identities are reflected more saliently than others — a distinction made apparent by the energy we invest in their examination."[9] As a Black woman, she explains, she has invested more time in thinking about what it means to be Black and female, in that order, than what it means to be heterosexual, able-bodied and middle class. This, she continues, is because these parts of her identity are most often reflected back to her as significant in the eyes of others. bell hooks relates that the forces of racism and sexism have been inseparable determining forces in her life.[10] Yet, unlike Black feminists, most white educators have invested little time in thinking about what it means to be White because it is reflected back to us by others as normal. To be White is to be Canadian, the standard, the universal measuring stick by which all others are measured. What we fail to understand, however, even though Black feminists have been telling us for decades, is just how oppressive this is for those who fall outside of the parameters of whiteness.

British writer Hazel Carby states that "the existence of racism must be acknowledged as a structuring feature of Black women's' relationship with White women."[11] She argues that Black women need to tell their own herstories through their lived realities and experiences of oppression, and that White women must write from their own experiences and acknowledge how they are simultaneously oppressor and oppressed. By doing so, we can explore the interconnections between the forces that shape our lives and the forces that shape Black women's lives; this, in turn, is key to shaping our respective worldviews. This understanding and perspective also shapes the relationships between Black students and their White teachers. It is essential that anti-racist educators understand the history of racism and how it has shaped Black–White relations over the decades, placing White in a position of privilege and power over Black. When we become aware of the power dynamics, we can change our perceptions of White as privileged and explore how White postionality affects the social construction of our knowledge, our understandings of ourselves, our world and our perception of the racialized Other. When we acknowledge that we speak, think and act from a privileged location, we break through White as normative and help to decentre White male authority — we can then grapple with how, as White women, we can oppress women of colour.

When we deconstruct white positionality, we unmask notions of liberal individualism that function to cover up power differences and maintain the status quo. bell hooks enthuses that Whites "have a deep emotional investment in the myth of 'sameness,' even as their actions reflect the primacy of whiteness as a sign informing who they are and how they think."[12] Through the ideology of individualism, many Whites tend to interpret racism as an individual belief rather than an institutional system supported by a collective worldview. Thus, it is common to hear Whites proclaim that we are all racist, meaning that we all have prejudiced attitudes. While the prejudiced attitudes of individuals cannot be denied, it is at once a denial of difference and of domination and feeds into the erroneous belief that equal opportunity exists.

Driven by a collective vision and a shared intellectual and political commitment, Black feminists are developing a Black women's standpoint that opposes the unjust practices and ideas of the White social hegemony. Patricia Hill Collins notes that "without a collectivity or group, there can be no critical social theory that aims to struggle with the realities confronting that group."[13] Many Black feminists attest to the strength and determination of Black women to give back to the community, to use their agency to create viable alternatives that reflect their Afrocentric worldviews. Heidi Safia Mirza states, "Valorizing their agency as subversive and transformative rather than as a manifestation of resistance, it becomes clear that black women do not just resist racism, they live 'other' worlds." She points to the strategy Black women in England use to do this — the creation of Black supplementary schools. The organization of these schools is a grassroots effort led mainly by Black women who want to resist mainstream schooling and provide an alternative way of being and knowing for Black students — a place where blackness "becomes the norm."[14] Their collective efforts are building social support networks that reflect the values, ideals and visions for redefining their world.

As educators we can participate in building links between the schools and Black communities. For example, an African-Canadian friend of mine is a yoga instructor who is working with Black youth in her community. She approached me about a Yoga for Youth program in my school. She had heard that yoga was being used in California with at-risk Black youth. Yoga strengthens the body and teaches breathing techniques and meditation that strengthen the students' abilities to concentrate and control anger. After a visit to the school to explain the benefits of yoga to both students and their parents, she began teaching yoga classes to ten and eleven year olds in the gym after school. Through storytelling and discussions, she stresses Afrocentric ideas; and through her program, she is building links with students in the school and the community.

Decolonizing the Mind

> Critically examining the association of whiteness as terror in the black imagination, deconstructing it, we both name racism's impact and help to break its hold. We decolonize our minds and our imaginations.
>
> — bell hooks,
> *Black Looks: Race and Representation*

Working from an anti-racist perspective involves readjusting the Eurocentric lens through which we view the world. It involves unlearning and relearning how we see, hear and read the world. We need to ask ourselves if we can recognize racist ideology when we hear it in conversations, when we see it in movies or read it in newspapers. If we can't recognize it in our everyday lives, we won't be able to recognize it when it emerges in the classroom, in the conversations of our students, in the films we view and in the textbooks we use. If we can't identify it, then we can't confront it, and it will continue to perpetuate in our classrooms. Not only do we, as teachers need to decolonize our thinking, we need to teach our students to decolonize theirs.

All of us who are White, even those of us who strive to be anti-racist, are affected by racist assumptions and thoughts. Becky Thompson contends that we are in fact "anti-racist racists" because we receive unearned privileges due to our whiteness, yet we are striving to become conscious of our racism and oppose White supremacy.[15] We need, as bell hooks asserts above, to "decolonize our minds and our imaginations." The first step in this process is to deconstruct our assumptions and viewpoints so we can better understand how racism and whiteness affect us as Whites and affect racialized Others. In this way, we may be able to understand our own complicity in an oppressive system; this insight is not meant to induce feelings of guilt or paralysis; it is meant to encourage us to open up to critical self-reflection.

In this process, it is important that we understand how Black women and Black students see us as White women and White educators. bell hooks argues that Whites have been "socialized to believe the fantasy that whiteness represents goodness and all that is benign and non-threatening." By contrast, Thompson asserts that in the Black imagination, whiteness is often associated with terror, "a power that wounds, hurts, tortures." She states that there is "a profound psychological impact of white racist domination" experienced by Blacks in response to the legacy of White domination. White people's inability to conceive of this terror, she holds, is itself an expression of White supremacy.[16]

White oppression extends beyond Black–White relations. Patricia Monture-Angus, an Aboriginal law professor, had to rush her eleven-month old son to the hospital when he fell and broke his arm. She was accused of child abuse by the doctors and separated from her son for eight days. When she explained to them that she was a law professor, she was laughed at by the doctors and questioned as to how frequently her husband beat her.[17]

As white educators we need to understand the power relations that exist in society and how these power relations have caused and continue to cause harm. To decolonize our minds is to understand how these power relations work. Issues of race, racism and whiteness are complex and deeply embedded in our everyday lives and social and political fabric. Nelson Rodriguez poses the question, "Do you really think it is possible to step fully outside of the history of racism, to remove ourselves from the way this history has inscribed itself on our bodies and in our very speech acts?"[18] Clearly, we can't. We can critique, challenge and deconstruct the colonized mind when we encounter it in ourselves and in the classroom, and we can teach our students to do the same. We can also do this by drawing on Black feminist thought and other anti-racist ideologies. By doing so, we are actively engaging in a more democratic and liberatory classroom practice.

Both Thompson and Rodriguez ask educators to rise to the occasion and reconceptualize a new curriculum that is inclusive and that challenges taken-for-granted Eurocentric and male-centred paradigms. To embark on such a project, I believe it is necessary to assess how we are situated in the colonial discourse and to ask ourselves in what ways we can engage in the transformative process of decolonizing our minds. We all choose different ways and avenues to engage in decolonization. I have chosen Black feminist theorizing as an entry point for my learning and teaching.[19]

Reconceptualizing Classroom Practice: Notes into Action

After teaching middle-school students for many years, I decided two years ago to teach younger students and accepted a position as a Grade 5 teacher in a public school, located in the north end of Toronto. I looked forward to working with younger students and to the challenge of developing an anti-racism curriculum in a multicultural school setting, and to creating a classroom that respected differences based on race, gender, class and sexuality.

Almost immediately, I began to moll over ideas of how best to deconstruct the ideology of racism with younger students and to develop in them a more critical consciousness. I wanted them not just to understand the historical roots of racism but to critically reflect on their own life experiences, and to apply their new learning to their own lives, thus deepening their awareness of themselves as multi-positioned subjects. As I began to work with the Grade 5 students, I was conscious that my anti-racism practice was privileging a male and mainly American perspective. I took on the challenge to make the curriculum more inclusive and to strengthen the focus on the Canadian context. I did this by infusing a Black feminist perspective and a stronger anti-racist feminist perspective into my everyday work.

Accomplishing this was much easier than I initially anticipated. There are many good resources available, and while there are teaching expectations that have to be met, there are no stipulations on the resources that can be used to meet these objectives. For example, a writing expectation is to have students write a non-fiction report based on their personal knowledge and information from a range of sources — the Internet, books, magazines and so on. I have purchased a variety of non-fiction books on Black history for my own classroom use, so that all students can research one Black historical or contemporary figure. Among these books are *Rosa Parks and the Montgomery Bus Boycott* by Teresa Celsi; *Mary Ann Shadd: Publisher, Editor, Teacher, Lawyer, Suffragette* by Rosemary Sadlier; *Brown Girl in the Ring* by Rosemary Brown; *A Picture Book of Sojourner Truth* by David A. Adler. While learning how to write a non-fiction report, students also learn of the struggles and history of Black women.

Another learning expectation for Grade 5 students is to identify a writer's or character's point of view. For this exercise, my students use *The People Who Hugged The Trees* by Deborah Lee Rose, based on a legend from Rajasthan, India. The legend tells the story of Amrita Devi and several hundred villagers who were the first tree huggers to protect their forests nearly three centuries ago. The students learn that the story is told from the village people's point of view. To explore another point of view, I ask, "What would be different about the story if it was told from the point of view of the Maharajah?" We discuss the fact that Amrita is the heroine of the story and if the story were told from the perspective of the Maharajah, then he would be the hero of the story and we would hear about his beautiful palace and his need for more wood. From his point of view, the villagers might be seen as unreasonable troublemakers, rather than brave people trying to protect their environment. By developing a power triangle that places the village people at the base of the triangle and the Maharajah at the apex, the students can see how the power structure of this society works.

Once the students understand perspective and point of view, I introduce the concept of non-violent protest and show that even though the villagers were poor, they used their collective power to oppose the Maharajah's army. This story is a good link to issues of non-violent resistance and to times in history when people have used their collective power to resist and change unfair state laws and practices. We study Gandhi, Martin Luther King and Rosa Parks during our unit on government, where we explore the theme of protest and resistance in more depth.

To bring in the perspectives of Aboriginal students, we study the novel *Indian Summer* by Barbara Girion. In this story a White family moves to Woodland Reservation for the summer. The two young girls in the story become instant roommates but not instant friends. Problems and conflicts unfold between them, based on their perceptions of each other's differences. While discussing the plot, setting and characters, I also introduce to the students the history of colonialism so that they can begin to understand how racism has worked in Canada. We discuss the European conquest, the taking away of land from Aboriginal peoples and the setting up of reservations. We explore racist stereotypes and look at how these racist images work in the media. Students are also introduced to Aboriginal beliefs, most notably, respect for the environment. When this novel study is finished, an Aboriginal guest speaker is invited to class to discuss such issues as Aboriginal spirituality, the *Indian Act* and residential schools in Canada.

I have found that teaching poetry is an effective way to present the work of talented, articulate Black authors — Maya Angelou, Margaret Walker and Langston Hughes — and to teach students to express themselves through this form. During the year, the students write rhyming couplets, limericks and diamonte poems in which they reflect on and express their own identity and culture. Before they write, however, we look at the different ways students can express their identity and then discuss how gender, race, culture, religion, language and class shape their sense of self. We take time to play with word combinations that express heritage and race.

For many students this is an opportunity to explore their diverse heritage. A student born in Guatemala, for example, might express her/his identity as Latina/o, Central American, Latin-American and Canadian. One student wrote that she was French Canadian, African-Canadian and Aboriginal. Aboriginal students identified by saying "I am Onieda," "I am Mohawk." Other students said they were of Cambodian, Vietnamese or Chinese heritage. For the White students, this exercise seemed strange and they simply said they were Canadian. I tried to help them deconstruct this category by pointing out that I was a White woman of British heritage and a Canadian. They then identified themselves as White Canadians, which can be seen as the taking of small steps towards politicizing whiteness and challenging its normality.

Exploring issues of racism through film has been very meaningful with the Grade 5 students. *For Angela,* a very powerful film that speaks directly to racism, is based on the real-life experience of a racial assault against an Aboriginal mother, Rhonda Gordon, and her young daughter Angela. While waiting at a bus stop, Angela and Rhonda are verbally attacked by a White male high school student, who attempts to amuse his friends as he hurls racial taints and slurs at them. The racial assault does not stop as they board the bus, while his friends respond with laughter, the passengers on the bus, visibly uncomfortable, witness the assault in steely silence. Angela cuts off her braids that night, no longer wanting to be seen as Aboriginal. Rhonda, tired of the relentless onslaughts and the negative affects on Angela, goes to the high school and with the assistance of the principal finds the main perpetrator, Ian. She confronts him in the principal's office and makes him listen to the devastating affects his actions have on Angela.

It is important to allow students time to discuss their feelings after the film.[20] We begin by reviewing the emotions felt by Rhonda, Angela, Ian, Ian's friends, the bus driver and the passengers on the bus. Then we explore Ian's actions and possible motivation for doing what he did. I make a connection between power and gender by asking the students if the racial assault would play out the same if the perpetrator was a female and the victims were male. Most students are quick to respond that they don't think it would; they think that a teenage girl would not assault a father and his son in this same way. We discuss the fact that Angela and her mother are victimized on the basis of both gender and race.

The silence of the bus driver and the people on the bus does not go unnoticed by students and they wonder why they did not act to stop Ian. Students also feel that the bus driver should have intervened in this situation and the police should have been contacted. In our discussion, we identify a stereotype as an untrue idea, prejudice as a negative attitude and discrimination as acting on untrue ideas and negative attitudes, and explore concrete examples of each. We look at how racist ideas, individual behaviours and systemic practices are linked to these definitions. Students quickly mention slavery, Jim Crow Laws, segregation and residential schools as examples of systemic racism that we have studied.

During Black History Month, we have an opportunity to explore the Underground Railroad and the role Black women played in this movement. In "The Lord Seemed to Say 'Go': Women and the Underground Railroad Movement," Adrienne Shadd documents the tremendous obstacles women faced when escaping north via the Railroad between 1815 and 1865. In addition, she explores both the formal and the informal networks they set up to aid escaping fugitives. These personal accounts and stories are brought to life and given voice, yet there are untold stories of courage and determination shown by Black women in working for freedom. Shadd argues that Harriet Tubman, who is synonymous with the Underground Railroad, is one of many women who resisted slavery and took part in the networks to help fugitives.[21] By bringing Black women into focus, Shadd makes them the subject of their own history.

♦

In reconceptualizing my classroom practice, I have challenged myself to meet certain goals. Incorporating a Black feminist perspective has been one of them. But to engage in effective anti-racism work requires that all oppressions are addressed in the classroom. When I discuss issues of race, racism and whiteness with my Grade 5 students, I am mindful that we must also discuss gay, lesbian and bisexual issues as well as homophobia and heterosexism in order to create a gay-positive classroom. When ethical clarity guides our anti-racism classroom practice, and when we see that we have the power to not only resist oppression but to transform classrooms into spaces for social and racial justice, then we will guide our students to do the same. Posing ethical questions, as Paulo Freire maintains, is at the heart of the debates about education.[22] Educators must continue to interrogate the Eurocentric knowledge base in classrooms, while at the same time interrogating their own power and privilege. Doing anti-racism work may not seem easy in these times of conservative restraint in education, yet, we must take a stand and work against the grain, for there is no middle ground in anti-racist work.[23]

NOTES

1. Nora Allingham, "Anti-Racist Education and the Curriculum: A Privileged Perspective." Keynote address to Wards 10 and 11, Toronto Board of Education, January 31, 1992, 1.
2. Becky Thompson, "Home/work: Antiracism Activism and the Meaning of Whiteness," in Michelle Fine, Lois Weis, Linda C. Powell and L. Mun Wong, eds., *Off White: Readings on Race, Power, and Society* (New York: Routledge, 1997), 357.
3. James Joseph Scheurich, "Towards a White Discourse on White Racism," *Educational Researcher* (November 1993), 9.
4. bell hooks, *Talking Back: Thinking Feminist-Thinking Black* (Boston: South End Press, 1989), 118.
5. Paulo Freire, "A Response," in Paulo Freire, ed., with James W. Fraser, Donaldo Macedo, Tanya McKinnon and William T. Stokes, *Mentoring the Mentor: A Critical Dialogue with Paulo Freire* (New York: Peter Lang, 1997), 315.
6. bell hooks, *Yearning: Race, Gender, and Cultural Politics* (Boston: South End Press, 1990), 15.
7. bell hooks, *Ain't I A Woman: Black Women and Feminism* (Boston: South End Press, 1981).
8. Peggy Bristow, Dionne Brand, Linda Carty, Afua P. Cooper, Sylvia Hamilton and Adrienne Shadd, *"We're Rooted Here and they Can't Pull Us Up": Essays in African Canadian Women's History* (Toronto: University of Toronto Press, 1994).
9. Beverely Daniel Tatum, "Lighting Candles in the Dark: One Black Woman's Response to White Antiracist Narratives," in C. Clark and J. O'Donnell, eds., *Becoming and Unbecoming White: Owning and Disowning a Racial Identity* (Westport: Bergin and Garvey, 1999), 60.
10. hooks, *Ain't I A Woman,* 12.
11. Hazel Carby, "White Women Listen! Black Feminism and the Boundaries of Sisterhood," in Heidi Safia Mirza, ed., *Black British Feminism: A Reader* (London: Routledge, 1997), 46.

12. bell hooks, *Black Looks: Race and Representation* (Boston: South End Press, 1992), 167.
13. Patricia Hill Collins, *Fighting Words: Black Women and the Search for Justice* (Minneapolis: University of Minnesota Press, 1998), xvii.
14. Heidi Safia Mirza, "Black Women in Education: A Collective Movement for Social Change," in Mirza, ed., *Black British Feminism,* 270, 273.
15. Thompson, "Home/work: Antiracism Activism and the Meaning of Whiteness," 357.
16. bell hooks, "Representing Whiteness in the Black Imagination," in L. Grossberg, C. Nelson and P. Treichler, eds., *Cultural Studies* (Boston: South End Press, 1991), 341.
17. Patricia Monture-Angus, *Thunder In My Soul: A Mohawk Woman Speaks* (Halifax: Fernwookd Publishing, 1995), 208.
18. Nelson M. Rodriguez, "Emptying the Contents of Whiteness: Towards an Understanding of the Relation between Whiteness and Pedagogy," in Joe L. Kincheloe, Shirley R. Steinberg, Nelson M. Rodriguez and Ronald E. Chennault, eds., *White Reign: Deploying Whiteness in America* (New York: St. Martin's Press, 1998), 43.
19. The literature on decolonization is extensive. For further reading, see M. Lazreg, *Decolonizing Feminism: The Eloquence of Silence: Algerian Women in Question* (London: Routledge, 1994); E. N. Saadawi, *The Nawal el Saadawi Reader* (London: Zed Books, 1997); S. Smith and J.Watson, *De/Colonizing the Subject: The Politics of Gender in Women's Autobiography* (Minneapolis: University of Minnesota Press, 1992); Ngugi Wa Thiongo, *Decolonizing the Mind: The Politics of Language in African Literature* (Oxford: Heinemann, 1986); Linda Tuhiwai Smith, *Decolonizing Methodologies: Research and Indigenous Peoples* (Dunedin: University of Otago Press, 1999); B. Ashcroft, G. Griffiths and H. Thiophene, *The Post-Colonial Studies Reader* (London: Routledge, 1995).
20. There are excellent suggestions in the after-viewing guide by Maureen Johns Simpson, *"Official Guide" For Angela.* National Film Board of Canada, 1993.
21. Adrienne Shadd, "'The Lord Seemed to Say 'Go'": Women and the Underground Railroad Movement," in Bristow et al., *"We're Rooted Here and They Can't Pull Us Up,"* 42.
22. Freire, "A Response," 314.
23. George Dei, *Theory and Practice: Anti-Racism Education* (Halifax: Fernwood Publishing, 1996), 26.

Chapter Seven

Carving out Critical Space: African-Canadian Women and the Academy

Njoki Nathani Wane

THERE IS A SENSE of awkwardness around me in my class. My guess is that this awkwardness stems from the fact that I am a woman and I am Black. I am the first woman from my family to go to graduate school. Many times when I talk during our seminars, other students say that I am angry and that I take things too personally or too seriously. Sometimes I get so discouraged when my colleagues constantly ask me to substantiate my theories or when my arguments are met with sympathetic expressions or expressionless faces. When I write or tell my stories during our seminars, I speak from the core of my heart. I tell my story to illustrate the invisible injury inflicted on us Black women and how this is transmitted through mutation from one generation to the next. I can articulate my story from different theories of oppression, but I choose to communicate from space — a woman's space

> defined by years of oppression and translation lost in theorizing.
>
> — Brenda

When Brenda joined my Black Women's Discussion Group,[1] she rarely spoke. Once in a while she would shake her head in agreement or disagreement when other women voiced their thoughts and opinions. Then one day, I asked her how her courses were going and the above quotation was her answer to my question. She had gotten back her end-of-term assignment and her professor had asked her to rewrite it if she did not want to fail the course. That was the day she talked about what it means to be a Black woman in the academy and how theorizing from a Black woman's perspective makes very little sense to many scholars.

As Black women in the academy carve out critical spaces from which to theorize, important questions arise. For example, What does it mean for Black women to inhabit the institutional space of higher education? How do Black women as intellectuals negotiate the relations of power involved when they try to include knowledge from the margins? How do they generate their own theories and practice from their own educational standpoints? What are some of the obstacles they encounter as Black women in the academy, and how is their work constructed? What strategies do they use to challenge their silencing? The answers to these questions are complex, but the questions themselves guide my examination of the challenges faced by Black women and the contributions their theorizing and their feminisms have made to the academy.

African-Canadian Women in the Academy

During the past two decades, there has been an unprecedented movement of progressive energy that has transformed higher education in North America. This transformation has increased the representation of people of colour, working-class people, gay and lesbians, and White women at all levels in the academy. At the forefront of the movement have been the traditionally marginalized groups that have demonstrated how the educational system has been locked into a paradigm of Eurocentrism, not only in terms of focus but also in terms of heritage, methodologies and conceptual structures.

In addition, Women's Studies, gender, ethnic and anti-racist studies have made great strides in integrating the realities and issues of marginalized groups to give a fuller understanding of how society functions. The analytical spaces provided by these fields of study challenge the development of critical knowledges and the simultaneous critique of knowledge itself. The task of excavating and validating the knowledge of traditionally muted subjects is by no means an easy one. For knowledge to be considered legitimate, it must be approved by the ruling class, which is constituted through the hegemony of White males who set the terms and criteria for what will be recognized as valid knowledge in our society. This hegemony is located within the "community of experts which is necessary to approve such thought and which is in constant action of refuting and suppressing the Other."[2]

Shelby F. Lewis eloquently captures this debate:

> Educational systems reflect the values and practices of the larger society. If the larger society is sexist, racist, and based on economic, cultural, and historical inequalities, it is unrealistic to expect educational systems to be devoid of these inequities. Educational systems, after all, are the formal, institutionalized, systematized vehicles through which the larger society socializes youth to the values held by the dominant or ruling group ... defining the very narrow dimension of the formal educational system as the arena within which a struggle for equity is concentrated raises strategic as well as theoretical questions ... alternative theoretical constructs must be developed for measuring,

> evaluating, and linking the causes, relationships, and consequences of inequality in the various dimensions of society.[3]

The dominant "community of experts" has the power to define an alternative community's credibility or lack of it even when that community of experts develops its own theoretical constructs. The knowledge produced by marginalized groups is subjugated by the dominant group and placed low on the hierarchy — far enough away from, and sufficiently non-challenging to, the mainstream. The exclusion of African-Canadian women scholars from mainstream academic discourse reveals how potent Euro-patriarchal knowledge production is. Feminist scholarship, however, has challenged the criteria that determines valid knowledge and has demonstrated that so-called universal objective knowledge is constructed by men and for men.[4] Challenging this dominant group has created major obstacles for both feminist scholars and scholars of colour.

Black women have a difficult time winning acceptance in colleges and universities, especially those that are predominantly White.[5] They have been excluded as definers, producers and conduits of knowledge about their own realities. Part of this exclusion is based on the misconception, as Nfah-Abbenyi points out, that for many decades "Black women writers did not exist … the black literary scene had historically been predominantly a male preserve … [and the] white, male-dominated publishing industry hadn't seen fit to publish the works of Black women writers." Nfah-Abbenyi refers to Ama Ata Aidoo who experienced first-hand the exclusionary practices of academics. Aidoo reports that she once challenged a White male professor who was presenting a lecture on African literature and had not mentioned African women's writings. When she pointed this out to him, he said he was sorry, but it had been so natural not to. It is that naturalness to omit or exclude African women writers that Black women in the North American academy have struggled to reverse.[6]

Black women scholars know how to resist, both individually and collectively, the imposed definitions and images of their racial and sexual being, not only through their writing but also through teaching. When Black women write, they bring to their work a critical self-consciousness about who they are and how they are defined by race, gender, class and ideology.[7] This is demonstrated by the works of Agnes Calliste, Dionne Brand, Linda Carty, Sylvia Hamilton, Nourbese Philip, just to name a few. Although their scholarship highlights marginalized spaces occupied by Black women, their works provide texts that faculty and students use to interrogate or rupture the lived experiences of African-Canadian women. These texts provide a conscious shift in which Black women become the centre of analysis, which gives scholars in the academy an opportunity to privilege the voices that have always occupied the margins. It is an opportunity that provides a space where misrepresentations can be corrected and where the achievements of Black women can be highlighted and celebrated.

Nagueylti is a Black woman scholar who uses an interesting strategy when she introduces the topic or writings by Black women. In her teaching, she lists all the stereotypes about Black women. Then, she engages the students in a dialogue by focusing the discussion on a series of questions: How are these images developed? How have they sustained themselves historically? How can these images be dismantled? This strategy helps to refocus students' impressions of Black women both intellectually and emotionally. I use a slightly different methodology. Instead of listing the various names that I use to refer to Black women, I show images of Black women and women of colour as portrayed by the media. Then I ask students to discuss among themselves, in groups of threes, how these images speak to them. I ask them to move beyond their preconceived notions and to challenge the status quo.

Not too long ago, one of my students, in a pre-service class, presented a critique of how Black and Asian women are represented in the media. She brought to class two images of Black and Asian women she had found in a woman's magazine. The first image was of a Black woman on her knees cleaning a sidewalk with a mop; two males were looking at her — one was Black and the other White. The second image was of an Asian woman touching her lips with very well manicured nails; a label across her chest read Man-Eater. She also showed clips of Hollywood films that portrayed Black women and women of colour in subservient positions and in domestic roles.

After her presentation she asked two questions: What can you tell from these images? What comes to mind when you see these images? The reactions from the class were quite amazing. Eighty percent of the students did not see anything wrong with these images. They felt these women were making good money posing for advertisements or acting in the films. Some said that these roles were roles from the past and were not how Black women and women of colour were portrayed today. In other words, they did not see anything wrong with these images. When I argued that these hurtful images drew on our colonial past — for example, explaining how the Vietnam War expanded the sexualization of women of colour in the popular media — it became evident that many of these students were not aware of even the basic facts of our colonial history. They questioned why this history was not taught in high school and why the media would be "allowed" to use images that perpetuate those stereotypes. It was, I argued with them, not a question of being "allowed" — many people do not want to think differently and by continuing to use such negative images is a way to undermine the meaningful role Black women and women of colour play in our society.

In another class, some students said they could not understand why there were so few women of colour in the academy. I remember one student saying that these people (African-Canadian people) need to work harder if they want to make it in our society. After a lengthy discussion, the students started to appreciate the systematic barriers inherent in our society that make it difficult not only for African-Canadian women but for all people of colour to find jobs in universities.

Teaching in the academy is one long educational moment. I

am continuously interrogating the stereotypes and challenging the biases I encounter. I also have to constantly explain who I am. During the first day in a new class, I tell the students a bit about my education, the number of degrees I have and the number of years I have been teaching. I have to legitimate and validate my position as an academic lest the students think I do not deserve to be there. Why do I have to explain myself? Why do I have to perform class? Why do I have to emphasize that I have a PhD? It is important to qualify that the question of my legitimacy does not only come from White students, it also comes from African-Canadian and students of colour.

In North American culture, men in any profession can be powerful, assertive, ambitious and achieving. Many people, however, are uncomfortable when Black or White women exhibit these traits. A woman's work is often not given the same credit as a man's; her accomplishments may be ignored or, conversely, scrutinized very carefully; she may be perceived as moving too fast. For Black women, gender and race intensify this perception.

African-Canadian women who enter the world of academia experience a tug-of-war in trying to balance professional with family and community responsibilities. They have a long tradition of managing these responsibilities, and have done so at a great psychological and professional cost.[8] They do less research and write fewer publications than their White male or female counterparts.[9] It is important to acknowledge that as an African-Canadian woman in the academy, my experiences are not comparable to an African-Canadian woman working as a nanny, a domestic or in a menial job. However, it is also important to note that maybe only a handful of African-Canadian women in the academy have not been subjected to employment in these areas. Zainabu, a participant in my Black Women's Discussion Group, confirmed this when she narrated her story about her aging mother:

> My mother is almost one hundred years old. She lives with me. My friends have been telling me to put her in a home. I

> cannot do that. I know this is North America and that is the practice, but I cannot do it. My grandparents lived with my parents until they died. I will not be the one to break our African tradition in my family. But then, this has had a toll on my family, my career and me. I cannot take a full-time teaching position. I would like to teach, but I do not think the climate in the academy would be very supportive of my family responsibility. The two years that I taught full-time were very gruelling years for me. By the way, do not misunderstand me. I do not shy away from hard work. But it is the climate, the isolation, the competitive nature that is built around the academic work. In my community we do a lot of collaborative projects — I know this happens in the academy — but I do not think everyone gets invited to these collaborative projects.

Zainabu's family responsibility is not uncommon. Other faculty members have similar situations, but I guess their priorities are different. In Zainabu's family, she was the only one with a graduate degree, and all her siblings looked up to her for guidance and direction on how to care for their ailing mother. As a result, she ended up teaching part-time and working in the corporate world three days a week. Family responsibilities can challenge African-Canadian women who want to pursue an academic career.

Another challenge facing African-Canadian women is the absence of collegiality, which can foster a sense of community as well as an atmosphere of creativity in which they can work and share their ideas. For many, this essential ingredient is missing from their professional experience. Their contributions are not always recognized or valued, and they are rarely invited to participate in joint research projects, to co-author papers or to provide sponsorship-mentoring that would give them greater access to more resources. Often, their research is trivialized and devalued if it focuses on African-Canadian issues. It is a known fact, although not publicly acknowledged, that if a Black scholar concentrates only on one Black issue — African history, for example — their scholarship is deemed narrow in scope. As a result, many Black women teach, write and research on a wide variety of issues. Rosemarie expressed it this way:

> When I got my first two-year contract I celebrated. I knew this would provide the opportunity to examine some of the issues in our community. I was interested in examining the issues of African immigrant women and their under-employment. I wrote a number of proposals, but received no funding from any of the funding agencies. I tried to solicit any of my colleagues to team up and write proposals together, but somehow, they had a nice way of turning down the offer without actually saying no. At the beginning it was difficult to get the message, but now I know: I am working on my own. Of course I have colleagues who have been extremely helpful, and I am grateful for their support, but these are the minority; I think we need to work on collegiality in the academy.

Listening to Rosemarie's comments has forced me to ask myself why the situation is the way it is. Why can't Rosemarie team up with other African-Canadian women or women of colour to do collaborative work? On close examination, however, I see that this is not possible because of the numbers: Rosemarie is the only Black woman in her department. She had tried to engage other women of colour from other departments, but none of them shared her interests. And, according to Rosemarie, "they are trying to survive, they have their own battles to fight, and since they have been here longer than me, they have a community of their own, so I do not think they are willing to open up a space for me in their circle."

Cleo narrated the dynamics among and between women of colour. She could not understand why women of colour are so caught up in their own battles that they cannot see the need to work together. "Sometimes," said Cleo, "we are our own worst enemies. We fight among ourselves, and we pull each other down. I do not see why we should complain about our White colleagues when we cannot deal with our group dynamics, which are not healthy at all."

Although the obstacles they face in the academy are daunting, African-Canadian women have not been silent and inactive. As more African-Canadian women enter the academy, the more they challenge the Eurocentric, androcentric and ethnocentric ways of thinking and knowing and the more positive influence their interaction with students and faculty have on many lives. They also address the absence of their voices from the literature, particularly in Women's Studies, ethnic studies and multicultural studies, and play a critical role in bringing works of silenced Black intellectuals into the discourse.[10] They have, as Ann duCille points out, opened up spaces within the academy for the study of Black women specifically and the study of women of colour more generally.[11]

The Question of Theory

As I discuss in chapter 1, African-Canadian women and marginalized groups have been accused of being incapable of producing interpretive, objective analytical thought that is accepted as valid theory in Western academies. Brenda's quotation at the beginning of this chapter illustrates this point. What is not understood is that African-Canadian women cannot separate theory and practice. Our everyday experiences inform our theory. For instance, we can analytically interrogate our lived experiences of racism, sexism and classism by examining the social, historical and economic construction of Black people as a race, and so we are in a position to come up with a theory of our oppression. Other marginalized groups are also capable of situating their lives in a particular theory. Even groups of people who have never experienced marginalization may theorize deprivation of privilege. But it is the historically disempowered groups that have been instrumental in bringing to light the ways in which dominant theory has been applied in a hierarchical ways and used to promote an academic elitism that embraces traditional structures of domination.[12]

It is interesting to note that this dominant theory has become a commodity that is used to determine not only if one is hired or promoted in academic institutions but whether one is heard at all.[13] Its pervasiveness in the academic hegemony is something African-Canadian women, people of colour and radical critics refuse to ignore. For these groups, the application of theory is not merely an occasion for discourse among scholars but essential nourishment for historically silenced groups. The development and discussion of the counter theory is an indispensable weapon in the struggle for legitimacy and visibility for oppressed groups because it provides certain kinds of insights that are a requisite if these groups are to act effectively.[14] Theory, then, must be understood as what Carol Boyce Davies refers to as "modes of intelligibility through which we make sense of structures, of values and beliefs which circulate in any given culture rather than a reified discourse for the privileged few."[15] Theories produced by, for and on behalf of Black women become vitally important in resisting oppression in the academy.

African-Canadian women working in the academy have voiced their concerns about the exclusionary nature of mainstream theory and about the shortcomings of a growing body of critical social theories. Although many of these critical social theories stem from seemingly progressive intentions, on closer examination we can see how their frameworks often replicate hierarchical structures, which undoubtedly have been the case for critical social theories like feminist theory or anti-racist theory, both of which continue to place Black women at the margins. bell hooks explains that social theories of difference used by intellectuals who are privileged within hierarchical power relations of race, class and gender may operate differently than comparable theories forwarded by intellectuals emerging from the centres of opposed groups or by those in what Patricia Hill Collins defines as "outsider-within locations."[16] According to Collins, theorizing from outsider-within locations reflects the multiplicity of being on the margin within intersecting systems of race, class and sexual and national oppression — they remain grounded and attentive to real differences in power and can produce distinctive oppositional knowledges that embrace multiplicities yet remain cognizant of power.[17] This can be achieved because of Black women's multiple locations in society, which challenge the notion that theory is owned by the elite and which problematize pedagogical practices within the academy in order to determine whose knowledge is valid.

Black feminism's entry into the discourse of anti-racism has shown that anti-racist theory has merely put a coat of paint on the issue of Black female subordination. In speaking and writing about sexism and racism, Black women have committed what Black male critics read as racial heresy.[18] Many Black women have been charged not only with historical inaccuracy but also with what Joy James refers to as racial infidelity. Racial infidelity, she argues, accuses Black women of putting their gender before their race and inventing historical functions that serve a feminist agenda rather than an anti-racist one. For Black women in the academy, membership in the sisterhood of feminists is often an unpardonable sin punishable by excommunication, if not from the race, certainly from the ranks of those who have authored the sacred texts of race.[19] Yet Black women must deal not only with the effects of racism but also those of sexism. Racism and sexism may be so fused in any given situation that it is difficult to tell which is which. Being Black and female cannot be separated. Each is an integral component of who Black women are. It is also important to note that Black women support and respect the experiences of Black men and the challenges they are subjected to in this society. Again, both are integral to who they are and cannot be separated.

Black feminist theory has been instrumental in illuminating

the contradictions in these critical theories, many of which reposition viewpoints within the context of professional politics inside the academy rather than creating links between struggles inside and outside the academy.[20] Furthermore, the language of much critical theory mystifies rather than clarifies, making it possible for a few people who know that particular language to control the critical scene.[21] It is not unusual to pick up a feminist text whose language is highly technical and inaccessible. Some scholars have fallen into the trap of mainstream knowledge production that produces knowledge for the elite. There is this mistaken notion that simplicity in communication is not as highly valued as the technical jargon of the academy. Mene eloquently described her experience:

> Being new in the academy can be very frustrating. People talk in a certain way. They use jargon that is familiar to them followed by a string of scholars in their line of argument. By the end of their argument you are left searching for anything meaningful they said. Please do not get me wrong — I just find theorizing in the academy is far removed from the community issues and especially my community, the Black community. When I joined the academy two years ago, I was silenced. I had a wealth of knowledge from my community but that was not valued. I felt people took me to be less of a scholar because I did not have a packaged theoretical framework from which to articulate my thoughts.

It is highly ironic that a certain kind of theoretical performance, which only a small group of people can possibly understand, has come to be seen as representing critical thought and has been given recognition within many academic circles.[22] Critics often ask for whom this material is written. As bell hooks points out, there are many different locations and spaces outside academic exchange where such theory would be seen not only as useless but also as politically non-progressive. Mene provided an example to illustrate this when she said:

> Sometimes I search for meaning in our post-structural or post-colonial theories and I find none. If I were to articulate these theories in my place of work where I am advocating for different marginalized groups, my colleagues would think I am not schooled at all in the school of life. The marginalized groups understand when you tell them how to find reasonably priced housing or how to find a good after-school program for their children.

Since mainstream and critical theories have not given priority to Black women or their scholarly works, African women in North American universities have collectively initiated and led a discourse that challenges their own adverse circumstances and, even more important, contributes to the recovery and analysis of the works they have produced. As a result of their exclusion from analyses of oppression and exploitation in traditional feminism, Black studies and mainstream academic disciplines, Black academics, independent scholars and activists have pioneered the field of Black feminist thought. Black feminist theory operates from a site of critical space and seeks to explain how positive and negative factors have been influenced by the intervention of Black women in their social structures as they challenge the hierarchy of power.

Black women and women of colour have made critical interventions to challenge and deconstruct the category of women by showing that gender is not the sole factor determining constructions of femaleness. These have led to a profound re-evaluation of feminist thought and have questioned the hegemonic feminist theory produced primarily by academic women, most of whom are White. Black women and women of colour have challenged the racist undertones in the feminist movement and have pointed out over and over again that sexism or classism are not the only issues to be fought for. But at the end of the day, the Black woman is still identified by her skin colour. Black women have also resisted attempts to be grafted into feminism in a tokenistic manner, as a colourful diversions to the real problems, and have made more than modest theoretical contributions to feminist and anti-racist theories. They have deconstructed these theories to determine their origin, intents and possibilities, yet their production of this knowledge has not been recognized.

Transformation through Decolonization

While Black Canadian writers such as Sylvia Hamilton, Linda Carty, Nourbese Philip, Agnes Calliste, Wanda Bernard, Afua Cooper, Peggy Bristow, Dionne Brand, Silvera Makeda, Adrienne Shadd and Althea Prince have gained greater visibility within the academy, their pedagogical and institutional practices and their relationship to scholarship have not been examined with care and attention. Although uncovering and reclaiming subjugated knowledges is one way to lay claim to alternative histories, these knowledges need to be understood and defined pedagogically as questions of strategy and practice as well as scholarship in order to transform educational institutions.[23] Teaching about histories of sexism, racism, imperialism, classism and homophobia poses fundamental challenges to the academy and its traditional production of knowledge, since it has often situated people of colour as populations whose histories and experiences are deviant, marginal or inessential to the acquisition of knowledge. Thus the task at hand is to decolonize disciplinary and pedagogical practices.

It is the responsibility of all educators, regardless of race, ethnicity, religious background or sexual orientation, to engage in decolonizing the colonial idea of supremacy that was conceived sometime in the fourteenth century or earlier and that sustains itself in the academy today. It is sometimes difficult to separate the colonizer and the colonized. Sometimes the colonized are at the forefront, implementing the same structures that have been oppressive for centuries — something they are able to implement because of historical amnesia. In order to decolonize the disciplines, all educators need to decolonize their minds,[24] which entails remembering how colonialism and imperialism impacted the lives of the colonizer and the colonized. In confronting the concepts and conditions of colonialism and neo-colonialism in the academy, our voices move beyond overworked metaphors of integration, multiculturation or cohesive living. An inquiry into the colonial idea brings together varied views, experiences, and perspectives, and sometimes disagreement or tension that are nevertheless bound into a frame of reference that exposes us all to a series of interrogations which we can no longer refuse or ignore.

Whether coming from another physical world, or this very familiar location, colonial and neo-colonial practices disturb and disorient our sense of race, class, gender, sexual orientation and ability. When I open up discussion on colonial thought using Black women as the referent point, what emerges are voices, desires and bodies of knowledge that reveal a sense of culture, of politics, history and identity that can no longer be referred to as old. The students in my classes are eager to address absences in history and to acknowledge the misrepresentations, especially of Black women. In my teaching, I am looking for a way to bring people together in the hope that the exercise will bring about transformation both at an individual as well as an institutional level.

As bell hooks suggests, decolonizing education practices requires transformation at a number of levels, both within and outside the academy. Within the academy, decolonization begins with the teachers who then integrate these practices into what they teach and how they teach it. For instance, you can implement other forms of learning — such as sitting in a circle instead of rows, teaching through storytelling or inviting non-academic scholars from the community to participate and teach in your class — to privilege multiple ways of learning and teaching. The next step is working on the resistance that you encounter from your students and your colleagues for being different. I remember one of my African-Canadian students commenting that sitting in a circle and using storytelling as pedagogy is not rigorous and scholarly enough. I did not fault her because all that she knew was the Eurocentric way of learning and teaching. bell hooks warns us that decolonizing pedagogical practices requires taking the relationship between knowledge and learning and student and teacher seriously.[25]

As an African-Canadian scholar teaching in the academy, I make it my priority to decolonize my classroom. For example, I tell students at the beginning of classes that each one of us is a teacher as well as a learner and the wealth of knowledge that we bring to our learning space will contribute tremendously to our classroom discussions, and that I encourage non-traditional methods of sharing information. Many times I bring a candle to class and light it before we begin. (Most of my traditional teachings were carried out around a fire — the candle helps me to centre my teaching and our learning.) Other times I bring an object (a piece of art or piece of cloth) from my culture and ask students to share with us how they see themselves in relation to the object. Some students see the object as something exotic and romantic, something that reminds them of the artifact they collected during their travels to faraway lands. Others cannot connect at all and shrug their shoulders, wanting to move on and learn something more concrete, more scholarly and more meaningful to them. But others see how exploring their relationship to other cultures can collapse boundaries and help them to appreciate the knowledge that cultures other than their own can offer them.

In my teaching, I acknowledge multiple centres and knowledges and I encourage my students to do the same. The goal for my participation as an educator is to contribute to a meaningful education — not only an education that will enable us to find employment but an education that engages our minds and souls. The results are often not immediate, however. I have had feedback from past students many months later about how I challenged them to think outside the box and to embrace diversity not in a narrow sense but a broad sense that incorporates the social and historical dimensions of our society.

I think that as a starting point, we need to take an inventory of the traces of colonialism that remain within us. This will help us develop an anti-colonial discursive framework. It is very important that we take note of the fact that our cultural apparatus is overwhelmingly European and that we acknowledge the fact that we occupy a privileged position in our society merely by being in the academy. As we interrogate the colonial experience, we need to constantly ask ourselves, whose voice, words, writings, do we privilege or reproduce? In whose theories do we situate our analysis and why? Are we writing as a reaction to or as promoters of the voices of marginalized people? Is there a particular moment in history that we can allude to as a starting point for anti-colonial educational thought? The notion of decolonizing ourselves should not be left to particular group of people or race, it should be an exercise for all individuals interested in creating a critical space not only for Black women but for all marginalized groups.

Carving Out Critical Space

As an African-Canadian woman in the academy, I encourage women to talk about their work and their realities. I want us to translate our experiences in the academy so that we can create a critical space for Black women in which our theory can thrive. How do we deconstruct a self-perpetuating pattern based on the values, interests and views of the oppressive power holders?

As African-Canadian women, it is important that we research, write and publish works that we use in our classrooms. We have the concepts and approaches that counter the negative thrust of history, and by writing and researching on issues that speak to Black people and their communities, we recognize and acknowledge the works and contributions of our mothers and grandmothers, our elders and teachers. Many of us fail to acknowledge these contributions in our publications, not realizing that it is because of what they did before us that we are able to stand today and challenge the distorted histories and the realities of our people. I have met many African-Canadian women who have written papers and speeches that remain unpublished. I ask them to send me their work so that I can help them publish it. Many agree to do so, but sooner or later they contact me and inform me that what they have is not good enough and, that furthermore, they are too caught up with their work to think about publishing at this time in their lives. Why do these women think their work is not good enough? Why is it that these women are so caught up with basic survival that they have no time to reflect and write and share their stories with the rest of the world?

These works need to be collected and published because they contain messages that are important to the struggles of African-Canadian women, not only within the walls of academe, but outside as well. When we use them in the academy, we contribute to our knowledge base and create a critical alternative theory. Black people have rich intellectual traditions, which should be brought to the fore. The importance of exploring the experience of ordinary African-Canadian women's writing is crucial because it enables us to re-tell our stories and to develop an overview and an analytical framework for understanding our lives.

In addition to writing and researching, it is also important that we design courses that examine issues pertaining to African-Canadian women's writing, spirituality, sexual violence, capitalism, social justice system, labour and health. Developing courses in these areas will involve the examination of African-Canadian women's issues at a deeper and more critical level.

There are many misconceptions that surround the status of African-Canadian women in the academy, in large part because there is very little research about us, about our contributions and the issues that concern us. Published research on minorities and women often ignores the experiences of Black women, which results in making Black women invisible. As a Black woman in academia, I encourage women to write and create texts that will contribute to various discourses in the academy. It is of great importance that we create a critical space for ourselves in which our theories can thrive.

Notes

1. My Black Women's Discussion Group was started two years ago and continues to meet monthly. It consists of students and women from the community. Brenda (not her real name) was one of them. All references are drawn from interviews with these participants who have chosen to use pseudonyms.
   In this paper, I use the terminology African-Canadian in reference to people of African descent. I also use the terminology Black interchangeably with African-Canadian.
2. Linda Carty, "Black Women in Academia: A Statement from the Periphery," in Himani Bannerji et al., eds., *Unsettling Relations: The University as a Site of Feminist Struggle* (Toronto: Women's Press, 1991), 20.
3. Lewis Shelby, "Africana Feminism: An Alternative Paradigm for Black Women in the Academy," in Lois Benjamin, ed., *Black Women in the Academy: Promises and Perils* (Gainesville: University Press of Florida, 1997), 41.
4. Barbara Smith, "Introduction: The Politics of Black Women's Studies," in Gloria T. Hull, Patricia Bell Scott and Barbara Smith, eds., *All the Women Are White, All the Blacks Are Men, But Some of Us Are Brave* (New York: Feminist Press, 1982), xvii–xxxii; Roxana Ng, "Teaching Against the Grain: Contradictions and Possibilities," in Roxana Ng et al., eds., *Anti-Racism, Feminism, and Critical Approaches to Education* (New York: Bergin and Garvey, 1991), 129–50.
5. Benjamin, ed., *Black Women in the Academy,* 39.
6. M.J. Nfah-Abbenyi, *Gender in African Women's Writing: Identity, Sexuality and Difference* (Indianapolis: Indiana University Press, 1997), 1.
7. Nagueylti Warren, "Deconstructing, Reconstructing, and Focusing our Literary Image," in Joy James and Ruth Farmer *Spirit, Space and Survival: African American Women in (White) Academe* (New York: Routledge, 1993), 99–117.
8. While conducting my research on Black feminist thought, it was very interesting to note how African-Canadian women have to balance their responsibilities between their immediate and extended family and members of the community.

Most of the women I talked to felt it was their responsibility to take up the issue of Black children's education. Many of them are involved in after-school activities and assist many children who may fall by the wayside either through counselling or academic work. Many women also complained of their loneliness in the academy and never seemed to have sincere working relationships with colleagues. If, for instance, they teamed up with non-Black colleagues, the Black colleagues would be very suspicious of their intentions – yet at the same time, these same colleagues did not hesitate to do collaborative work with non-Blacks. Most of the Black women I spoke with felt their colleagues had double standards which made it a difficult workplace.

9. Benjamin, ed., *Black Women in the Academy.*

10. Yohanda Moses, "Black Women in Academe: Issues and Strategies," and Nellie Y. McKay, "A Troubled Peace: Black Women in the Halls of the White Academy," in Benjamin, ed., *Black Women in the Academy.*

11. Anne duCille, "The Occult of True Black Womanhood: Critical Demeanor and Black Feminist Studies," *Signs: Journal of Women in Culture and Society* 19, no. 3 (Spring1994), 591–629.

12. Annette Henry, *Taking Back Control: African Canadian Women Teachers' Lives and Practice* (Albany, NY: State University of New York Press, 1998).

13. Barbara Christian, "Black Feminism and the Academy," in Les Back and John Solomos, eds., *Theories of Race and Racism: A Reader* (New York: Routledge, 2000), 462–72.

14. Henry, *Taking Back Control.*

15. Carole Boyce Davies, *Black Women, Writing and Identity: Migration of the Subject* (London: Routledge, 1994), 18.

16. bell hooks, *Teaching To Transgress: Education as the Practice of Freedom* (NewYork: Routledge, 1994), 79; Patricia Hill Collins, *Fighting Words, Black Women and the Search for Justice* (Minneapolis: University of Minnesota Press, 1998), 126.

17. Collins, *Fighting Words.*

18. Anne duCille, *Skin Trade* (Cambridge, MA: Harvard University Press, 1996), 64.

19. Joy James, *Shadowboxing: Representations of Black Feminist Politics* (New York: St. Martin's Press, 1999), 64.

20. Christian, "Black Feminism and the Academy."

21. Collins, *Fighting Words,* 143.

22. Ibid.

23. Chandra Mohanty, "Under Western Eyes," in Back and Solomos, eds., *Theories of Race and Racism,* 203–23.

24. Ngugi Wa Thiongo, *Decolonizing the Mind: The Politics of Language in African Literature* (Oxford: Heinemann, 1986); Linda Tuhiwai Smith, *Decolonising Methodologies: Research and Indigenous Peoples* (New York: Zed Books, 1999).

25. hooks, *Teaching to Transgress*, 49.

Part III

The Social Gaze

Chapter Eight

Images in Black:

Black Women, Media and the Mythology of an Orderly Society

Erica Lawson

BLACK WOMEN ARE marked as racial outsiders in neo-colonial societies. Their bodies are associated with degeneracy and promiscuity in ways that support systems of oppression. Negative representations of these racialized bodies are perpetuated in the media, which play a role in Black women's subordination. The media stigmatizes Black women as "mammies," "whores," "hoochie mamas" and "welfare queens" who exploit the state's financial "generosity." These constructed images and accompanying discourses have political, social and economic currency that justifies the exploitation of Black women's labour and sexuality. Moreover, sexualized and servile images of Black women are widely disseminated in popular culture.

This essay is divided into three interconnected sections. In the first section, I examine how media can shape and direct opinions about national identity. In the second section, I examine contemporary media discourses and images about Black women in Canada by analyzing interviews with five African-Canadian women. I explore their comments in the context of the media's exploitation of Black women's sexuality and the material implications of Black women's subordination. In so doing, I attempt to identify and discuss how Black feminist consciousness influences the strategies that Black women use to critique and resist popular media stereotypes. The third section analyzes a strip-search incident involving a Black woman, how she was talked about in the mainstream media and what the coverage revealed about how Canada is imagined. The arguments that I make are centred on the context of the media's attempt to establish a collective white Canadian identity at the expense of racialized bodies.

Media and the Mythology of an Orderly Society

Media (print, radio, television and video) are powerful tools that shape opinions about oppressed peoples. Although media practitioners lay claim to objectivity, they routinely construct "reality" based on professional or personal ideologies, corporate interests, organizational norms, values and priorities.[1] The print media in particular play a central role in the development of a national identity, thereby creating a sense that complete strangers belong to a community of shared norms and values.[2] Racialized minorities who are outside of what is considered "normal" are often constructed as social deviants. Moreover, since white elites in the media are interested in maintaining their own power through the media, they generally favour a negative representation of minorities and a positive representation of the white group.[3] In some instances, there are noticeable connections between negative media representations and changes in the law under the guise of protecting the country's population from internal or external threats. A collective investment in an imagined Canadian identity, largely viewed as white and European, lies at the heart of the collusion between media and other elites who feel threatened by racialized peoples.

For example, on April 5, 1994, three Black men entered the Just Desserts Café at the corner of Davenport and Avenue Roads in the heart of the Annex, a wealthy Toronto neighbourhood. According to news reports, the men intended to rob the restaurant. In the process, one of the assailants shot and fatally wounded Georgina Leimonis, a young white woman who later died from her injuries. The loss of this young woman's life as well as the trauma caused to others in the café at the time was undeniably tragic. The crime shocked Toronto residents and the public used the local newspapers to express their grief and outrage. It quickly became apparent that the African-Canadian community was expected to take responsibility for the crime. Collective blame on the basis of race was evident in an article in *The Globe and Mail* that provided a chilling glimpse into how African Canadians and people of colour are perceived. The journalist, Michael Valpy, began by stating that:

> The Barbarians are inside the gate … if you live in any metropolitan city … you thought about the way you conduct your life, about the safety of familiar surroundings, about the mythology of Canada as an orderly society. Maybe in reality, maybe only in perception our little country passed some sort of benchmark these last few days. We have been brought face to face with an alien slaughter, something that is not supposed to happen here. Getting robbed in the Annex is alien enough … But who expects a murder in exchange for an act of hitherto normal Canadian behaviour: telling the robbers no, you can't have my money? You expect maybe to get pushed around, maybe punched, but killed? [4]

I propose that this article illustrates a common national story that goes like this: Canada is a nation of law-abiding white citizens whose norms and values derive from a proud European tradition. The citizens and their peaceful way of life are constantly under threat from uncivilized barbarians who are outsiders within. Being a generous multicultural society, Canada is obliged to tolerate these outsiders. However, the state must pass laws to keep these barbarians in check; the state must also reserve the right to remove them when they break the law. This commonsense narrative erases the reality that Canada is a white settler society:

> A white settler society is one established by Europeans on non-European soil. Its origins lie in the dispossession and near extermination of Indigenous populations by the conquering Europeans. As it evolves, a white settler society continues to be structured by a racial hierarchy. In the national mythologies of such societies, it is believed that white people came first and that it is they who principally developed the land; Aboriginal peoples are presumed to be mostly dead or assimilated. European settlers thus become the original inhabitants and the group most entitled to the fruits of citizenship. A quintessential feature of white mythologies is, therefore, the disavowal of conquest, genocide, slavery, and the exploitation of the labour of peoples of colour. In North America, it is still the case that European conquest and colonization are often denied, largely through the fantasy that North America was peacefully settled and not colonized.[5]

Valpy's reference to "getting robbed in the Annex" as being an "alien" experience reveals that racialized bodies ought not to cross borders that demarcate "white only" boundaries because of the disruption that these bodies create. The news story also points to the continuation of segregative practices, now more covert than in the past, but still crucial to maintaining safe spaces for white settlers. Thus, spatial theory becomes useful for understanding how whiteness is conveyed in a variety of seemingly less pernicious ways:

> consider for example, how the geographies of white Canada set an implicit (and frequently explicit) norm around which belonging is constructed. The residential geographies of Afro-Caribbean immigrants in Canadian cities have frequently been described in terms of "ghetto" or "near-ghetto" imagery, but the same descriptors have never been attributed to the even more "segregated" but entirely normalized geographies of white Canadians living in the distant suburbs of Toronto or Montreal.[6]

Although Michael Valpy makes no direct reference to race or colour, the use of the word "Barbarians" to describe the perpetrators draws on existing discourses about Black people in general and Black men in particular. In other words, the author tapped into stereotypical language about African peoples that is prevalent in Eurocentric societies and used it to frame the way that Canadians ought to think and talk about the incident. The journalist's descriptive use of barbarity is further illustrative of how racist discourse is increasingly coded with more "acceptable" signifiers of difference.

The Just Desserts incident involved a Jamaican man who was previously ordered deported but had been granted a stay on appeal. The intense media coverage of the incident resulted in a link between crime and immigration in the public's mind and a call to strengthen the country's immigration laws. As a result, the federal government introduced a provision to deport landed immigrants who have been convicted of a crime for which a penalty of ten years or more is available and who are deemed to be a "danger to the public." This change in the law effectively removed the right to appeal to the Immigration Appeal Division. Therefore, far from being a passive mouthpiece, the media plays a crucial role in the reproduction of contemporary racial inequality including its influence in areas of law and social policy. Moreover, media is one of a network of institutions that work together to protect dominant group interests. What emerges is a picture of the sophisticated ways in which white supremacy is maintained with help from the media, and the ongoing challenges that racialized bodies pose to the state and to Canadian nationalism. How are Black women configured in these oppressive arrangements? And how do they resist these negative portrayals and discourses?

Black Women in the Media

Except for community newspapers that profile their progress, Black women are largely invisible in Canadian mainstream media. This invisibility symbolizes a collective forgetting of genocide, slavery and xenophobia that shaped Canada's past and present, and the ways in which racialized bodies are configured in systems of power. It also speaks to how people become racialized and simultaneously erased from the Canadian landscape so that while they exist, they are not seen:

> Variously labeled as "violent immigrants" or "just off the boat," the construction of people of colour as outside the nation places them as negative disruptions of the Canadian landscape. In the national imaginary the "real" Canada — Canada as the great white north — lies beyond the nation's largest cities in the countryside and small towns (also overwhelmingly white).[7]

When they are made visible, images and discourses about Black women reveal more about the ways in which they are disembodied to strengthen a Euro-Canadian identity.

In the interviews I held with five African-Canadian women, each woman was asked a series of questions, the first one being: When you think of images of Black women on television, in videos, in magazines, or newspapers, what comes to mind?[8] Rachael, a thirty-two-year-old graphic designer and a new mother, responded that "it really depends on what type of media." Rachael went on to outline her description of the various forms of media and how she reacts to them:

> *Television:* Talk shows being one of the worst. I cringe when I hear and see the slew of loud, obnoxious, inarticulate Black women who are encouraged to display their anger and hostility towards one another. Worst kind of Black female exploitation by the white media.
>
> *Videos:* Worst kind of Black female exploitation by our own community. The "scantily-clad gyrating stripper" video formula has become the norm. Women are used as mindless sexual objects. This infuriates me.
>
> *Newspaper/Magazines:* Of all the types of media, this one is less likely to offend me which could also be due to the fact that we are rarely featured in the print media, unless it's a Black owned publication geared towards Black people.
>
> *Films/Television Shows:* They may have gravitated away from the sexual stereotyping to a certain degree, but there's this perpetuation of the angry Black woman (they would have you believe it's a display of the "strong Black woman"). She is usually sassy, lippy and sarcastic. It's boring and one-dimensional.

Other women in the study responded similarly to this question and pointed to the ways in which these representations continue to be manifested. For example, the respondents critiqued the images of the strong, hardworking Black woman who holds the family together as provider and nurturer; the single-minded career woman who strives to succeed in white mainstream society, such as Oprah and Whoopi; and the single welfare mother with many children from different men. Roslyn, a graduate student, expressed her concern as follows:

> *The Jerry Springer Show* typifies this (welfare) image. She is an uneducated crack addict who depends on the state to care for herself and her children. Then there is the sex-pot, the "hoochie" mama who is "loose" and uncontrollable, who

> exploits others for easy money. She blurs the line between stripper and hooker. I find that rap videos exploit this image. To a large extent, the images are ambivalent, almost as if the media are unsure of where to place Black women.

The fact that the participants pointed to the pervasive images of Black women in popular American culture further underscores the invisibility of African-Canadian women and the general lack of multidimensional and positive images. These negative representations have universal applicability differing only to the extent that particular social and political conditions shape Black women's lives. Moreover, they have intersectional currency since they are used to serve overlapping dominant interests. For example, the Black female domestic who is constructed as the "Mammy" is also the "whore" who is susceptible to sexual assault by her employer. This is evident in the experience of Black domestic workers in the homes of white Canadians who have been harassed by male employers.[9]

In recent years, hyper-sexualized images of Black women have come to dominate popular culture. The prevalence of rap music videos, to which Roslyn refers, and their exploitation of Black women's sexuality was a recurring theme in the responses to the questions. Lorraine, a thirty-year-old employment recruiter, argued that in hip-hop culture

> the Black female is portrayed as the sexual object of male fantasy — this viewpoint is mainly reinforced through music videos. This is largely constructed by males, both Black and white, in a music industry that has replaced "sex, drugs and rock and roll" with "sex, hip hop and Benjamins."[10] The Black female has become the "groupie" to the male star — willing to do anything because he is famous (and rich). There aren't enough Black female artists gaining prominence to counteract this trend, and the boyz seem to be adding their own posse of females that seem to reinforce the images

even more. Girlz like Lil' Kim are in effect saying, "I like being a 'Ho,' as long as it brings dough."

Lorraine's view reflects Patricia Hill Collins's argument that Black and white men have been involved in finding ways to profit from Black women's bodies. This exploitation is articulated by Brother Marquis from the group 2 Live Crew, who, in an interview with cultural critic Lisa Jones, stated that

> I'm not gonna try to disrespect you and call you all those names like I do on those records. I would never do that to a young lady, especially a sister. I'm degrading you to try and get me some money ... And besides, you let me do that to you. You got pimps out here who are making you sell your body. Just let me talk about you for a little while, you know what I'm saying? And make me a little money.[11]

In assessing Brother Marquis's logic, Collins opines that his explanation displays familiar rationalizations in that he divided women into two categories of good girls and "hoochies." In his mind, if Black women are devalued within prostitution already, what harm can it do to talk about debasing Black women, especially if he can profit from such talk? Collins further explains that Brother Marquis's logic denies that images of Black women as "jezebels" and "hoochies" is a form of violence against Black women. In reality, these controlling images are vital to the intersecting oppressions to which Black women are subjected.

Lorraine's observation of Lil' Kim, one of the few Black women who has penetrated the male-dominated hip-hop market, raises questions about how Black women participate in systems of oppression. There are female rappers who would argue that, rather than being exploited, using their sexuality for profit is a form of empowerment and resistance to patriarchy and racism. However, arguing that the sexualized Black woman is economically empowered in a culture that feeds on her exploitation is a seductive participation in Black women's oppression.

Furthermore, it is a perspective that does not challenge or transform the systems that rely on Black women's subordination. Wendy, a thirty-year-old public relations consultant, addresses this sentiment:

> As images, these portrayals of Black women and of other visible minority women often represent how easily assimilated or comparable with white women we are. This is done for the benefit of whomever created the image. So in contemporary culture, whereas we were excluded before, we can now view ourselves drinking Second Cup coffee, driving the latest Chrysler car or wearing Calvin Klein jeans.

Similarly, Karen, a thirty-three-year-old actress, expresses the uses of Black women's bodies in capitalist culture by articulating that

> it's all about what sells. Give people what they want. Only in this case, "people" refers exclusively to whites who allegedly have no interest in seeing fully clothed Black women living civil, well-rounded lives ... The purpose is to sell products. The interests served are those of whites. I also think the larger purpose is to keep things as they are ... don't inspire change, because no one, meaning whites, likes change.

Thus, the sexualization of Black women in popular culture reinforces their subordination rather than materially and symbolically facilitating their full participation in the social, political and economic structures of North American society.

Sexualization and Servitude: Limited Opportunities for Black Women

The connection between sexualized representations and Black female bodies is an indication of the centrality of sexuality in hegemonic systems of oppression. Sexuality is one of the points of intersection of relations of social, economic and cultural power. Furthermore, as Kay Ferres articulates, "class, gender, and race are systems of difference which take hold of and produce particular kinds of sexualized bodies,"[12] something the media, popular culture and film are good at doing. Similarly, Londa Schiebinger argues that representations of bodies are bound up in colonialism, scientific racism and sexism, and with a desire to prove that women are irrational beings.[13] And Lorraine O'Grady tells us that "a kaleidescope of not-white females, Asian, Native American, and African, have played distinct parts in the West's theater of sexual hierarchy, but it is the African female who, by virtue of color and feature and the extreme metaphors of enslavement, is at the outermost reaches of 'otherness.'"[14] Therefore, a reading of the uses of female sexuality in the media must be examined through a race lens to fully determine their unique and intersecting manifestations and how these work to control Black women's bodies and limit their opportunities.

Negative images of Black women in the media have serious effects on the life chances of Black women. Indeed, media images that portray Black women in positions of servitude perpetuate their subordination in the everyday world. This is particularly the case with Black women's labour, which historically has been and currently is being used for the benefit of others. Philomena Essed argues that images today can be used flexibly to rationalize the exploitation of women as workers.[15] Furthermore, the range of discriminatory practices creates glass ceilings and brick walls for women of colour who aspire to social and economic mobility. In Canada, women of colour are overrepresented in manufacturing, in the service sector such as cafeterias, restaurants and healthcare, and in domestic work. Tania Das Gupta points out that "one-third of Metro Toronto's workers of colour are nursing attendants in homes for the aged. More than half are Black and 93 percent are women."[16] I argue that negative images of Black women as peripheral helpers and sexualized commodities are contributing factors to their subordination in ghettoized spheres and to their invisibility in "spaces that matter."

The underrepresentation or absence of Black women in decision-making positions within institutions of power also has social impacts, particularly with respect to mentoring other women. Lorraine spoke strongly to this point in the interview:

> Who are young African-Canadian girls looking up to? Do they realize that real power is on those business pages, not Black Entertainment Television? Do they know what their mothers/aunts/sistahs struggle against everyday in the workplace? What visions of success do they have? Other than Oprah, I rarely see another Black female mentioned in the business pages. Does Zanana Akande sit on any board of directors, how about Bev Mascoll?[17] These are two prominent, successful women in Toronto. I've never seen them publicized outside of *Share* magazine. While it is widely acceptable to disseminate sexualized or otherwise subordinate images of Black women, it upsets the status quo to show us in positions of authority.

In this vein, Lorraine captures the importance of making connections between the absent or negative representations of Black women in the media, the impact of their ability to gain professional credibility, and the loss of mentors for young Black women in a competitive society.

RESISTANCE TO NEGATIVE REPRESENTATIONS: CONTEXTUALIZING BLACK WOMEN'S FEMINISMS

Yet the women who were interviewed revealed that they were not consciously influenced by negative media images and discourses to the extent that their sense of self was destabilized. While the women enjoyed some aspects of media and its transmission of popular culture, they did not speak of media as a significant factor in shaping their worldviews and identities, or in influencing their relationships with other women. Instead, they pointed to the importance of family, community, friends and partners in helping them to live holistically. I read the women's critical analysis of the media in the context of Black feminist thought and what it offers for understanding how Black women engage in practices of resistance.

Black feminist praxis interrogates the sites at which and the ways in which Black women have resisted subordination throughout history from differing geographical locations. As a discipline, Black feminist thought engages in examining context-specific sites of knowledge production that are crucial to Black women, though not necessarily valued by mainstream society. Thus, although the media is a crucial pedagogical site of socialization for Canadians and a source of knowledge about the Other, the women in the study are also exposed to subjugated knowledges about their histories and their identities. In this regard, emerging African-Canadian feminisms are grounded in the lived realities of African-Canadian women and in the relationships that matter to them. For example, the women noted that families and communities are central pedagogical sites that offer empowering perspectives to counteract the negativity that frames Black women's lives in media and popular culture. Lorraine explained that

> my family has definitely had the biggest impact on my identity. Growing up in Calgary, with the exception of one teacher in junior high, the Black women I learned from were my mother and my aunts. I think I was very fortunate that the women who surrounded me were well educated, were in relatively solid relationships, and even when there were troubles we were always able to laugh. No high drama. I also have to say that my father and uncles had a big impact as well — they never hesitated to tell me I was beautiful and to encourage me. My father's relationship with my mother was always very affectionate and loving — a good example of how relationships between Black men and women should be.

Similarly, Rachael stated that her involvement in the life of her younger sister and her connection to other politically conscious Black women is crucial to how she is able to critically analyze and challenge stereotypical representations of Black women:

> Having a younger teenage sister has made me particularly aware of negative, stereotypical images. Talking about these issues with her has helped solidify my views. I am lucky to have beautiful, strong, politically and socially aware female friends who encourage a level of consciousness. You tend to gravitate towards those that are either like-minded and/or have an ability to develop certain characteristics in you that you desire.

Whether or not they articulate their experiences as Black feminist thought or African-Canadian feminism, Black women across the globe have always engaged in various forms of resistance borne out of the socioeconomic and political conditions under which they live. The circumstances that give rise to these experiences are remarkably similar.

Filomina Steady argues that the capitalist mode of production is largely responsible for the massive dispersal of African women from the continent. And the motive of capital and its transformation over time have brought the production and reproduction of African women into unified oppression on the basis of sex and race.[18] Therefore, for Black women globally, perhaps more than any other group of women, feminism must discursively emerge out of a politics that is connected to reclaiming cultural identities and challenging racism within capitalist structures.

It is within the above paradigm that I further read the women's resistance and reclamation of positive identities in the face of a media system that supports elite interests. I also make connections between the struggles for positive spaces and identities in Canada to the common experience of Black women in other oppressive societies, and the supportive influence of personal/familial relationships in this struggle. Other women also spoke to the importance of choosing friends who reflect their values and ability to live healthily. For example, Wendy noted that "my friends through example have proven to be the most positive, reliable sources for balanced Black female identity."

In addition to finding their identities and experiences positively reflected in the people they value, the women spoke to personal choices they make in their everyday lives to challenge racist and sexist images. Their actions ranged from making conscious choices about their economic buying power to engaging in critical conversations about how to assess negative stereotypes:

> I resist these images with my economic power. I will not subscribe to Black Entertainment Television. I will change the channel when I see an offensive video on MuchMusic. I threw a Snoop album in the garbage (I won it at a networking function) because after the first listen I found it offensive. I will buy *Elle* magazine with Alek Wek on the cover to make up for all the lost sales that these magazines say they lose when they feature a Black model on the cover. (Lorraine)

> I refuse to contribute my money to films, magazines, newspapers, et cetera, that I believe contribute to these racist, sexist images. (Rachael)

> My husband and I have conversations almost daily about the negative images on television regarding Blacks on the whole so he knows exactly where I stand. Sometimes he initiates the conversation and we talk about how we would deal with Black identity when we have children. I have three nieces in the education system. One goes to the University of Toronto, another hopes to start there in September, while another is in advanced classes in high

> school. We have conversations about body image, about Black students in the school system and about boyfriends. I try to give advice to empower them when handling themselves in the larger society ... By and large, I think that it is working because my nieces are becoming involved in community volunteer work. I have a five-year-old niece for whom I buy books with Black characters and stories. (Roslyn)

As mentioned earlier, the views of the women interviewed for this essay emerged out of the corporeal experience of being Black and from the proliferation of American media representations of Black women. But the Canadian media engages in its own peculiar form of racial and patriarchal violence against Black women. Whereas the second section of this essay examined Black women's perspectives with respect to media and popular culture, the following section explores an incident involving the strip searching of a Black woman and the problematic ways in which it was taken up in the media. By moving from the general perspectives and critiques offered by Black women to scrutinizing the particularities of the incident in question, I wish to broaden the scope of understanding the ways in which white Canadians are invested in the subordination of Black women.

The Audrey Smith Incident

On August 10, 1993, Audrey Smith, a Jamaican woman on a visit to Toronto, was approached by two (male) police officers in Parkdale, a mixed-income neighbourhood in the west end of the city, a site that is constructed as a space for prostitution and drug activities. The officers had been tipped off that Smith, described as "a heavy-set black woman in an orange outfit,"[19] had crack cocaine in her underwear. Because male officers are not allowed to strip-search female suspects, Constable Tracey Peters was called to the scene to search Smith for drugs. When she arrived, Peters's two male colleagues reported that she was wearing latex gloves.[20] The female officer, carrying a flashlight, went behind a bank at the corner of a public intersection with Smith. What happened next came down to Smith's word against Peters's.

According to Smith, the officer asked her to unbutton the top of her jump suit, which she did. Constable Peters then pulled down Smith's panties and asked her to bend over.[21] Smith never denied agreeing to be searched, but said that she had expected it to happen in private at the police station, not in a public place. According to Peters, to her surprise, Smith pulled down her own clothes then turned around voluntarily and bent over at the waist. Smith's actions, from Peters's perspective, were meant to embarrass her to stop the search.[22] No drugs were found on Audrey Smith's body. Some months later, the incident was heard before a police tribunal to determine the facts of the case.

The police officer's lawyer accused Smith of exhibitionism, and stated that it was typical of Jamaican women to flash their bottoms at authority figures as a sign of disrespect.[23] Roger McTair, a Black journalist, suspected that this information was first leaked to the media by the police who, fearing controversy, sought to discredit Jamaicans in general and Smith in particular. McTair argues that the police response is typical of trying to discredit other cultures and out-groups to justify inappropriate behaviour towards them. And, given the high level of support that police enjoy from white middle-class Canadians, it is not in the elite media's interest to take their actions to task.

Toni Morrison argues that in white supremacist capitalist societies, the police are the praetorian guards for the white middle-class population who sometimes have to violate the law to enforce it.[24] For whites to consider police corruption as systemic rather than occasional is to place themselves in the untenable position of being shielded by, rather than protected from, chaos. Police officers admit to routine strip searches to protect themselves and the suspect from harm. For example, Craig Bromell, president of the Toronto police union, has admitted to carrying "out hundreds of strip searches when he was a uniformed officer at 51 Division in Regent Park."[25] In Ontario, there has been a public outcry against the abusive ways in which strip-searches have been used, not for protection but for humiliation and the abuse of power. It is likely that what happened to Audrey Smith, as with many other cases, would have gone unnoticed except that the search was conducted in a public place. This is against the *Police Services Act* of Ontario, which specifies that strip searches must be carried out in a private setting.[26] However, what concerns me here is how the incident provided insight into how Black female bodies are configured in xenophobic and racist notions that informs white Canadian identity.

Legal experts and journalists have wondered out loud that if Tracey Peters intended to do a pat-down search as she insisted, then why was she wearing latex gloves? Although she denied wearing gloves as reported by the other officers at the scene, the contradiction threw doubt on Peters's version of the incident. Is it possible that the gloves symbolized the deeply held view that Black bodies are diseased units of contamination? Do they serve to remind us that this young white officer, sympathetically described as a "real innocent"[27] in the incident, needed to be protected from filth and dirt associated with the Black body? Richard Dyer opines that "non-white people are associated in various ways with the dirt that comes out of the body, notably in the repeated racist perception that they smell."[28] I suggest that the gloves offered some protection against complete contact with such filth, leaving whiteness unmarred by the experience. I argue further that Smith's racially marked Black middle-aged Jamaican body highlighted the Canadian cultural narrative of Tracey Peters's whiteness. Smith, as the figure of "the prostitute" who is habitually regarded as a source of disease, needed to be approached with caution. And for Peters, a pair of latex gloves was all that stood between her and the fear of infection, not just of her physical body, but the infection of the purity of her whiteness.

When no drugs were found on her person, the narrative

shifted and Smith, who could not clearly explain why she was sitting on a park bench in the early hours of the morning — except to say that she was waiting for someone named "Rick"[29] — was accused of waiting for a john. The story continued that since Smith was a married woman with a husband in Jamaica, she was embarrassed to admit that "Rick" was not merely someone whom she had met on the subway as she claimed. The mystery as to why she was sitting in the park at that time of the morning in an area associated with drugs and prostitution has never been solved. But the search for an answer, albeit speculative, could only be explored in the context of the enduring image of the criminalized Black woman who is also promiscuous, thereby erasing the violence to which Smith was subjected.

Sherene Razack argues that "bodies in degenerate spaces lose their entitlement to personhood through a complex process in which the violence that is enacted is naturalized."[30] The media stories revealed a Black body that was gendered, raced, sexualized and classed, one that represented chaos and disease in the pristine, orderly society that is Canada, and one that needed to be punished for crossing the border (Jamaica to Canada) and finding itself in a known criminalized space (Parkdale). The way in which Smith's body was racialized in media coverage by two white female journalists, Christie Blatchford, formerly with *The Toronto Sun*, and Rosie DiManno with *The Toronto Star*, was revealing in terms of how white women participate in nationalism and in the oppression of women who are Othered.

Rescuing the Racialized Subject: Reading Blatchford and DiManno

Advocating for the upliftment of lesser women is one of the ways in which many European women were able to participate in empire building. It was also a rite-of-passage for laying claim to citizenship and a meaningful identity in a white male dominated project. For example, the Suffragist Movement, which advocated for the vote for (white) women, was aligned with racist ideologies espoused by their male counterparts, and pioneering feminists generally failed to make a connection between their oppression and the oppression of Black and Aboriginal women. I contend that, for the most part, this remains the case today. White female journalists like Christie Blatchford and Rosie DiManno continue to espouse racist views to prove that they have earned the right to participate in the nation's affairs, still firmly controlled by elite white males.

True to her reputation as being hostile to the African-Canadian community, Blatchford begins one of her articles about the strip searching of Smith by stating, "There's only one question left, it seems to me, in the Audrey Smith matter, and that's this — is this an example of white justice?"[31] Her lead-in came out of comments made by Peter Abrahams, Smith's lawyer, to *The Toronto Star* that Blacks should not try to "seek justice from the police unless [they] have a video tape."[32] Abrahams articulated a widely held view among African-Canadians and other people of colour who are constantly harassed by the police and whose complaints are routinely dismissed. However, it is a view that apparently irritated Blatchford who abides by an uncritical understanding of liberal democratic principles. Her statement is also indicative of the frustration that white Canadians feel towards African Canadians who insist on being ungrateful by talking about racism.

Using language that reflects the perceived innate untrustworthiness of racialized and sexualized Black bodies, Rosie DiManno declared that she believed Smith's version of the truth because the woman was simply too stupid to lie:

> [T]here's no way to put this kindly, but Smith, in her appearance before a police board of inquiry ... came across as patently incapable of constructing such a contrived falsehood, one that could withstand the brutal scrutiny of lawyers Harry Black and J.J. Burke ... Smith is a bovine woman. Her simpleness, as it turns out was her strongest

> asset at the inquiry … Sometimes truth doesn't shine brightly. Sometimes it just sits there like a lump on a log.[33]

No doubt DiManno believed that showing Smith's alleged simplicity was for her own good, as it offered a way to garner her some degree of sympathy. However, DiManno's attempt to rescue Smith ends up portraying the Jamaican woman as little more than a dull animal in her confrontation with the two male lawyers, whom I assume are white. DiManno's statement is an example of what Mary Louise Pratt refers to as anti-conquest. Pratt uses anti-conquest to describe the "strategies of representation whereby European bourgeois subjects seek to secure their innocence in the same moment as they assert European hegemony."[34] In other words, DiManno's point of view is an attempt to "save" the subordinated subject with a move that simultaneously oppresses her.

In one of her articles about the incident, Christie Blatchford describes Audrey Smith as a "rather sad, unsophisticated woman" who "is capable of a little politicking."[35] She goes on to say that there were moments during the inquiry "when the heart wins out, and she (Smith) looks, in her lacy pink dress and bright yellow sweater, alone and quite scared; there are other moments when the mind triumphs and she seems not so much beguiling as full of guile."[36] I read Blatchford's descriptions, especially about Smith's clothes, as an attempt to paint her as the childlike native, yet one who is cunning, unpredictable and untrustworthy.

Blatchford and DiManno do not critically interrogate the reasons Smith was strip searched in the first place. Nor do they use their respective positions of power and privilege to challenge or disrupt the racist system within which Smith became entangled. Furthermore, the kinds of images about Black women that Blatchford and DiManno conjure up through language already exist as part of the national story, and needed only a few well-placed lines in widely circulated newspapers to tap into the reader's imagination. The result is that both women get to assert their allegiance to white supremacy and to a white Canadian identity. These assertions are, however, a form of violence against Black women.

As noted earlier, Benedict Anderson argues that print media plays a role in developing a national identity and in creating a sense that complete strangers belong to a community of shared values. The ways in which the Audrey Smith incident was covered by Blatchford, DiManno and other journalists illustrate Anderson's point. The media functioned to remind white Canadians that they live in a national community of shared Eurocentric values, and that these values must be protected from outsiders. The organization of racism in patriarchal states like Canada socializes women to engage in competing interests, so it is not surprising that Blatchford and DiManno were unable to critically read Smith's experience as one that is an affront to all women. Ruth Roach Pierson writes that "in cultures in which 'asymmetric race and class relations are a central organizing principle of society,' one may also 'become a woman' in opposition to other women."[37] Nor would it have been in their best interest to tell the story from a subversive position aimed at disrupting racism and patriarchy. Indeed, a subversive approach is almost unimaginable when we consider the ways in which the official Canadian story is told to deny genocide and racism and to declare white Canadians as innocents. From this perspective, the violence to which Audrey Smith was subjected behind the bank in Parkdale became completely erased from media stories that relied on old colonial narratives about racialized Others.

♦

A critical reading of media and popular cultural representations of Black women's bodies allows us to unmask the oppression that is otherwise normalized. By understanding the everyday violence to which Black women are subjected through media images and discourses, we are better positioned to interrogate how systems of oppression support each other to protect dominant group interests. Rather than merely being informed or entertained, it is my hope that a critical reading of the media will empower all of us to hold the media to higher standards of public accountability.

Notes

1. Teun Van Dijk, *Elite Discourse and Racism* (Newbury Park, CA: Sage Publications Inc., 1993), 243.
2. Benedict Anderson, *Imagined Communities: Reflections on the Origin and Spread of Nationalism* (London: Verso, 1983).
3. Van Dijk, *Elite Discourse and Racism,* 248.
4. Michael Valpy, "Face to Face With a New Violence," *The Globe and Mail,* 7 April 1994.
5. Sherene Razack, "Introduction," Sherene Razack, ed., *Race, Space, and the Law: Unmapping a White Settler Society* (Toronto: Between the Lines, 2002), 1–2.
6. Linda Peake and Brian Ray, "Racializing the Canadian Landscape: Whiteness, Uneven Geographies and Social Justice," *Canadian Geography* 45, no. 1 (Spring 2001), 180.
7. Ibid.
8. The other questions I asked were: 1b. How are these images constructed and what accounts for their perpetuation? 2a. What do these images mean to you? 2b. To what extent do you think these images reflect who we really are? 3. How do they affect how you relate to other Black women? 4. What purpose(s) and whose interests do these images serve? 5. How do they affect or shape how you see yourself as a Black woman? 6. How has your family, community and your peers influenced your Black female identity? 7. What role do you think Black men, intimate partners, co-workers, friends, family play in re-inscribing negative images? 8. Are there connections between images of Black women and (a) racism? (b) sexism? (c) capitalism? 9. How would you describe the differences between the images of Black women in the media compared to how they live their daily lives? 10. How do you think these images affect the larger Black community in Canada? 11. What are some of the ways in which Black women can resist negative representation? 12. What are some of the things that you do in your daily life to challenge how Black women are represented?

9. Makeda Silvera, *Silenced: Makeda Silvera Talks with Working Class West Indian Women about their Struggles as Domestic Workers in Canada* (Toronto: Wallace-Williams, 1983).

10. Benjamins refer to the picture of Franklin Benjamin on US $100 bills.

11. Patricia Hill Collins, *Black Feminist Thought: Knowledge, Consciousness, and the Politics of Empowerment* (New York: Routledge, 2000) 143–44.

12. Kay Ferres, "Written on the Body: Jean Devanney, Sexuality and Censorship," *A Woman's Interdisciplinary Journal* 20, no. 1 (1994) 123–34.

13. Londa Schiebinger, "Theories of Gender and Race," in Janet Price and Margrit Shildrick, eds., *Feminist Theory and the Body: A Reader* (New York: Routledge, 1999) 21–31.

14. Lorraine O'Grady, "Olympia's Maid: Reclaiming Black Female Subjectivity," in Joanna Fruen et al., eds., *New Feminist Criticism: Art, Identity, Action* (New York: Harper Collins Inc., 1994), 152–70.

15. Philomena Essed, "Towards a Methodology to Identify: Converging Forms of Everyday Discrimination." *United Nations. Women Watch. Division for the Advancement of Women.* <http://www.un.org/womenwatch/daw/csw/essed45.htm>. July 2002.

16. Tania Das Gupta, *Racism and Paid Work* (Toronto: Garamond Press, 1996), 7–8.

17. Sadly, Beverly Mascoll, a prominent business woman in the Black community, died of cancer in 2001.

18. Filomina Chioma Steady, *The Black Woman Cross-Culturally* (Rochester: Schenkman Books Inc., 1990), 27.

19. Kris Rushowy, "Smith Probe 'Obstructed,' Officer Says Strip-Search Investigator Hits Out at Top Brass," *The Toronto Star,* 26 July 1995, A7.

20. Rosie DiManno, "Smith's Simple Testimony Blunted Lawyer's Barbs," *The Toronto Star,* 22 September 1995, A6.

21. Gay Abbate, "Woman Describes Strip-Search Done by Police," *The Globe and Mail,* 27 April 1995, A9.

22. DiManno, "Smith's Simple Testimony Blunted Lawyer's Barbs."

23. Roger McTair, "Common Practice and Common Slander," *The Toronto Star,* 29 September 1995, A23.

24. Toni Morrison, "The Official Story: Dead Man Golfing," in Toni Morrison and Claudia Brodsky Lacour, eds., *Birth of a Nation'hood: Gaze, Script and Spectacle in the O.J. Simpson Trial* (New York: Pantheon Books, 1998), vii–xxviii.

25. John Duncanson, "Proposed New Police Rules Okay By Union: Boss Says Changes Won't Greatly Alter Officers' Routine," *The Toronto Star,* 14

November 1998, A4.

26. In *Ian Vincent Golden v. Her Majesty the Queen,* the Supreme Court of Canada recently ruled that in addition to reasonable and probable grounds justifying the arrest, the police must also establish reasonable and probable grounds justifying the strip search. The ruling, which further outlines strict conditions for carrying out a search, effectively prevents the police from using strip search as a means to humiliate detainees.
27. Christie Blatchford, "Justice Is Neither Black Nor White," *The Toronto Sun,* 22 September 1995, 5.
28. Richard Dyer, *White* (London: Routledge, 1997), 75–6.
29. Abbate, "Woman Describes Strip-Search Done By Police."
30. Sherene Razack, "Gendered Racial Violence and Spatialized Justice," Razack, ed., *Race, Space, and the Law,* 155.
31. Blatchford, "Justice Is Neither Black Nor White."
32. Ibid.
33. DiManno, "Smith's Simple Testimony Blunted Lawyers' Barbs."
34. Mary Louise Pratt, *Imperial Eyes: Travel Writing and Transculturation* (London: Routledge, 1992), 7.
35. Christie Blatchford, "Search for the Truth," *The Toronto Sun,* 27 April 1994, 5.
36. Ibid.
37. Ruth Roach Pierson and Nupur Chaudhuri, eds., With the Assistance of Beth McAuley, *Nation, Empire, Colony: Historicizing Gender and Race* (Bloomington: Indiana University Press, 1998), 3.

Chapter Nine

Spirit-Murdering the Messenger: The Discourse of Fingerpointing as the Law's Response to Racism

Patricia J. Williams

Windows and Mirrors

BUZZERS ARE BIG in New York City, favored particularly by smaller stores and boutiques. Merchants throughout the city have installed them as screening devices to reduce the incidence of robbery. When the buzzer sounds, if the face at the door looks "desirable," the door is unlocked. If the face is that of an "undesirable," the door stays locked. Predictably, the issue of undesirability has revealed itself to be primarily a racial determination. Although the buzzer system was controversial at first, even civil rights organizations have backed down in the face of arguments that the system is a "necessary evil,"[1] that it is a "mere inconvenience" compared to the risks of being murdered,[2] that discrimination is not as bad as assault,[3] and that in any event, it is not all blacks who are barred, just "17-year-old black males wearing running shoes and hooded sweatshirts."[4]

Two Saturdays before Christmas, I saw a sweater I wanted to purchase for my mother. I pressed my brown face to the store window and my finger to the buzzer, seeking admittance. A narrow-eyed white youth who looked barely seventeen, wearing tennis sneakers and feasting on bubble gum, glared at me, evaluating me for signs that would pit me against the limits of his social understanding. After about five seconds, he mouthed, "We're closed," and blew pink rubber at me. It was one o'clock in the afternoon. There were several white people in the store who appeared to be shopping for things for their mothers.

I was enraged. At that moment I literally wanted to break all the windows in the store and take lots of sweaters for my mother. In the flicker of his judgmental grey eyes, that saleschild had reduced my brightly sentimental, joy-to-the-world, pre-Christmas spree to a shambles. He had snuffed my sense of humanitarian catholicity, and there was nothing I could do to snuff his, without simply making a spectacle of myself.

I am still struck by the structure of power that drove me into such a blizzard of rage. There was almost nothing I could do, short of physically intruding on him, that would humiliate him the way he humiliated me. His refusal to let me into the store was an outward manifestation of his never having let someone like me into the realm of his reality. He saw me only as one who would take his money and therefore could not conceive that I was there to give him money.

In this weird ontological imbalance, I realized that buying something in that store was like bestowing a gift: the gift of my commerce. In the wake of my outrage, I wanted to take back the gift of my appreciation, which my peering in the window must have appeared to be. I wanted to take it back in the form of unappreciation, disrespect, and defilement. I wanted to work so hard at wishing he could feel what I felt that he would never again mistake my hatred for some sort of plaintive need to be included. I was quite willing to disenfranchise myself in the heat of my need to revoke the flattery of my purchasing power. I was willing to boycott this particular store, random white-owned businesses, and anyone who blew bubble gum in my face again.

The violence of my desire to have burst into that store is probably quite apparent to the reader. I wonder whether the violence and the exclusionary hatred are equally apparent in the repeated public urging that blacks put themselves in the shoes of white store owners[5] and that, in effect, blacks look into the mirror of frightened white faces to the reality of their undesirability; then blacks would "just as surely conclude that [they] would not let [themselves] in under similar circumstances."[6]

This essay will consider how the rhetoric of increased privatization, in response to racial issues, functions as the rationalizing agent of public unaccountability and, ultimately, irresponsibility. I will analyze the language of lawmakers, officials, and the public in order to present racial discrimination — so pervasive yet so hard to prosecute, so active yet so unactionable — in a new light. To this end, I will examine the death of Eleanor Bumpurs, an elderly black woman shot by police in the Bronx.

The second purpose of this essay is to examine racism as a crime, an offence so deeply painful and assaultive as to constitute something I call "spirit-murder." Society is only beginning to recognize that racism is as devastating, as costly, and as psychically obliterating as robbery or assault; indeed, they are often the same. It can be as difficult to prove as child abuse or rape, where the victim is forced to convince others that he or she was not at fault, or that the perpetrator was not just "playing around." As in rape cases, victims of racism must prove that they did not distort the circumstances, misunderstand the intent, or even enjoy it.

Crimes Without Passion

Eleanor Bumpurs and the Language of Lawmakers

On October 29, 1984, Eleanor Bumpurs, a 270-pound, arthritic, sixty-seven-year-old woman, was shot to death while resisting eviction from her apartment in the Bronx. She was $98.85, or one month, behind in her rent. New York City mayor Ed Koch and police commissioner Benjamin Ward described the struggle preceding her demise as involving two officers with plastic shields, one officer with a restraining hook, another officer with a shotgun, and at least one supervising officer. All the officers also carried service revolvers. According to Commissioner Ward, during the course of the attempted eviction Eleanor Bumpurs escaped from the restraining hook twice and wielded a knife that Commissioner Ward says was "bent" on one of the plastic shields. At some point, Officer Stephen Sullivan, the officer positioned farthest away from her, aimed and fired his shotgun. It is alleged that the blast removed half of her hand, so that, according to the Bronx district attorney's office, "it was anatomically impossible for her to hold the knife."[7] The officer pumped his gun and shot again, making his mark completely the second time around.[8]

Since 1984, Mayor Koch, Commissioner Ward, and a host of other city officials repeatedly have described the shooting of Eleanor Bumpurs as completely legal.[9] At the same time, Ward has admitted publicly that Bumpurs should not have died. Koch admitted that her death was the result of "a chain of mistakes and circumstances" that came together in the worst possible way, with the worst possible consequences.[10] Ward admitted that the officers could have waited for Bumpurs to calm down, and that they could have used tear gas or mace instead of gunfire. According to Ward, however, these observations are made with hindsight. As to whether this shooting of a black woman by a white police officer had racial overtones, he stated that he had "no evidence of racism."[11] Ward pointed out that he is sworn to uphold the law, which is "inconsistent with treating blacks differently,"[12] and that the shooting was legal because it was within the code of police ethics.[13] Finally, city officials have resisted criticism of the police department's handling of the incident by remarking that "outsiders" do not know all the facts and do not understand the pressure under which officers labor.

The root of the word "legal" is the Latin word *lex,* which means law in a fairly concrete sense — law as we understand it when we refer to written law, codes, and systems of obedience.[14] The word *lex* does not include the more abstract, ethical dimension of law that contemplates the purposes of rules and their effective implementation. This latter meaning is contained in the Latin word *jus,* from which we derive the word "justice."[15] This semantic distinction is not insignificant. The law, whether statutory or judicial, is a subcategory of the underlying social motives and beliefs from which it is born. It is the technical embodiment of attempts to order society according to a consensus of ideals.

Cultural needs and ideals change with the momentum of time; redefining our laws in keeping with the spirit of cultural flux keeps society alive and humane. In the Bumpers case, the words of the law called for nonlethal alternatives first, but allowed some officer discretion in determining which situations are so immediately life endangering as to require the use of deadly force.[16] This discretionary area was presumably the basis for the claim that Officer Sullivan acted legally. The law as written permitted shooting in general, and therefore, by extension of the city's interpretation of this law, it would be impossible for a police officer ever to shoot someone in a specifically objectionable way.

If our laws are thus piano-wired on the exclusive validity of literalism, if they are picked clean of their spirit, then society risks heightened irresponsibility for the consequences of abominable actions. We also risk subjecting ourselves to such absurdly empty rhetoric as Benjamin Ward's comments to the effect that both Eleanor Bumpurs's death and racism were unfortunate, while stating, "but the law says ..."[17] The law thus becomes a shield behind which to avoid responsibility for the human repercussions of both governmental and publicly harmful private activity.

A related issue is the degree to which much of the criticism of the police department's handling of this case was devalued as "noisy" or excessively emotional. It is as though passionate protest were a separate crime, a rudeness of such dimension as to defeat altogether any legitimacy of content.

But undue literalism is only one type of sleight of tongue in the attainment of meaningless dialogue. Mayor Koch, Commissioner Ward, and Officer Sullivan's defense attorneys have used overgeneralization as an effective rhetorical complement to their avoidance of the issues. For example, allegations that the killing was illegal and unnecessary, and should therefore be prosecuted, were met with responses such as "The laws permit police officers to shoot people."[18] "As long as police officers have guns, there will be unfortunate deaths."[19] "The conviction rate in cases like this is very low." The observation that tear gas would have been an effective alternative to shooting Eleanor Bumpurs drew the dismissive reply that "there were lots of things they could have done."[20]

"Discrimination Doesn't Hurt as much as Being Assaulted" or "A Prejudiced Society Is better than A Violent Society"

The attempt to split bias from violence has been this society's most enduring and fatal rationalization. Prejudice does hurt, however, just as the absence of prejudice can nourish and shelter. Discrimination can repel and vilify, ostracize and alienate. White people who do not believe this should try telling everyone they meet that one of their ancestors was black. I had a friend in college who, having lived her life as a blonde, grey-eyed white person, discovered that she was one-sixteenth black. She began to externalize all the unconscious baggage that "black" bore for her: the self-hatred that is racism. She did not think of herself as a racist (nor had I), but she literally wanted to jump out of her skin, shed her flesh, and start life over again. She confided in me that she felt "fouled" and "betrayed." She also asked me whether I had ever felt this way. Her question dredged from some deep corner of my suppressed memory the recollection of feeling precisely that, when at the age of three or so, some white playmates explained to me that God had mixed mud with the pure clay of life in order to make me.

In the Vietnamese language, "the word 'I' (toi) ... means 'your servant'; there is no 'I' as such. When you talk to someone, you establish a relationship."[21] Such a concept of "self" is a way of experiencing the other, ritualistically sharing the other's essence, and cherishing it. In our culture, seeing and feeling the dimension of harm that results from separating self from "other" require more work.[22] Very little in our language or our culture encourages or reinforces any attempt to look at others as part of ourselves. With the imperviously divided symmetry of the marketplace, social costs to blacks are simply not seen as costs to whites,[23] just as blacks do not share in the advances whites may enjoy.

This structure of thought is complicated by the fact that the distancing does not stop with the separation of the white self from the black other. In addition, the cultural domination of blacks by whites means that the black self is placed at a distance even from itself, as in the example of blacks being asked to put themselves in the position of the white shopkeepers who view them.[24] So blacks are conditioned from infancy to see in themselves only what others who despise them see.[25]

It is true that conforming to what others see in us is every child's way of becoming socialized.[26] It is what makes children in our society seem so gullible, so impressionable, so "impolitely" honest, so blindly loyal, and so charming to the ones they imitate. Yet this conformity also describes a way of being that relinquishes the power of independent ethical choice. Although such a relinquishment can have quite desirable social consequences, it also presumes a fairly homogeneous social context in which values are shared and enforced collectively. Thus, it is no wonder that Western anthropologists and ethnographers, for whom adulthood is manifested by the exercise of independent ethical judgment, so frequently denounce tribal cultures or other collectivist ethics as "childlike."

By contrast, our culture constructs some, but not all, selves to be the servants of others. Thus, some "I's" are defined as "your servant," some as "your master." The struggle for the self becomes not a true mirroring of self-in-other, but rather a hierarchically inspired series of distortions, in which some serve without ever being served, some master without ever being mastered, and almost everyone hides from this vernacular domination by clinging to the legally official definition of "I" as meaning "your equal."

In such an environment, relinquishing the power of individual ethical judgment to a collective ideal risks psychic violence, an obliteration of the self through domination by an all-powerful other. In such an environment, it is essential at some stage that the self be permitted to retreat into itself and make its own decisions with self-love and self-confidence. What links child abuse, the mistreatment of women, and racism is the massive external intrusion into psyche that dominating powers impose to keep the self from ever fully seeing itself.[27] Because the self's power resides in another, little faith is placed in the true self, that is, in one's own experiential knowledge. Consequently, the power of children, women, and blacks is actually reduced to the "intuitive" rather than the real; social life is necessarily based primarily on the imaginary. Furthermore, because it is difficult to affirm constantly with the other the congruence of the self's imagining what the other is really thinking of the self, and because even that correlative effort is usually kept within very limited family, neighborhood, religious, or racial boundaries, encounters cease to be social and become presumptuous, random, and disconnected.

The Gift of Intelligent Rage

OWNING THE SELF IN A DISOWNED WORLD

While I was in grammar school in the 1960s, a white man acting out of racial motives killed a black man who was working for some civil rights organization or cause. The man was stabbed thirty-nine times, a number that prompted a radio commentator to observe that the point was not just murder, but something beyond.

Taking the example of the man who was stabbed thirty-nine times out of the context of our compartmentalized legal system, and considering it in the hypothetical framework of a legal system that encompasses and recognizes morality, religion, and psychology, I am moved to see this act as not merely body murder but spirit-murder as well. I see it as spirit-murder, only one of whose manifestations is racism; cultural obliteration, prostitution, abandonment of the elderly and the homeless, and genocide are some of its other guises. I see spirit-murder as no less than the equivalent of body murder.

One of the reasons that I fear what I call spirit-murder, or disregard for others whose lives qualitatively depend on our regard, is that its product is a system of formalized distortions of thought. It produces social structures centered around fear and hate; it provides a tumorous outlet for feelings elsewhere unexpressed. I think we need to elevate what I call spirit-murder to the conceptual, if not punitive level of a capital moral offense.[28] We need to see it as a cultural cancer; we need to open our eyes to the spiritual genocide it is wreaking on blacks, whites, and the abandoned and abused of all races and ages. We need to eradicate its numbing pathology before it wipes out what precious little humanity we have left.

Mirrors and Windows

My life experiences had prepared me better to comprehend and sympathize with the animating force behind the outraged, dispossessed knife wielding of Eleanor Bumpurs. What I found more difficult to focus on was the "why," the animus that inspired such fear, and such impatient contempt in a police officer that the presence of six other heavily armed men could not allay his need to kill a sick old lady fighting off hallucinations with a knife. It seemed to me a fear embellished by something beyond Bumpurs herself; something about her enlarged to fill the void between her physical, limited presence and the "immediate threat and endangerment to life" that filled the beholding eyes of the officer. Why was the sight of a knife-wielding woman so fearfully offensive to a shotgun-wielding policeman that he felt that blowing her to pieces was the only recourse, the only way to preserve his physical integrity? What offensive spirit of his past experience raised her presence to the level of a physical menace beyond real dimensions? What spirit of prejudgment and prejudice provided him with such a powerful hallucinogen?

However slippery these questions may be on a legal or conscious level, unresponsiveness to them does not make these issues go away. Failure to resolve the dilemma of racial violence merely displaces its power. The legacy of killing finds its way into cultural expectations, archetypes, and "isms." The echoes of both dead and deadly others acquire a hallucinatory quality; their voices speak of an unwanted past, but also reflect for us images of the future. Today's world condemns those voices as superstitious and paranoid. Neglected, they speak from the shadows of such inattention, in garbles and growls, in the tongues of the damned and insane. The superstitious listen, and perhaps in the silence of their attention, they hear and understand. So-called enlightened others who fail to listen to the voices of demonic selves, made invisibly uncivilized, simply make them larger, more barbarously enraged, until the nearsightedness of looking glass existence is smashed in upon by the terrible dispossession of dreams too long deferred.

Notes

Patricia J. Williams, "Spirit-Murdering the Messenger: The Discourse of Fingerpointing as the Law's Response to Racism," *University of Miami Law Review* 42, no. 1 (1987). Reprinted with the permission of the University of Miami Law Review. American spelling has been retained in this article.

1. Gross, "When 'By Appointment' Means Keep Out," *The New York Times,* 17 December 1986, B1.
2. Ibid.
3. Michael Levin and Marguerita Levin, Letter to the Editor, *The New York Times,* 11 January 1987, E32.
4. Ibid.
5. Gross, "When 'By Appointment' Means Keep Out."
6. Levin and Levin, Letter to the Editor. The fact that some blacks might agree with the store owners shows that some of us have learned too well the lessons of privatized self-hatred and rationalized away the fullness of our public, participatory selves.
7. *The New York Times,* 12 January 1987, B2.
8. *The New York Times,* 27 February 1987, B1.
9. Benjamin Ward (Police Commissioner of New York City), Remarks at City University of

New York (CUNY) Law School (November 1985) (audiotape on file at CUNY).

10. *The New York Times,* 21 November 1984, B3.
11. Ibid.
12. Ward, Remarks at CUNY.
13. Raab, "Ward Defends Police Actions in Bronx Death," *The New York Times,* 3 November 1984, paragraph 1, p. 27.
14. *Webster's Ninth Collegiate Dictionary* (1983), p. 682.
15. Ibid.
16. Laws requiring police officers to use nonlethal alternatives are prevalent in this country. Nationwide, a majority of the states have specific provisions governing the use of deadly force. As a general proposition, efforts to control the use of deadly force have not fared too well over time. For example, the Missouri legislature rejected the suggestion of its advisory committee to limit the use of deadly force when he or she "reasonably believes" such force is necessary. Of the states evaluated, over half dealt with the issue of the use of force, but few adhered to the standard of the Model Penal Code concerning the police decision to use force. The approach of the legislatures evaluated has to be described as one of maintaining extensive discretion in the use of force – not of limiting it. Patricia Williams, "The Politics of Police Discretion," in C. Pinkele and W. Louthan, eds., *Discretion, Justice, and Democracy* (Ames: Iowa State University Press, 1985), 23.
17. Ward, Remarks at CUNY.
18. Raab, "Ward Defends Police Actions in Bronx Death."
19. Ibid.; Ward, Remarks at CUNY.
20. Ward, Remarks at CUNY. See also, *The New York Times,* 21 November 1984, B3 (Mayor Koch's description of the Bumpurs incident).
21. D. Berrigan and T. Nhat Hanh, T*he Raft Is Not the Shore* (Boston: Beacon Press, 1975), 38.
22. See generally, J. Lacan, "Aggressivity in Psychoanalysis," in *Ecrits: A Selection* (New York: W.W. Norton, 1977), 23-4, challenging the tendency of our language to equate "I" with the subject.
23. The starkest recent example of this has been the disastrous delay in the response to the AIDS epidemic; as long as AIDS was seen as an affliction affecting Haitians, Hispanics, Africans, and other marginalized groups such as intravenous drug users and homosexuals, its long-term implications were ignored. "Health Experts Fault U.S. on Response to AIDS," *The New York Times,* 12 August 1987, A20, col. 1.
24. Levin and Levin, Letter to the Editor.
25. See generally, K. Clark, Dark Ghetto (Middletown, CT: Wesleyan University Press, 1965); K. Clark, *Prejudice and Your Child* (Middletown, CT: Wesleyan University Press, 1955); J. Comer and A. Poussaint, *Black Child Care* (New York: Simon and Schuster, 1975); W. Grier and P. Cobbs, *Black Rage* (New York: Basic Books, 1968).
26. See generally, Selznick, "Law, Society and Moral Evaluation," in P. Schuchman, ed., *Readings in Jurisprudence and Legal Philosophy* (1979), 931, 947–49.
27. See generally, A. Miller, *The Drama of the Gifted Child* (New York: Basic Books, 1984).
28. See, for example, Delgado, "Words that Wound: A Tort Action for Racial Insults, Epithets and Name-Calling," *Harvard C.R.-C.L. Law Review* 17 (1982), 133.

Chapter Ten

Transgressive Whiteness:

The Social Construction of White Women Involved in Interracial Relationships with Black Men

Katerina Deliovsky

When I became openly involved in an interracial relationship with an African-Jamaican man my life changed significantly. The rapid and sudden change created feelings of disorientation and terror. I was forced to leave my parents' home with nothing but the clothes on my back. My family members expressed outrage and disappointment in many forms — both physical and psychological. Life became very burdensome and stressful, and I never knew when I would be forced to confront some form of anti-interracial sentiment. I lived in fear of what might happen. When I became pregnant with my first child, my father ordered me to abort "or else." I feared the "or else." I lived in trepidation that a family member would find me and kick my pregnant belly, causing me to spontaneously abort and be rid of this "so called" contagion. I experienced what I identify as psychic injury — or spirt-murder as Patricia Williams refers to it[1] — an injury to the spirit that felt like a heavy weight around my heart.

In the early part of my relationship with my partner, I would often wonder how we were going to survive. There were times we did not cope well. The external pressures were difficult to bear and sometimes we took it out on each other. But over the years life became a little easier and I became a different person. The negative energy that strangers hurl at me is less frequent now and does not touch me as painfully as it once did. The reason is that I now understand there is a history that preceded my relationship with my partner: a history of miscegnation, relationships of love surrounded by a hate and fear that I knew only too well.

For example, from the 1850s into the 1900s, it was the unspoken presumption that no upstanding White woman would freely consent to an interracial relationship with a Black man. Given the racist depictions of Black men as dangerous sexual predators, such unions were an affront to White common sense. Indeed, if there were Black male–White female relations, it was the Black man who was accused of wrongdoing. In 1908, a Black Canadian man living in Chatham, Ontario, was punished, ostensibly, for "luring a [young] White [woman] from her home."[2] The man was given a five-year jail sentence and forty lashes. In another incident, a mob of White citizens surrounded a Black man's house yelling "hang the nigger"[3] for reportedly "forcing" a young White woman to carry his child. Colin Thomson in *Blacks In Deep Snow: Black Pioneers in Canada* argues that these incidents are only a few of the "many which indicated the Canadian taboo on interracial sexual relations," a view shared by the first prime minister of Canada.[4] In a letter written in 1868, Sir John A. Macdonald wrote:

> We still retained the punishment of death for rape ... We have thought it well ... to continue it on account of the frequency of rape committed by negroes, of whom we have too many in Upper Canada. They are very prone to felonious

> assaults on White women: if the sentence and imprisonment were not very severe there would be a great dread of the people taking the law into their own hands.[5]

For a long time before I understood this history, my family's and society's response made little sense to me. Why was I living on the brink of homelessness just because I loved an African-Jamaican man and was carrying our child? What was I doing that was so morally and ethically reprehensible? What was it about our baby growing in my womb that needed to be destroyed? What was it about my partner's body that made him dangerous *a priori* to any contact with him?

These questions stayed with me over the years and I began to search for answers, a search that was really a solitary quest, only sometimes shared with my partner. As an undergraduate student I eagerly read any book that might give me some clues. The most insightful were those by Black feminists and anti-racist scholars such as bell hooks, Hazel Carby, Franz Fanon and Paul Hoch. Their work sent me on a journey towards understanding how powerful are the meanings and representations inscribed on the bodies of White women and Black men. But I didn't share my new-found knowledge with anyone outside my intimate circle. Too many of my social experiences were hostile and disturbing, and because I could only anticipate more negative responses, I silenced myself. I didn't feel strong enough to share my knowledge with the world. But as I became stronger, more confident in my quest for self-understanding, I developed a sense of the importance of giving voice to my experiences.

I came to understand that in being silent I was hurting myself. And I began to talk, perhaps timidly, but talking nonetheless. It was an act of personal liberation, and the more confident I became, the more I realized that not only did my experiences need a forum for expression, but so did the experiences of other White women in interracial relationships with Black men. And so this is where I find myself today — *speaking* about these experiences.

This essay is an attempt to legitimate my voice and those of women who are in similar relationships. Equally, this essay serves to open fresh discussion about interracial unions and the social context in which they exist. I attempt to illustrate how the experiences of White women in interracial unions with Black men can illuminate stark social inequalites based on race, class and gender, and to better understand how White women in interracial relationships with Black men are historically and currently perceived through the lens of whiteness.

In "The Multicultural Wars," Hazel Carby writes: "[E]veryone in this social order has been constructed in our political imagination as a racialized subject."[6] As such, all people living in North America have a place in the social and racial hierarchy. However, for the most part, it has been racialized communities which have been viewed and constructed as racial objects to be examined. In comparison, White people in relation to their Whiteness have been left unexamined. As Richard Dyer points out:

> The invisibility of Whiteness as a racial position in White discourse is a piece of its ubiquity ... In fact for most of the time White people speak about nothing but White people, it's just that we couch it in terms of "people" in general ...Whites are everywhere in representation. Yet precisely because of this and their placing as norm they seem not to be represented to themselves *as* Whites but as people who are variously gendered, classed, sexualized and abled. At the level of racial representation, in other words, Whites are not of a certain race, they're just the human race.[7]

My goal, then, is to draw attention to racial constructions of White women's bodies. My reasons are guided by two factors. First, it is important to acknowledge that White women's bodies are also raced bodies. Because of the structural advantage of whiteness, which universalizes White people, race has been constructed to be the stigmatized transcendental property of racialized women. The failure to see White women as raced has created a situation where the *burden* of race primarily falls on the bodies of racialized women. But, if everyone is constructed as a racialized subject, as Carby writes, how then are White women racialized? How do they experience their "raced" bodies, particularly in the context of interracial relationships? Second, by establishing that White women are raced in the first place, this acknowledgement allows for the critical elaboration of the conditions that bring this "raceness" into focus. My experiences in an interracial relationship suggest that one of those times might be when White women transgress the appropriate codes of conduct in White patriarchal society and involve themselves in interracial relationships with Black men.

Constructing Whiteness

When an interracial couple, consisting of a Black man and a White woman, walk down any North American street they are not simply "a man and a woman" walking down the street. As raced and sexed subjects, their bodies are interwoven into a system of meaning and representation that existed prior to their entry on to the street. Race, as it is practised in the West, is a way of categorizing different types of human bodies. By assigning characteristics to certain bodies and skin colour, differences are systematized and assigned human value and worth. The value and worth of White femininity is generally positive and affirming, while the value and worth of Black masculinity is negative and pejorative. Heterosexuality is the means of ensuring as well as endangering the reproduction of these differences.[8] Consequently, Black men and White women exist not only in a "saturated field of racial visibility," as Judith Butler would argue, but an optic saturated with racial and sexual visibility.[9] Therefore when they walk down the street they are not just simply a man and a woman, they are a Black man and a White woman. Their union, perceived through a field of racial and sexual visibility, produces a hypervisibility which does not allow them the normalcy given to same-race couples. But in order to comprehend how White women exist in a field saturated with racial and sexual visibility, it is important to understand how representations of whiteness and blackness have been mapped onto the bodies of both White women and Black men.

The construction of White femininity and Black masculinity, according to Paul Hoch in *White Hero Black Beast: Racism, Sexism and the Mask of Masculinity*, is as old as class structure in Western societies.[10] In Western class-stratified societies, masculinity is often established through various forms of competition between men for domination over other "less worthy" men and for domination over all women. White men have established dominance over racialized men through imperialism, slavery and colonialism. Alongside these methods of conquest came the creation of cultural myths, which helped to establish and maintain dominance. One of the widely circulated myths in Western society is the conquest of White manhood over the Black villain whose evil and unrestrained sexuality is a threat to White women, or "the White Goddess."[11] In White cultural mythology, Hoch explains, "[t]he White Goddess [is] clearly in danger; [and usually] her would-be attackers [are] super-masculine black beasts."[12] The goal for White men, then, is to save the "White Goddess" from the super-masculine Black beasts.

In a similar explanation, bell hooks illustrates how a historical narrative of pornographic sexual projection of fantasy and fear was displaced onto Black men. This narrative, fabricated by White men, depicts the "desperate longing Black men have to sexually violate the bodies of White women."[13] The central character in this story is the Black male rapist who is constructed as a dangerous menace to White society. A historical image which is today manipulated by the media to manufacture the belief that a "Black menace" is at large and the only viable means of safety is repression and violent domination. Representations of the Black male body in current popular culture are still informed by these constructions of masculinity. Not only has the mass media manipulated these images, so too have politicians, government officials and entertainers. Much of the intent for using this cultural currency is to deflect from the actual material, economic and moral consequences of perpetuating White supremacy and its traumatic, life-altering impact on Black men and women and others in capitalist society.[14]

Black sexuality, bell hooks contends, has been historically and socially constructed in a negative image as opposed to the positive image of innocent White womanhood. In the nineteenth century, there was a shift away from fundamentalist Christian doctrine that perceived women as a sexual temptress and a new image was constructed that depicted White women "as a goddess rather than sinner; she was virtuous, pure, innocent, not sexual and worldly."[15] This new idealization of White womanhood served as an act of exorcism, transforming her image as a "fallen woman" to that of a virtuous woman. Once the American White female was cleansed of the curse of forbidden sexuality, she became mythologized as pure and virtuous. It was then that she became worthy of love, worship and respect. The curse of forbidden sexuality became fully displaced onto the bodies of Black women. This idealization, however, did not alter the fundamental misogyny White men felt towards White women. hooks contends that in a White supremacist sexist society all women's bodies are devalued. However, White women's bodies are considered more worthy than other women's bodies.

Similar to Hoch and hooks, Richard Dyer explains how the idealization of White femininity converges with aesthetic standards informed by White supremacy. In *White*, he writes, "The White woman as angel ... [is] both the symbol of White virtuousness and the last word in the claim that what [makes] Whites special as a race [is] their non-physical, spiritual, indeed ethereal qualities."[16] However, to sustain these unique qualities, the White woman must not betray her role in the White masculine order. When White women do transgress the cardinal rule of White male supremacy there is indeed a dilemma, for as Dyer explains, "interracial heterosexuality threatens the power of Whiteness because it breaks the legitimation of Whiteness with reference to the White body ... if White bodies are no longer indubitably White bodies ... then the 'natural' basis of their domination is no longer credible."[17]

Supporting Dyer's contention, Ruth Frankenberg, in *White Women, Race Matters: The Social Construction of Whiteness*, found during her interviews with thirty White women that the construction of whiteness and gender were most visible in the area of heterosexual interracial relationships. She suggests that White women who crossed the boundaries of colour and race no longer fit neatly into the racial order of North American society. Symbolically, these women's inclusion into their "rightful" place in the racial hierarchy was altered due to their interracial transgressions. For such women the "range of possible meanings of White femininity ... [was] transformed in interracial contexts."[18] White women in relationships with racialized men were frequently reduced to sexual beings, as well as constructed as less bound by social controls. Frankenberg also suggests that these women experienced a phenomenon she identifies as a "rebound effect," which is a "force that owes its existence and direction to an earlier aim and impact, yet retains enough force to wound."[19] The impact of racism on these White women originates from, and is shaped by, their intimate involvement with a Black man. However, the effect is "neither identical nor merely a weaker version of the original impact: it is qualitatively new."[20]

In a study conducted in the late 1970s in the United States, Ernest Potterfield found it common for young White women who dated Black men to be sent to mental institutions or psychiatrists or to be disowned by family members.[21] Evidently, in White society's view, only psychologically unstable White women would date Black men, and those White women who could not be saved from themselves were either institutionalized or subjected to social and familial sanctions.

Transgressive Whiteness and Stigma Transference

Given the historical significance of White women's and Black men's symbolic representation, how do White women in interracial relationships with Black men fare in contemporary Canada? Does the "rebound effect" Frankenberg identified suggest that these women's lives are marked with emotional and physical violence? Are their identities spoiled due to their racial transgressions and therefore their whiteness is deemed null and void? How do society, family and friends perceive, construct and react to these women's intimate relationships? To answer these questions, I draw on a life history study I conducted between 1997 and 1999 with six White women in interracial relationships with Black men. The women interviewed had a variety of characteristics, which included differences in age, ethnicity and class. Three women were of English background while the other three were of Czechoslovakian, Ukrainian and Italian backgrounds. Their ages ranged from twenty-two to forty-nine. Five of the women were unknown to me prior to the interviews and came primarily by word-of-mouth, and one was a casual acquaintance. The interviews were based on forty questions and lasted anywhere between forty-five to ninety-five minutes. My criterion for choosing the women was that they had to have had an intimate involvement with a Black man which they defined as committed and serious. While it was not necessary that they were at the time involved with Black men, I required that their relationship spanned at least six months. The rationale for this six-month criterion was that it allowed for the possibility of diverse and varied experiences.

On the basis of the data, I distilled categories that showed how social constructions of White femininity and Black masculinity informed aspects of these women's lives and "spoiled"[22] their social identities. I also define and elaborate on a unique and primary feature of these women's experiences I refer to as stigma transference.

Once You Go Black, You Never Go Back

In the time I have associated with Black men, I always felt there was a very strange and exaggerated response from my family members, friends and the public. Over the course of fifteen years with my partner, I have heard numerous times that "once you go Black you never go back." It was always said with a grin, a chuckle or a wink. Did they know something that I didn't? Invariably questions followed this comment: "Is it true?" they would ask. Until chastened by experience, I would innocently respond, "What is *it*?" "You know, *it* — his penis. Is it really as big as they say? Is sex with a Black man better?" Initially dumbfounded, I came to sarcastically respond, "I wouldn't know. I haven't screwed every Black man on the planet to find out." What I learned from these experiences was that my association with Black men was interpreted through an eroticized discourse of sexual pleasure and penis size.

My experiences particularly resonated with Barbara. At the time of the interview, Barbara, of British descent, was a forty-nine-year-old woman working as a market researcher. She believed that White men are sexually intimidated by Black men:

> I think that White men are totally intimidated by Black men, anyway from a sexual point of view. I think they sort of resent the fact that you might not find them attractive because you hung out with Black guys, therefore that is your standard of attraction and so you wouldn't be attracted to them, and they resent that.

In my discussion with Barbara, I related my experience with Andrew, an Italian-Canadian whom I had been dating years before my involvement with my current partner. Andrew and I had a casual dating relationship. On one occasion while driving to the corner store, he decided to make a personal confession. Being a co-worker with my ex-boyfriend, Andrew told me that he was aware that I had been seriously involved with a Black man. In light of this, he thought it only fair to tell me that he had a small penis. I was stunned by his disclosure and thought I had misheard him. Not understanding the reasons that had compelled his disclosure, I asked him why he would feel a need to tell me such a thing. He said he felt it was an important issue because I had been with a Black man and in the eventuality of us having sex, I would not be terribly disappointed by his size. When I relayed my story to Barbara, she laughed all the while nodding in recognition. She exclaimed at the end of my narrative,

> Exactly! I think there is a lot of penis focus from White guys, "once you go Black you never go back." You must have heard that a million times ... It's wild, eh? It's because White men have tiny little penises, very small [she says sarcastically]. When you are in a society that has developed penis enhancers, you know you are in big trouble.

After speaking with other women, it was evident that the association with Black men and large genitalia was not exclusive to our experiences. It was a common mythology about Black men that was known to the other women. Donna, for example, commented on the same point when she spoke about what she believed shaped her father's response to her interracial relationship. She said,

> My father acts as if my partner has a super huge penis and so, I think, [that my father] thinks, and all other White men, that I am being fucked real good. Excuse my vulgar language. But I really think that is what goes through their minds. When they see me with him, they see lots and lots of wild insatiable sex.

Whether it be sexual or more generally relating to culture, there is something about "blackness" that is framed as overpowering and hence, when "you go Black, you never go back." The implication is that "going Black" is like a drug addiction. And like a drug addict, White women in interracial relationships crave the drug. The Black male is equated to the drug — addictive, but pleasurably overpowering, and to be avoided because there is "no point of return."

The myth of Black men as evil and beast-like was a driving force behind Marina's family's reactions. Marina identified herself as a twenty-seven-year-old Italian Canadian. As an example, she described how her sister-in-law protects her nephew when she visits by pinning a "horn" pendant to the baby, "As if I'm gonna, like, curse my nephew ... they [don't] even let me hold [him]." Her family acts this way "because Jonathan is Black and ... they think I'm going to put some 'Black' on [my nephew]." The horn, she explains, is a Mediterranean and Eastern European symbol that has power to ward off evil. In other words, the pendant provides protection against the blackness to which Marina has succumbed or which has contaminated her. Not only is the association between blackness and evil present, so too is the idea that all Black people are prone to engage in lascivious and immoral behaviour. In this respect, Marina explains that her family believes that "all Black people are druggies, are robbers, are cheaters, cannot have a family." As Marina's boyfriend was permanently marked by an evil, she too, by virtue of her relationship with him, was also marked as lascivious and prone to evil.

Barbara, who has been in an interracial relationship for over twenty-five years and had previously dated men from various "racial" groups, also described this social perception of White women who date Black men:

> The fact that you were going out with Black men made you somehow out of that norm, way more than anyone else. Your friends may have slept with fifteen guys, but if you slept with one Black guy it was way worse than anything else you could have done ... Somehow you are much more promiscuous, much more loose ... than some little White woman in a White-only relationship who screws everything that moves.

Donna described the exaggerated response she received because of her involvement with Sean. At the time of the interview, Donna, a Czechoslovakian Canadian, was thirty-two years old and just completing her PhD:

> No matter what. No matter how many degrees I have, whether I have Doctor in front of my name, behind my name, whether I am driving a BMW — I am with him and my kids are mixed — *I am stained.* (Emphasis mine.)

She explained how some people treat her because of this stain: "[You] get treated like there is something wrong with you. I can't explain it. It is like people don't want to touch you, they don't want to look at you too long. If they look at you somehow it will *rub off* on them." (Emphasis mine.) Barbara referred to a similar idea of contagion, "People don't want to get too close to you because they don't want to get tarnished. You find you don't have many female friends — that's how it translates." Similarly, Donna commented that she has not made friends because of her association with Black men, "I think that I have probably not made friends because of it. In part because I want to protect myself."

RACIAL TRANSGRESSIONS

What is it about blackness and those associated with it that make some White people act as though it were a contagion, something that will rub off or tarnish them? Clues to these questions lie in the women's narratives themselves. Marina's family associated blackness with evil. Barbara's experiences illustrate that society associates blackness with some kind of metaphysical power that overtakes women who are involved with Black men. As well, the narratives illustrate that Black men are associated with large genitalia and sexual potency. None of these discourses are new or surprising. The association of Black people with evil and lascivious behaviour has a long history.

For example, in Western societies between the seventeenth and nineteenth centuries, the "Great Chain of Being" was a widely known model that categorized all life on a hierarchical scale. Naturally perceiving themselves masters of the world, elite White men were on top and Black people oscillated between the bottom of the human scale and the top of the animal kingdom.[23] Within this hierarchy, Black men and women were constructed as embodying all that was "lower" and "sexual"; Black men represented the dark bestial forces of lust and were prone to raping White women.[24] The conception of the Black male was constructed in predominantly genital terms — he was a "walking phallus." He was thought to be endowed with large genitalia, and in a Eurocentric world that had a phallocentric idealization of masculinity, the Black male reigned supreme. Here was a paradox: the Black man became simultaneously the model of super masculine potency and absolute debasement.

Foregrounded by this history, when these women did not guard the sanctity of their whiteness and involved themselves with Black men, White society and family members were quick to point out their transgression. They were called names like "White slut," "nigger lover" and "White trash." Barbara said, "When I was in my twenties people would shout out of the car windows 'nigger lover' and stuff like that." More recently, Marina had a similar experience: "We were downtown going to the hair dresser holding hands, a car drives by and only White guys [are in the car and they yell out,] 'Hey you nigger lover.'" Marina also experienced verbal responses that most of the other women did not. She recalled her father's response when he found out about her partner Jonathan, "You are a whore, you are a slut, you are White trash ... you are worse than dirt." Verbal assaults like these were not restricted solely to Marina's family relations. Her former boss verbally attacked her character on the job: "Nigger lover. White trash. We don't need White trash working in our store." In an all too familiar narrative, Donna says, "You get really tired of being called a nigger lover, White slut, White trash, White bitch."

The defining characteristics of these verbal assaults are meant to degrade the women and put them in their "place" for their "transgressions." The instability and conditionality of White femininity hint at what Erving Goffman calls "spoiled identity," a conception which supports Frankenberg's contention that White women experience a "rebound effect" for their "racial transgressions." Like the double consciousness of W.E.B. Dubois, one private and one public,[25] Goffman suggests that a discrepancy exists between a person's virtual and actual identity. Through various means, society categorizes people and categorizes complimentary attributes deemed appropriate for those people in each category. Likewise "social settings establish the categories of persons likely to be encountered there."[26] The routines of daily living in those established settings allow people to handle "anticipated others" without much thought. When a "stranger" comes into an established setting it is the initial appearance of the stranger that enables people to anticipate the stranger's category and attributes — meaning her/his social identity. People lean on these anticipations and transform "them into normative expectations, [and] into righteously presented demands."[27] When a stranger possesses an attribute that marks her/him as different from others in relation to the normative expectations or categories, he/she is reduced from a whole and "usual" person to a tainted, discredited person.

Goffman calls this attribute of being marked and devalued a *stigma.* It is the apparent stigma that causes the discrepancy between one's virtual and actual social identity. Goffman states that a stigma such as "race" can be transmitted through lineage and equally contaminates all family members. I argue this transmission of race suggests that White women's involvement with men who have the stigma of race contaminate them and consequently discredit their virtual social identity. When a White woman transgresses racial boundaries, her discrepancy becomes socially apparent and spoils her social identity. This transgression "has the effect of cutting [her] off from society and from [herself] so that [she] stands a discredited person facing an unaccepting world."[28] Thus White women who involve themselves with Black men experience a discrepancy between their virtual and actual identities, which amounts to the spoiling of their social identities.

However, there needs to be a more aggressive deconstruction and analysis of the consistent responses they receive from White society. For example, why the emphasis on White in "White slut, White trash, White bitch"? Why not just slut or bitch? When a White woman involves herself with a Black man she is constructed as promiscuous and immoral. But why is she a "White slut" and not just a "slut"? Why even call a woman who is involved with a Black man "slut"? When strangers drive by a White couple do they yell out the car window "White slut," let alone "slut"? When a father learns that his adult White daughter is in love with a White man does he call her "White trash"? The answer in each case is no. These questions seem almost absurd. But we need to go to the absurd to understand and deconstruct this phenomenon.

I believe we must attend to the association and relationship between whiteness, blackness and sexuality in this society. In order to understand the association, it is helpful to ask the question, How does a White person know they are "White" and not "pink" or "beige"? A White person knows they are White because they are *not* "Black." In the same vein, how does a man know he is a man? A man knows he is a man because he is *not* a "woman." These binary opposites are not just colour or sex designations, they are social definitions and symbolic manicheanisms that mark the boundaries of power, privilege and belonging in Western society. In a long and complex history, which I cannot elaborate on here, White people have constructed a racial category called "White."[29] The racial appellation of "White" is not only constructed as a unique category belonging to White people, it is also ideologically juxtaposed to blackness or darkness.[30] As such, it is part of a referential system that signals for White people "the production and reproduction of dominance rather than subordination, normativity rather than marginality and privilege rather than disadvantage."[31]

While not all White individuals have absolute privilege, any more than all males have absolute privilege, individuals whose ascribed characteristics include Whiteness (and maleness) will find the benefits of that ascription accruing to them. Overlaying the racial appellation are gender distinctions, which mark the boundaries of acceptable conduct and appropriate behaviour. In this context of racial and gender significance, when a White woman takes a Black man for a lover/husband, her whiteness, femininity/sexuality and conduct come into being and therefore into question. The power of whiteness lies in its invisibility, in it *not* being distinctive in its corporeality.[32]

A White woman's whiteness remains non-distinctive, as long as she is with a White man which, by extension, means her whiteness is mediated by the person with whom she forms intimate attachments. Her whiteness and sexuality are commodities used for their exchange value — the reproduction of whiteness (and maleness) and therefore White, male, racial dominance. This fact never comes into question when she remains "in-house." So when she transgresses the colour line she is not only a slut, she is a "White slut." She has closed off her womb to White racial reproduction and, therefore, she is to be publicly degraded — made to be a spectacle by the "appellation"[33] of her transgressive White femininity. In the appellation, she is hailed as an object of transgressive virtue and, in being made a spectacle, she serves as a disciplinary example to other would-be transgressors.

Social Stigmatization

While these discourses play a central role in how these women experience their interracial relationships, what is revealing is the extent to which these women are stigmatized. In the attempt to conceptually capture the depth and complexity of their experiences, I borrow from Erving Goffman the concepts of "discredited" and "discreditable" social identities and extend his concept of "courtesy stigma."[34] Goffman's definition of courtesy stigma applies to "spouses and offspring of [psychiatric] patients, families of [developmental challenged] children, and convicted felons, parents of gays and others who are required to share the discredit assigned to the stigmatized individual."[35] While White women in interracial relationships with Black men do experience a social liability, the concept of "courtesy stigma" does not capture the depth and complexity of their social experience. Consequently, I have developed the idea that in extraordinary circumstances, such as Black male–White female relationships, stigma can be situationally transferred.

As with "courtesy stigma," *stigma transference* in this case lies in White women's association with what Goffman defines as a *discredited* person (a Black man), which as a result makes the White woman a *discreditable* person. The difference between the discredited and discreditable, Goffman explains, is that the discredited are known to the world as stigmatized and it is not something that can be concealed. The discreditable have the ability to "pass" because the stigma may not be immediately perceivable to society.[36] In this context, White women who date Black men, are *discreditable* and only become *discredited* situatonally in the presence of their Black partners, who are stigmatized by "race," or when their relationship becomes publicly known.

Where Goffman's concept of "courtesy stigma" differs from my concept of *stigma transference* is that the White women are condemned for their *choice* to be with a stigmatized individual. In the case of spouses and offspring of alcoholic parents or psychiatric patients, although they experience stigma, they are not socially condemned for having made a *choice* in their associations. In point of fact, they also experience pity and compassion. After all, they themselves are not the ones stigmatized.

White women in interracial relationships are seen as making a choice, a choice that marks them as traitors to their race and willful enactors of female agency. White women do not experience this stigma as a "courtesy"; rather, they experience a stigma that resembles the racism associated with their partners' blackness. A further distinction arises when race is complicated by whiteness as a structural location of social power and advantage. Because whiteness is a location of social power and advantage, White women do not possess the stigma of race and therefore can oscillate between being a discreditable and a discredited person. Simply put, these women do not possess the stigma of "black" skin. They are White women. The actual visibility and perceived knowledge of their association to the stigmatized Black male is the pivotal factor in the phenomenon of *stigma transference*, and it is that which spoils their social identities. If they were to separate and close off all attachments to their Black partners, there is a possibility that they would lose the social stigma and be redeemed, as long as their previous "transgression" was not known. Once the Black male is absent there is no visible cue to their "transgression," unless there is an interracial child involved or some lingering social knowledge of their past transgression.

Although family members and people in close proximity to their lives (friends, neighbours and work associates) may still fault them for their involvement, their access to the benefits accrued to them for their White skin remains intact. Consequently, the White skin privilege lost or altered due to their involvement is reinstated. Their access to housing, their risk of physical and psychological injury, their overall quality of life will *not* be negatively affected by their involvement with a stigmatized male. In addition, family members who previously condemned them for their choice to become intimately involved with a Black male may rethink their position and allow them their one transgression — as long as it is the *only* "transgression." They cannot be repeat offenders.

Stigma transference is complex because of the fluidity with which personal and structural power operate. The fact that the White women may not always be damned for their "transgression" and that the privilege of whiteness remains intact as long as the Black man is absent indicates the power, privilege and fluidity of whiteness that operates both at the individual and structural level. In this context, whiteness as a location of structural advantage and of race privilege signals the production and reproduction of dominance and power. However, given that it is a relational category, it is mediated by other categories of class, gender, ethnicity and sexuality.[37] In this context, as White women, they have access to the benefits and privileges accrued as a consequence of their whiteness, but as White women in interracial relationships with Black men, their benefits and privileges are mediated by *stigma transference.* The complex relationship between personal and structural power and their relationship to stigma transference is embedded in the narratives of my research participants. For example:

> *Donna*: When I am by myself, and that is not to say I get treated wonderfully when I am by myself, I think being a woman kind of marks you as well, but overall I am treated well in terms of shopping [and being serviced]. People don't gawk at me. People don't stare at me. People don't call me "White slut." I think there is a privilege I get at just being White — doors will open. I will get served. People will greet me. When I am with my children or my partner, there is a funny response.
>
> *Tammy*: I don't get the hassles ... the fact of the matter is that I am *White* and I will still have it *easier* than Black [women] and especially Black [men]. (Her emphasis.)

Diminished Desirability

The phenomenon of *stigma transference* echoes the point made by Dyer that whiteness, as a cultural signifier of privilege, is not a fixed and stable category. Its stability is maintained by its continued reproduction and perpetuation. However, for this to occur, White reproduction must go undisturbed. These White women have ceased participating in the continued reproduction of whiteness and, consequently, their intimate association with their Black partners symbolically signals to the (White) world that they are no longer available for White physical and cultural reproduction. Some of the anti-interracial discourse they identified centred on their reproduction of mixed-race children and revolved around two central issues. One issue was the question of what would happen to the children growing up in a racially hostile environment. The sentiment was that it would not be fair to bring children into a world hostile to them. The other issue revolved around the belief that mixed-race children would somehow be confused at best, and defective at worst. There was a belief that a mixture of White and Black genes would produce a congenitally undesirable specimen.

Marina's father held this belief. "He told me that if Jonathan and I get married and have children that our children would become retarded." Kelly also noted that it was when the issue of children came up that she noticed "other people [would start] saying to me, 'My goodness, think about your children.'" In a similar, yet slightly different context, Donna identified how her union was perceived when she had mixed-race children: "It kinda legitimated our union, but at the same time it was [rejected] because it was a permanent marker of our interracial violation." What these statements reveal is that the physical reproduction of whiteness is an essential part of the collective White consciousness. Jesse Daniels in *White Lies* identifies this point in her analysis of White supremacist discourse:

> The penultimate affront to White men's control over White women's sexuality and reproductive lives is a White woman who chooses to not only have sex with, but also bear children with, a Black man.[38]

These issues around reproduction become amplified when these White women are young and approximate stereotypical notions of female beauty. For example, Barbara commented:

> I am not especially a great sex symbol. I am forty-eight. You may be some sort of sexual prize when you are young but that starts to diminish as you get older. I think there is a lot of animosity for younger women in interracial relationships, particularly if they are not three hundred pounds.

In addition to age, Donna's narrative suggests that class also indicates attractiveness and desirability. She commented on White society's image of who dates Black men:

> I think the popular notion is that only the leftovers of society, only the ones nobody wants, date Black men— fat, unattractive White women. But I also think White women are portrayed as having something psychologically wrong with them — like the poorest working class or underclass. They are perceived as having something filthy about them, something dirty about them.

These accounts illustrate that youth, stereotypical good looks and class location are a primary designator of desirability and attractiveness, but they are also the indicators in the amplification of anti-interracial response.

Naomi Wolfe in *The Beauty Myth* states that "beauty is a currency system like the gold standard. Like an economy, it is determined by politics."[39] Assigning value to women's bodies based on culturally imposed physical standards of beauty is an expression of White masculine power relations in which women are ultimately the losers. Wolfe states that this assignment of value placed on "beauty" creates a vertical hierarchy in which women must compete. Importantly, she notes that the characteristics or qualities defined as beautiful are really only symbols of *behaviour* defined as appropriate. Therefore beauty is actually about behaviour and not physical appearance.

In this context, White women's behaviour designates them as "race traitors" and patriarchical rule violators. The discourse against White women who involve themselves with Black men suggests that they are objects to be regulated in service of and for the pleasures of White men. What this reveals is that the desirability of White women is not a positive and individually self-referential beauty. It is beauty only when connected to White masculinity. When this connection is broken, especially by the presence of Black masculinity, White women's desirability diminishes.

In the diminishment of their desirability, the Black man is what brings the White woman's Whiteness into being. Ideologically, his "race" is what *particularizes* her identity and uncovers whiteness as a social construct of power and privilege. Yet in his absence, her whiteness is non-particular, and it is this non-particularity that makes White domination difficult to grasp in terms of the characteristics and practices of White people. As Dyer points out, "Whites must be seen to be White, yet Whiteness as race resides in invisible properties and Whiteness as power is maintained by being unseen."[40] In this context, the *stigma transference* identified in this research makes White women visible and consequently disempowered or empowered in their in/ability to support White racial reproduction and domination. Indeed, Donna's life experience validates Dyer's assertion:

> It's funny because I now see myself as White although I recognize that I am Czechoslovakian ... what is different now is that I see myself as White whereas I didn't before. I just was. But now that I am with my Black partner, it has been made so clear to me that my Whiteness is some kind of currency that I am suppose to guard.

Prior to Donna's involvement with her partner she "just was," she was not visibly marked by her whiteness. Her relationship with a Black man brought her whiteness into sharp focus. This illustrates that the blackness of their partners brings the women's whiteness into distinction. In the absence of their partners their whiteness is non-particular. However, as pointed out, the *stigma transference* is not a permanent stigma. If they were to sever their intimate involvement with their partners, they could lose their discredited status and regain their White status in full. What this suggests is that White women can travel a continuum of whiteness. Kate Davy in "Outing Whiteness" suggests that,

> White women's privilege can be understood in terms of her mobility; by virtue of race, she has the potential to

> travel this continuum, moving ever further away from savagery toward enlightenement. Insofar as she is White, heterosexual, and of middle-to-upper-class status, she moves ever closer to the civilized end of the sociosymbolic order.[41]

Constructing Social Identity and Relations of Ruling

While never fully inhabiting the full spectrum of whiteness, which is reserved for White men, White women can signify and enact whiteness in a way that no other female can, especially if she is paired up with a White male.

To fully grasp the implications of *stigma transference*, attention must be drawn to how the social identity of Black men has been constructed. Blackness, as the antithesis to whiteness, conveys an image in White supremacist society of evil, disease, filth, sexuality and inferiority. Jessie Daniels in *White Lies* comments on this point:

> The portrait painted of Black men is, almost without exception, that of the Black man as "threat." Black men are seen as threats to the White social order in a series of arenas: as criminals, as economic and political threats and in terms of their sexuality.[42]

A Black man's "blackness" and "maleness" are interwoven in such a way that makes him not just *a man who happens to be Black* but *a Black person who happens to be a man.* His personhood is defined by his blackness, which is seen as embodying all that is negative. This connection is important to understand because it this "historical schema"[43] of blackness that allows for the comprehension of the exaggerated responses to the bodies of Black men and consequently to the White women who are intimately involved with them. The explicit combination and association of feminine whiteness to masculine blackness evokes particular responses of anger, rage and sometimes violence. We in Canada, with our mystique of historical generosity and its modern variant multiculturalism, wrongly supppose anti-interracial animus to be peculiar to the United States. We need only recall the case in Hamilton, Ontario, of Greek immigrant Andreas Mouskos who conspired unsuccessfully to have his daughter's Jamaican fiancé murdered.[44]

The crucial point is that whiteness as a social currency carries the most cultural weight in juxtaposition to blackness. In this context, how the bodies of White women are socially constructed plays a pivotal role in the responses and experiences of these women. As White women, imbued with pure White womanhood, they either guarantee or threaten the perpetuation of White supremacy — this is a lot of power that must be controlled and subdued for White male interests. It is their whiteness and consequently race loyalty that comes into question when they are with a Black man. Therefore, when their whiteness comes into question so too does their femininity. When they transgress the colour line they become sexually immoral race traitors who are to be punished. The violation of their social and cultural inheritance as reproducers of Whiteness and commodities to White men grant society and family members permission to impose punishment on them. Part of the punishment lays in the social stigmatization that they suffer, as well as the loss of material and emotional privilege. This *stigma transference* is also what causes the potentially dangerous or intimidating situations from male family members and White male strangers. It is also the primary reason that some of these women may experience a diminished quality of life.

Ethnicity appeared to play a role as well. The women who were of Czechoslovakian, Ukrainian and Italian background experienced more violent opposition from family members. One of the research participants suggested that the reasons may have had something to do with how these ethnic groups organize their families along patriarchal lines and how they, as former immigrants, experience and guard their Whiteness. She states:

> [My mother] and my father wanted to shed the mark of being an immigrant. After years of being in Canada they have become somewhat [Anglo-identified]. My bringing a

> Black man and a Black baby, to boot, to their front door, has ruined their climb up the Anglo ladder, if you know what I mean. It took them so long not be defined by their immigrant status and here I am bringing a "nigger" into their home. They felt that I "blackened" their image.

This essay has sought to speak to the lives of six women in interracial relationship with Black men. It is in their relationship with Black men that their Whiteness comes into distinction and shifts the social world they live in. But what does it say about the larger society? I think my research sheds some light on the existence and intensity of racial, ethnic and sexual hierarchies in Canada. Can these six women share similar experiences of *stigma transference* without it being endemic to others like them in the larger society? It seems unlikely so. For these six women to experience the "spirit-murder" and the threat of physical violence because they are involved with Black men suggests that prevailing notions of gender, race and White supremacy exist and act as "relations of ruling" in southern Ontario specifically, and in Canada more generally.

Notes

1. Patricia Williams, "Spirit-Murdering The Messenger: The Discourse of Fingerpointing as the Law's Response to Racism," *University of Miami Law Review* 42, no. 1 (1987). Reprinted in this volume, as chapter 9.
2. Colin Thomson, *Blacks in Deep Snow: Black Pioneers in Canada* (Don Mills, ON: J.M. Dent and Sons Ltd., 1979), 46.
3. Thomson, *Blacks in Deep Snow: Black Pioneers in Canada,* 47.
4. Ibid., 46.
5. Constance Backhouse, *Petticoats and Prejudice: Women and Law in Nineteenth-Century Canada* (Toronto: Women's Press, 1991), 98.

6. Hazel Carby, "The Multicultural Wars," in Gina Dent, ed., *Black Popular Culture* (Seattle: Bay Press, 1992), 193.
7. Richard Dyer, *White* (London: Routledge, 1997), 3.
8. Ibid., 20.
9. Judith Butler, "Endangered/Endangering: Schematic Racism and White Paranoia," in Robert Gooding-Williams, ed., *Reading Rodney King, Reading Urban Uprising* (London: Routledge, 1993), 17.
10. Paul Hoch, *White Hero Black Beast: Racism, Sexism and the Mask of Masculinity* (London: Pluto Press, 1979), 43.
11. Ibid.
12. Ibid., 51.
13. bell hooks, *Black Looks: Race and Representation* (Toronto: Between the Lines, 1992), 58.
14. bell hooks, *Yearning: Race, Gender, and Cultural Politics* (Toronto: Between the Lines, 1990), 61.
15. bell hooks, *Ain't I A Woman: Black Women and Feminism* (Boston, MA: South End Press, 1981), 31.
16. Dyer, *White,* 127.
17. Ibid., 25.
18. Ruth Frankenberg, *White Women, Race Matters : The Social Construction of Whiteness* (Minneapolis: University of Minnesota Press, 1993), 136.
19. Ibid., 112.
20. Ibid.
21. Ernest Potterfield, *Black and White Mixed Marriages* (Chicago: Nelson-Hall, 1978).
22. Erving Goffman, *Stigma: Notes on the Management of Spoiled Identity* (New York: Prentice-Hall, Inc., 1963).
23. Winthrop Jordon, *White Over Black: American Attitudes Toward the Negro, 1550–1812* (New York: W.W. Norton, 1968). Jordon states that the "Great Chain of Being" has deep roots in classical Greece, however it was not thought to be imbued with a racial hierarchy. Rather, it was a way of systematizing creation. It was later in the eighteenth century that European scientists, such as Edward Topsell, imbued the chain with a racial hierarchy.
24. Hoch, *White Hero Black Beast,* 52.
25. W.E.B. Dubois, "The Souls of Black Folks," in John Hope Franklin, ed., *Three Negro Classics* (New York: Avon Books, 1965), 215.
26. Goffman, *Stigma,* 2.
27. Ibid.

28. Ibid., 19.
29. Matthew Frye Jacobson, *Whiteness of a Different Color: European Immigrants and the Alchemy of Race* (Cambridge: Harvard University Press, 1998).
30. Franz Fanon, *Black Skin White Mask* (New York: Grove Press Inc., 1967).
31. Frankenberg, *White Women, Race Matters,* 237.
32. Dyer, *White.*
33. Lois Althusser, *Lenin and Philosophy and Other Essays* (London: NLB, 1971).
34. Goffman, *Stigma,* 30.
35. E.H. Pfuhl and S. Henry, *The Deviance Process* (New York: Adline de Gruyter Inc., 1993), 178.
36. Goffman, *Stigma,* 4.
37. Deborah King, "Mulitple Jeopardy, Multiple Consciousness: The Context of a Black Feminist Ideology," *Signs: Journal of Women in Culture and Society* 14, no. 1 (1988).
38. Jesse Daniels, *White Lies: Race, Class, Gender and Sexuality in White Supremacist Discourse* (New York: Routledge, 1997), 81.
39. Naomi Wolfe, *The Beauty Myth* (London: Chatto and Windus, 1990), 12.
40. Dyer, *White,* 57.
41. Kate Davy, "Outing Whiteness: A Feminist/Lesbian Project," *Theater Journal* 47, no. 2 (1995), 197.
42. Daniels, *White Lies,* 81.
43. Fanon, *Black Skin White Mask.*
44. There were several news articles about this incident in *The Hamilton Spectator*: Doug Lefaive, "Man Wanted Hired Gun to Kill Daughter's Fiancé," 9 March 1993; Paul Legall, "Sentencing in 'Greek Tragedy' Hit-Man Case Slated for June 4," 15 May 1993; and Barbara Brown, "Father Jailed for Murder Plot," 5 June 1993.

Chapter Eleven

Brief Reflections toward a Multiplicative Theory and Praxis of Being

Adrien Katherine Wing

> we're anything brighter than even the sun
> (we're everything greater/than books/might mean
> we're everyanything more than believe
> (with a spin/leap/
> alive we're alive)
> we're wonderful one times one
>
> — e.e. cummings, *1 x 1*

Since Feeling Is First

In an earlier stage of being, I used to be a poet. But studying the law killed my muse. At this point, it does not really matter, because another poet, e.e. cummings, has said it better anyway — one times one equals one.[1] The purpose of this reflection is to put forth the proposition that the experiences of black women, whether in legal academia or elsewhere, might reflect the basic mathematical equation that one times one truly does equal one. This reflection will then briefly propose how we might utilize this theoretical knowledge to construct a concrete legal program benefiting black women.

Several prominent female legal academics of color, such as Mari Matsuda, Kimberlé Crenshaw, Judy Scales-Trent, and Angela Harris, speak of multiple levels of consciousness to characterize our existence – shifting back and forth between our consciousness as persons of color and "the white consciousness required for survival in elite educational institutions."[2] The constant shifting between levels of consciousness "produces sometimes madness, sometimes genius, sometimes both."[3] This multiple consciousness can include "a sense of self-contradiction" or even a sense of "containing the oppressor within oneself."[4] It can produce a feeling of ambiguity and frustration as well. In my own case, these levels of consciousness combine to make me a young black, female, wife, mother, international lawyer, professor, and activist.

On a daily basis, I feel subjected to subtle or overt discrimination on one or more of these levels. An example is illustrative. Recently, I passed through the San Francisco Airport on my return home to Iowa after a hectic six-day trip. I had attended a Critical Race Theory conference in Madison, Wisconsin, and recruited prelaw students in Los Angeles, San Bernardino, and Berkeley.

I handed my return ticket to the reservation agent, a white woman in her forties, and waited to be upgraded to first class as a frequent flier Gold Privilege customer. After holding my ticket for what seemed like ages, she said, "May I see some picture ID, please?" Now, in the hundreds of thousands of miles I have traveled by air, I have never had an agent ask me for identification on the return portion of a domestic flight for a ticket that was already in my possession. Suddenly, all kinds of thoughts ran through my head. "Do I look like a scam artist or some kind of thief standing here at the TWA first class counter of San Francisco Airport?" As Patricia Williams put it, "[N]o matter what degree of professional or professor I became, people would greet and dismiss my black femaleness as unreliable, untrustworthy, hostile, angry, powerless, irrational and probably destitute."[5] I laid my Iowa picture ID driver's license, along with my faculty ID card, TWA Gold Privilege card, and gold American Express card on the ticket counter. After looking at the gold and silver plastic in front of her for a while, the agent finally returned my ticket and boarding pass.

Resentful but resigned, I queried, "Why did you ask for my picture

ID? I've never had that happen before." Her words said it all: "Well, you just didn't look like you could be Professor A. Wing."

On the plane, I replayed the scene in my head. I realized that this experience could be interpreted in several different ways. What if I had not been black? Well, I was still a woman. What if I had not been young? Well, I was still black. Somehow I thought that one of my white male colleagues would not have been challenged in the same way, even if he were in blue jeans.

To some people, such incidents of micro-discrimination may appear trivial and not worthy of discussion. After all, I should be thankful that I haven't been raped, beaten, or lynched as were countless numbers of my people. Yet the cumulative impact of hundreds or even thousands of such incidents has been devastating to my spirit.

Spirit Injury

I have finally come to the realization that black women are lifelong victims of what Patricia Williams has so aptly called "spirit-murder."[6] To me, spirit-murder consists of hundreds, if not thousands, of spirit injuries and assaults — some major, some minor — the cumulative effect of which is the slow death of the psyche, the soul, and the persona. This spirit-murder affects all blacks and all black women, whether we are in the depths of poverty or in the heights of academe. The following examples are only a few of the numerous experiences that have occurred in my life.

The injury to my spirit was almost fatal when I was just nine and my beloved father — a brilliant, articulate medical doctor, the first black on the research staff of a major drug company, honor graduate of the New York University Medical School, Phi Beta Kappa graduate of the University of California at Los Angeles and the Bronx High School of Science, survivor of the Harlem streets, one of ten children — committed suicide. My interpretation of the death of this "model Negro" was that he had finally gotten sick and tired of being treated as a second-class citizen. After he was terminated from his job, his spirit withered and died. He fell into a profound depression and finally took his physical life.

Time passed; outwardly I flourished — honor roll, athlete, class president — in my predominantly white, all-girls prep school. Yet inside, the ongoing injury to my spirit was apparently so profound that I wrote a poem about nihility as a ninth-grader in 1970. By the end of high school, the nihilist had changed: the good Negro girl had become the militant Afro-American, wearing as much of an Afro as my long wavy hair would permit. I often ended up in discussions with darker-skinned blacks with "real afros" who would claim that no "high yellow girl" with "good hair" going to some fancy white private school wearing a uniform was really black.

Recently, I have discovered that my spirit injury reaches back down to the roots of my family's existence in America. In October 1990, I attended the National Conference of Black Lawyers Convention in New Orleans. It was my first trip to the City of Jazz, and I viewed it with some excitement because some of my ancestors hail from there. New Orleans is also the home of the historic landmark known as the Beauregard Mansion, named for the famous Confederate general who fired on Fort Sumter, Pierre Gustave Toutant Beauregard. My relatives had said I must see this famous tourist attraction.

I took the one-hour tour of the carefully preserved "city cottage" conducted by a woman in antebellum dress. She showed us what she had characterized as the "lovely" pictures of the general's "lovely" wife and his "lovely" daughters and the bedrooms where they all lived. As we walked out onto the back balcony, we gazed on an open courtyard fenced in by some buildings that looked like stables or storage space. As the only one of the small group asking questions, I said, "What are those small buildings?" The guide responded in her "lovely" Southern drawl, "Why, those were the slave quarters, of course. But we've renovated them and rented out the upstairs, so we won't be seeing inside them." I was riveted to the floor by the offhand manner in which she casually dismissed the bondage and confinement of human beings in such a small space, not historically worthy of the careful restoration and preservation of the main house. "And how many slaves lived there?" I queried, dreading the answer. "Well, we're not exactly sure, but the only census ever done indicates twenty-nine." I was dumbfounded. Twenty-nine black people cramped together to serve the needs of four white people living in a two thousand-square-foot "city cottage." "Of course, there were lots more living in the countryside plantation," the tour guide added.

At the end of the tour I purchased Beauregard's biography and paid a dollar extra for a sheet detailing his family tree. The tour guide said, "You certainly asked a lot of questions, young lady. Do you have a particular interest in our general?" I responded, "Not exactly. It's the general who has an interest in me — a property interest. General Beauregard was my great-great-grandfather." The intake of breath was audible. "Those pictures of his children on the wall, those were only his white children. The general had black children as well, including my maternal great-grandmother Susan," I said, repeating a fact that had been passed down in my family for generations. Our gracious guide did not even blink: "Well, we'd heard rumors that the general was like the other Southern gentlemen of his time. But we're not allowed to discuss it."

For the rest of the day an image continued to haunt me. It was of the long-dead general sneaking out of the main house, across the courtyard, to the slave quarters. Did he rape my great-great-grandmother Sally Hardin there?[7] Maybe it occurred on the plantation. Despite my extensive academic knowledge of slavery, actually seeing the *place* where my slave ancestors may have been raped, conceived, or born, the place where they may have loved, worked, or even died had a profound effect on me.

The Multiplier Effect

Constant overt and covert discrimination, both individual and institutional, augments the lifelong spirit injury of black women. "I find I am constantly being encouraged to pluck out some one aspect of myself and present this as the meaningful whole, eclipsing or denying the other parts of self."[8] I am also not the "essential" (white) woman discussed by many white feminists. I am not a white woman "leached of all color and irrelevant social circumstance — a process which leaves black women's selves fragmented beyond recognition."[9] My experience cannot be reduced to an addition problem: "racism + sexism = straight black woman's experience."[10] I am not a "white woman plus."[11] I am an indivisible black female with a multiple consciousness.

In this society, the law does not know how to characterize my experience as a black woman. For example, in *DeGraffenreid v. General Motors,* a Maryland district court granted partial summary judgment in favor of the defendant in a suit brought by five black women challenging the seniority system.[12] The court stated that they were entitled to bring a suit for "race discrimination, sex discrimination, or alternatively either, but not a combination of both."[13] The court found that there was no case stating that "black women are a special class"[14] to be protected in and of themselves.

If black females do not constitute a class in and of themselves, then surely they should be allowed to represent classes containing all females or all blacks. Yet in another case, the court would not let a black female represent white females. In *Moore v. Hughes Helicopter*, the Ninth Circuit affirmed the district court's refusal to certify Moore, a black woman, as the class representative in the sex discrimination complaint on behalf of all women at Hughes.[15] "Moore had never claimed before the EEOC that she was discriminated against as a female, but only as a Black female ... [T]his raised serious doubts as to Moore's ability to adequately represent white female employees."[16] If black females cannot represent themselves or all women, than surely they should be able to represent all blacks. Yet in *Payne v. Travenol*, black women could not represent all blacks.[17] The Mississippi district court refused to let the black female plaintiffs represent black men in a suit alleging race discrimination at a pharmaceutical plant.

We, as black women, can no longer afford to think of ourselves or let the law think of us as merely the sum of separate parts that can be added together or subtracted from, until a white male or female stands before you. The actuality of our layered experience is multiplicative. Multiply each of my part together, 1 x 1 x 1 x 1 x 1, and you have one indivisible being. If you divide one of these parts from one you still have one.

Negativity/Positivity Dialectic

Once the existence of this multiplicity affecting our being is acknowledged, another issue arises. What is the nature of this multiplicity? Is it negative or positive or both? I think it is becoming increasingly easy for at least certain sectors of society, including us ourselves, to see black women as victims subjected to multiple layers of oppression. A disproportionate number of black women are on welfare, in poverty, among the working poor, unemployed, underemployed, or underpaid. The majority of black families are now headed by women, predominantly single women. A disproportionate number of black men are dead, in jail, or unemployed.[18] It is estimated that less than 50 percent of all black men are actually in the workforce.[19] The life expectancy of black men is actually declining.[20] I realize how few black men I know are over the age of sixty.[21] The scourges of Drugs, Crime, AIDS, Homelessness, and Joblessness are wreaking havoc on our already weakened communities.

Yet I want to assert affirmatively to the legal academy, and to ourselves as well, that we black women are more than "multiply burdened"[22] entities subject to a multiplicity of oppression, discrimination, pain and depression. Our essence is also characterized by a multiplicity of *strength, love, joy* (with a spin/leap/alive we're alive), and *transcendence* that flourishes despite adversity.

Rather than let ourselves be defined by those who see the world in a unilinear fashion, we are beginning to celebrate our own multiplicative definition of self. Rather than seeing ourselves as distorted white males, we are beginning to see ourselves in our multiplicative, multilayered wholeness. We are beginning, "collectively and individually, to distinguish between mere speaking that is about self-aggrandizement, exploitation of the exotic 'other'; and that coming to voice which is a gesture of resistance, an affirmation of struggle."[23] Imagine a world where the richness of our experience and vision was the standard. Imagine God as a Black Woman.

Translating Theory Into Praxis

We must not only talk about our multiplicity, but act on it in ways that may not translate into entries on our résumés. On a micro level, black women law professors can transcend the negativity affecting our people. Whether married or not and whether we have children or not, we must mentor, inspire, nurture, and adopt, literally and figuratively, the black children and young people out there. We must regard all of them as our children and our responsibility. We can literally borrow other people's children for an afternoon or a week or a month. We can also fund prizes at local schools or our own alma maters to inspire students. We can do these things even though we may be in an environment where there are not many black children.

Multiplicative Legal Praxis

On a macro level, we must use our legal skills to push toward forging social policy that allows black women to capitalize on their richness and strength by giving them the financial and educational tools to meet their true multiplicative potential. For instance, current poverty laws and programs (vastly underfunded as they are) "treat the nuclear family as the norm and other units as aberrant and unworthy of societal accommodation."[24] They are designed predominantly by white, male, elite, unilinear thinkers who have never personally experienced the problems that are the subject of the legislation they pass. If these men had to raise their children singlehandedly (without the support of housewives, spouses, or servants) plus work full-time, many would crack within a week.

A solution may be found in a comprehensive, multifaceted program that would link child care, health care, nutrition, education, job training, and positive emotional support together to enable women (and men) to leave poverty and contribute to society. The key elements of such a project are that it be (1) designed by the people affected, including women of color; (2) responsive to their multiple needs as defined by them; and (3) adequately funded.

It is my fervent hope that readers of this reflection will be motivated to care and to act because they are morally concerned about the plight of black women. But even if America is not intrinsically interested in saving black souls and bodies, according to Derrick Bell's self-interest paradigm,[25] it should nonetheless be interested in becoming globally competitive with Japan and united Europe in the 1990s. It cannot do that without the assistance of the 85 percent majority of the workforce who will be white women and people of color.[26] Thus, waging this war to save the souls and bodies of black women and the poor will result in saving America.

In conclusion, I am asserting that the experience of black women must be seen as a multiplicative, multilayered, indivisible whole, symbolized by the equation one times one, *not* one plus one. This experience is characterized not only by oppression, discrimination, and spirit-murder, but by strength and love and transcendence as well.

All of us with multiple consciousness must help society address the needs of those multiply burdened first. Restructuring and remaking the world, where necessary, will affect those who are singularly disadvantaged as well. By designing programs that operate on multiple levels of consciousness and address multiple levels of need, we will *all* be able to reach our true potential to the benefit of ourselves, our families, our profession, our country, and the world.

For the blood of all people
runs within me
(Africa, Asia, Europe, Middle East and the Americas too)
I respect them
I embrace them
I transcend with them
For blood has only one color
(can you tell black white brown yellow blood apart?)
Red
For Love.
— The earth mother beckons
Save the world!! she says.
Love my children.

Well what do you know. My muse returns.

NOTES

* Adrien Katherine Wing, "Brief Reflections toward a Multiplicative Theory and Praxis of Being." © 1990 by the *Berkeley Women's Law Journal*. Reprinted from the *Berkeley Women's Law Journal* 6, no. 1, pp. 181–201, by permission of the University of California, Berkeley. American spelling has been retained in this chapter.

1. The title of this section is from another cummings poem, e.e. cummings, *is 5* (originally published in 1926), pt. 4, poem 7, in *Complete Poems, 1913-1962* (New York: Harcourt Brace Jovanovich, 1980), 290: "since feeling is first/who pays any attention to the syntax of things/will never wholly kiss you."
2. Mari Matsuda, "When the First Quail Calls: Multiple Consciousness at Jurisprudential Method," *Women's Rights Law Report* 11 (1989), 7, 8.
3. Ibid.
4. Angela P. Harris, "Race and Essentialism in Feminist Legal Theory," *Stanford Law Review* 42 (1990), 581, 608. See Patricia Williams, "On Being the Object of Property," *Signs* 14 (1988), 5, on coming to terms with the fact that her white slavemaster ancestor, Austin Miller, who raped her eleven-year-old great-great-grandmother, Sophie, was a lawyer. When Williams went to law school, her mother told her, "The Millers were lawyers, so you have it

in your blood." Ibid., p. 6.

5. Patricia Williams, "Alchemical Notes: Reconstructing Ideals from Deconstructed Rights," *Harvard C.R.-C.L. Law Review* 22 (1987), 401, 407 (footnote omitted).
6. Patricia Williams, "Spirit-Murdering the Messenger: The Discourse of Fingerpointing as the Law's Response to Racism," *University of Miami Law Review* 42 (1987) 127, 129. See chapter 9 in this volume.
7. During slavery, the rape of a black woman by any man, white or black, was simply not a crime. Jennifer Wriggins, "Rape, Racism, and the Law," *Harvard Women's Law Journal* 6 (1983), 108, 118.
8. Audre Lorde, "Age, Race, Class, and Sex: Women Redefining Difference," in Lorde, *Sister Outsider: Essays and Speeches* (Trumansburg, NY: Crossing Press, 1984), 114, 120.
9. Harris, "Race and Essentialism ...," 592. This problem in feminist literature can be summed up by the book title *All the Women Are White, All the Blacks Are Men, But Some of Us Are Brave,* Gloria T. Hull, Patricia Bell Scott and Barbara Smith, eds. (Old Westbury, NY: The Feminist Press, 1982).
10. Harris, "Race and Essentialism ...," 588, citing Deborah K. King, "Mutliple Jeopardy, Multiple Consciousness: The Context of a Black Feminist Ideology," *Signs* 14 (1988), 42, 51. See also Elizabeth Spelman's chapter "Gender and Race: The Ampersand Problem in Feminist Thought," in her *Inessential Woman: Problems of Exclusion in Feminist Thought* (Boston: Beacon Press, 1988).
11. Harris, "Race and Essentialism ...," 598.
12. 413 F.Supp. 142 (E.D. Md. 1976).
13. Ibid.
14. Ibid.
15. 708 F.2d 475 (9th Cir. 1983).
16. Ibid., 480.
17. 416 F.Supp. 248 (N.D. Miss. 1976).
18. Eloise Salholz, "Short Lives, Bloody Deaths," *Newsweek,* 17 December 1990, 33 (footnote omitted).
19. U.S. Department of Commerce, Bureau of Census, "Employment Status of the Civilian Population 16 years and Over by Sex, by Race, and by Hispanic Origin: 1960–1988," in *Statistical Abstract of the U.S. 1990,* table 628, page 380. See also James D. Williams, ed., *The State of Black America* (1979), 26–27.
20. Philip J. Hilts, "Life Expectancy for Black in U.S. Shows Sharp Drop," *The New York Times,* 29 November 1990, A1.
21. According to my informal survey, very few black children that I know, including my own, have any living grandfathers.
22. Kimberlé Crenshaw, "Demarginalizing the Intersection of Race and Sex: A Black Feminist Critique of Antidiscrimination Doctrine, Feminist Theory and Antiracist Politics," *U.C.L.F.* (1989), 139, 140.
23. bell hooks, *Talking Back: Thinking Feminist, Thinking Black* (Boston: South End Press, 1989), 18.
24. Crewnshaw, "Demarginalizing the Intersection of Race and Sex," 165n.72.
25. Derrick Bell, *Race, Racism and American Law,* 2nd ed. (Gaithersburg, MD: Aspen Law and Business, 1980), 7, 10, 25, 41.
26. U.S. Bureau of Labor Statistics, "Civilian Labor Force – Employment Status by Sex, Race, and Age: 1988: Employment and Earnings Monthly," in *S tatistical Abstract of the U.S. 1990,* table 618, page 386.

Part IV

Indigenous Connections

Chapter Twelve

African Women and Spirituality:

Harmonizing the Balance of Life

Njoki Nathani Wane

This short excerpt is taken from *Expanding the Boundaries of Transformative Learning: Essays on Theory and Praxis*, and is based on "African Women and Spirituality," a work in progress. It is not an analysis of what was or was not done to African women. Instead, it explores the realm of possibility and gives voice to the unspoken strength of African women and their spirituality.

The other two essays in this section invoke the spirit of indigenous knowledge. Brenda Firman's essay explores Aboriginal people's ways of teaching and learning. Barbara Waterfall's essay evokes the spirit of creation and acknowledges the centrality and sacredness of women's spirit. All three essays acknowledge women's multiple ways of knowing, notions of creation and the centrality of land.

— N.W.

African Women and Spirituality: Revisiting My Birthplace and the Embu Rural Women

The culture of our ancestors was spiritual rather than religious. Religion is modern whereas spirituality is primordial.[1] Spiritual immersion was the mode of existence, a view that empowered our ancestors. They did not entertain any doctrine of salvation by proxy, and every member of society was responsible and accountable for his or her actions. The women of my birthplace, Kenya, and the Embu rural women,[2] who participated in my research work, exemplify a cohesion of thought that was previously disregarded by some scholars. From my personal observations and textual documentation, the foundation for understanding African women and spirituality has been strengthened.

In my village in Embu, Kenya, a neighbour, Waitherero, whom I have known since I was a small child, had a reputation for talking to herself all the time. This exercise was most noticeable in the mornings, while she was working on the farm, and in the evenings. She talked to the plants, cows, sky and all natural living objects. When I returned to my birthplace to carry out my research on the daily routine of Embu women in relation to their food processing activities, I asked Waitherero about her daily routine.

> I wake up before sunrise, give thanks to Ngai [Creator in Kiembu] for giving me another day to celebrate my life, my gifts from the land, and my relations with my family, friends, neighbours and strangers. I always remember those people who are travelling, the sick and those who have no food. Every morning when I stand at my threshold, I look at the rising sun, at Mount Kenya, at the sky, and then look down and touch the soil and any plants around me and say thank you out loud … With that one breath, I am ready to begin my day. When I do this, I rekindle my energies within me.

Waitherero was not the only woman I spoke to who practised morning or evening "rituals." Rukiri, a sixty-year-old Embu woman, also practised her daily morning and evening rituals by conversing with nature. "I always 'talk' with the rising sun and to the setting sun," she told me.

Although uttered more than five years ago, the words of these women had not disclosed any significant meaning to me until recently. Waitherero's words underline her connection with Earth, the universe, the Ngai's creation. She maintains a strong connection to her land and expresses her gratitude to the Creator through her thoughts, speech, and deeds. Land is considered sacred for these women, all of whom live off the land. They understand that a reciprocal relationship of harmony and reverence maintains a balance between life-sustenance and loss.

For Waitherero and Rukiri, their expressions of gratitude also enrich their spirituality. Land, universe and creation are treated as rare commodities. By honouring these commodities through simple words of gratitude, they feed their own spirit, which is the source of their strength. Although not succinctly expressed in terms such as "honouring the land" or "feeding my spirituality," their words of reverence for natural creations are expressions of their spirituality. Their exhortations are neither forced nor exploitative. …

By its very nature, spirituality is a personal enterprise. An understanding of spirituality cannot be obtained from books. As one visiting Embu elder explained, upon reading the words of Waitherero and Rukiri, spirituality is part of the natural process of life. It is evident that these rural women have much to share that can enrich our collective psyche. They share the same ancient Nubian traditions. These traditions can teach all people to connect with the land and to have meaningful rather than exploitative relationships with the universe and other creations.[3]

I believe these words indicate that spirituality is not something out there, something that you read in your books, something that you can learn in your university. It is in your heart, it is in you. Spirituality is when you wake up in the morning and call on Ngai to guide you and to be with you. Spirituality is when you stand on your threshold and acknowledge the land you are standing on, the air you breathe, the creation surrounding you. Spirituality is when you give thanks before you eat or drink to Ngai first and to your ancestors, and to the land. In those brief moments when you pour a libation and welcome people to share what you have. For me that is spirituality.

Owing to spirituality's intangible and nebulous qualities, defining it is extremely difficult. To facilitate an understanding, what it means, it is better to view it in the context within which it is sustained and cultivated. Land, for the Embu rural women, is recognized for its tangible importance. From land and nature the women connect and nourish their spirituality. To most Embu elders, land is sacred.[4] One of the elders, Mukuru, once said to me: "Walk cautiously on the land. Walk like a chameleon. When you do that, you watch where you are going, you do not kill any of Ngai's creation and you do not 'abuse' the land. Never bite the hand that feeds your body and spirit …" These words carry multiple meanings. Mukuru could have been cautioning me about my interactions with people or could have been telling me to honour that which feeds my psyche and surrounds me. They sky above and the earth beneath, the rivers, the moon, the changing seasons, the birds on the bush, sunrise and sunset — all are woven into a rich and sustainting "tapestry" that speaks continuously of the glory of the Creator. What surrounds us communicates a wonderful sense of time, almost a sense of timelessness.[5]

The bond between nature and spirituality is strong for those who work intimately with the land. To this day, I remember the moment at which our family land was taken away and given to another family. I can still remember the pain in my mother's eyes, the unspoken questions, and the many times she touched the soil and the plants. I can still remember my mother shaking her head as if asking herself whether the new owners would have the same reverence for this land as she had or as her ancestors had had for generations; also, whether the new owners would ever know the land as well as her family did. …

In summary, the Embu women enjoy an intimate relationship with nature and its processes. The women enhance and sustain their spirituality both by expressing simple words of gratitude on a daily basis and by returning to the land a portion of what they have taken. This reciprocal relationship suggests the importance of continuous reverence for the balance of life and the harmony of spirituality.

Notes

*This excerpt is taken from Njoki Nathani Wane, "African Women and Spirituality: Connections Between Thought and Education." © Edmund O'Sullivan, Amish Morrell, Mary Ann O'Connor. *Expanding the Boundaries of Transformative Learning: Essays on Theory and Praxis* by Edmund O'Sullivan, Amish Morrell, Mary Ann O'Connor. Reprinted with permission of Palgrave Macmillan.

1. Queen Afua and Helen O. Robinson, *The Sacred Woman: A Guide to Healing the Feminine Body, Mind, and Spirit* (New York: Ballantine, 2000); Caroline Shola Arewa, *Opening to Spirit: Contacting the Healing Power of the Chakras and Honoring African Spirituality* (London: Thorsons, 1998).
2. The Embu is a group of people belonging to the Bantu-speaking people. They occupy the slopes and surrounding areas of Mount Kenya. Although the Embu are comprised of different clans, they unite together for social and defence purposes. Bantu is one of the languages of Kenya and is used to denote the people who speak the language. Bantu is composed of approximately six hundred dialects.
3. Afua and Robinson, *The Sacred Woman.*
4. Njoki Nathani Wane, "Indigenous Knowlwedge: Lesson from the Elders — A Kenyan Case Study," in G. Dei, B. Hall and D. Goldin-Rosenberg, *Indigenous Knowledges in Global Contexts: Multiple Readings of Our World* (Toronto: University of Toronto Press, 2000), 95–108.
5. John J. Riordian, *Celtic Spirituality: A View from the Inside* (Dublin: Columbia Press, 1996).

Chapter Thirteen

Living Well Within the Context of Indigenous Education

BRENDA FIRMAN

WITH THIS ESSAY, I embark on a new journey — my first attempt at sharing my voice in a published collection. In this context, we share a responsibility as writer and reader. As Celia Haig-Brown wrote in "Choosing Border Work," it is important to remember that the "usefulness, cohesiveness, truthfulness" of words and texts "lie with the readers as well as the writer."[1] While studying at the University of British Columbia, which sits on the traditional lands of the Musqueam and Coast Salish peoples, I learned the importance of showing respect for one's hosts. Whenever I travel to speak at another place, my first thoughts are about how to respectfully acknowledge the peoples of that place. As you read this chapter, I am invited to *your* place as a guest. I thank you for hosting me and respectfully acknowledge the ancestors of your place and their traditional relationship with the place in which I am a visitor.

When I travelled to Toronto to present the thoughts included in this chapter, I learned that *Toronto* is a Wyandot/ Haudenausaunee word for *gathering place* — a centre of trade between all of the nations in that area before settlement. I was told that these nations lived by the laws of "great peace," which they shared in common. In the gathering place of this book (as it is written and as it is read), many nations — both authors and readers — meet to share knowledges. At the same time, however, one nation has had the power to privilege its own sense of truth and legitimate knowledge over all other epistemologies and ways of being. By birth and ancestry (born to parents who are "White, Anglo-Saxon, protestant), by appearance (fair-skinned and blond hair) and in many other ways, I belong to this powerful nation. I am fortunate that life experiences over the last twenty years have provided me with opportunities to become aware of and acknowledge responsibility for "White privilege."[2] At the same time, I have been offered glimpses into life lived within what might be called "Indigenous philosophy" or an "Indigenous mind."[3] Living both within and between two cultures, I am conscious of the message given by Dennis McPherson and J. Douglas Rabb that "[p]hilosophy is a thoughtful interaction with the world … the outsider examines Indigenous philosophy by thoughtfully interacting with the Indigenous philosopher."[4]

In the academy, my life circumstances situate me in what Haig-Brown refers to as "border work." I am blessed with two Anishnabe grandchildren who live on a remote reserve in northwestern Ontario and another grandchild born into and living in "white privilege." I am also a full-time mother to a grandchild of mixed ancestry whose great-grandfather lived as a traditional Anishnabe. I have a lifetime of experience in and passion for "education of, by, and for the people." Given all this, where else would I situate myself in the academy?

The Indigenous presence in the academy has helped me to validate and formalize many of the experiential understandings I have gained by learning within another culture. In Sty-wet-tan at UBC, the late Musqueam Elder Tsimilano (Dr. Vincent Stogan, Sr.) reminded us of the tradition of reaching our hands back to seek help from those who went before us, and extending our hands forward to offer assistance to and share these teachings with those who are following us. In this way, we form a circle of "caring and sharing."[5] As I reach my hands forward to my grandchildren, my "hands back" reach to the ancestors who continue to give me their teachings.

Some time ago, I sat with a small circle of people on Squamish land under the Lion's Gate Bridge in Vancouver. We listened to Chief Dan George's son, Bob George, a respected Elder of the Tsleil-Waututh First Nation, reminisce about his childhood. He spoke of his grandfather telling him how to be a good speaker[6]: "Fill your heart with love for all, and the words will come out." The Elder also spoke of hearing the ancestors talking, reminding us all to be good to one another, to take care of one another. He spoke of his own language, in which there are no words to use to be mean to another person, and he reminded us that we cannot be mean to just one person, because we are all connected.[7]

Now that you know a little about "who I am, and where I come from," let's explore a very simple concept. Children have a right to learn with, from and about their own people, in their own language. For children on a northern Ontario reserve, this means learning how to live *menobimosehwin* (walking the good way), according to the philosophies of their ancestors' way of being,[8] *before* they learn how to use the tools of another people. Furthermore, children and their parents have a right to decide and influence the "what, when, where, why and how" of learning the tools of another people. In the small Anishnabe community where two of my grandchildren live, I acknowledge responsibility for the continuing existence of an education system that prevents this from happening.[9] This responsibility, combined with my accountability to the future generations of *all* my grandchildren, demands that I contribute to the efforts being made to transform the present-day reality.

The writings and efforts of many scholars and educators have contributed to an improved understanding of the historical and continuing reality of education for the Indigenous peoples of Canada. In "First Nation Control of Education: The Path to Our Survival as Nations," Dianne Longboat describes the effects of an imposed education system on Aboriginal peoples:

> The education provided to First Nations ... has been an important element in an overall policy of assimilation. It has been a means of replacing Native languages, religions, history and cultural traditions, values and worldviews with those of the European settler nations and of modifying the values of the Indian nations through their children — those who are weakest and can offer least resistance. Education has worked as an agent of colonial subjugation with the long-term objective of weakening Indian nations by causing the children to lose sight of their identities, history, and spiritual knowledge.[10]

Marie Battiste describes the transformation that is necessary today:

> ... the educational processes of Indian education should strengthen First Nations languages and cultures, build upon the strong foundations of ancestral heritage and culture, and enlist the invaluable advice and assistance of elders. The very tenets of Indian education [have] to change from accepting acculturation and cognitive assimilation as final ends to revitalizing and renewing language and cultural identity and dignity.[11]

The combined effects of the responsibility inherent in recognizing White privilege and my accountability to the future of all my grandchildren lead me to ceaselessly explore possibilities for "making a difference" in one small Anishnabe community. My explorations are fuelled by Stan Wilson's challenge to "shift our attention to what it was that kept our ancestors in harmony with their environment" and by Peter Hanohano's conviction that "for Natives, sense of place anchors their being and identity in who they are and their relationship to Mother Earth, and the places that have special meaning for tribal groups and members."[12] Verna Kirkness reminds me that "our Elders ... are the keepers and teachers of our cultures. It is our responsibility to ensure that the ties between the Elders and the youth are firmly entrenched," and George Erasmus warns me that "[t]he future of our people in Canada and the survival of our cultures, languages, and all that we value are directly linked to the education of our children."[13]

The opportunity to learn from Marie Battiste in person attracted me to the BAITWorM 2001 Conference in Toronto.[14] During my years of learning from the Anishnabe culture, I have come to appreciate the teachings of the circle and to know that an action at any point on the circle will have a transforming effect throughout the circle. The conference's focus on environmental education led me to consider environmental education as an entry point for "making a difference" in my circle. At the conference, I spoke of possibilities for environmental education that enable a lived relationship among people, education and the land; an education that encourages all involved to experience a relationship with Mother Earth, as envisioned by Chief Dan George:

> The beauty of the trees,
> The softness of the air,
> The fragrance of the grass,
> Speaks to me.
>
> The summit of the mountain,
> The thunder of the sky,
> The rhythm of the sea,
> Speaks to me.
>
> The faintness of the stars,

The freshness of the morning,
The dew drop on the flower,
Speaks to me.

The strength of fire,
The taste of salmon,
The trail of the sun,
And the life that never goes away,
They speak to me.

And my heart soars.[15]

Chief Dan George's poignant words encourage me to believe in environmental education as a possible site of transformation. Maori scholar Graham Smith refers to a "utopian vision," which he believes gives direction to transformation.[16] My own utopian vision includes a curriculum for "healing through learning," which draws on the strengths and gifts of the land and the people of the community to develop the strengths and gifts of the youth who, in turn, will determine the community's future. In this vision of an education controlled by the community it serves and involving the community in all aspects of the curriculum process, students would learn through lived experience, following a curriculum that is organized around the activities and interactions of "everyday life" on the land and in their own community. In a dynamic learning process that is directly connected to Anishnabe worldviews and ways of being in the world, students would learn from their own people in their own language. Following tradition, they would also share with others by using this new knowledge to provide learning experiences for younger students. This vision of transformed education promotes education as a preparation for total living within an holistic approach that is practical, reality-based and ecologically sound. It is based on the recognition that to live means to be whole and to be firmly connected to the past, the future, the earth (including all relations) and each other.

Now, these are all very wonderful words — but how can they transform reality? The "real world" is controlled by a "white privilege" that frequently greets my vision with charges of "romanticism." Michael Marker points out just how difficult transformation is when we are working so closely with a bureaucracy whose goals and understandings are so different from ours:

> One of the central shortcomings of too much of the writing about Native education is the exclusionary focus on "Indians" without looking at the non-Native bureaucrats, administrators, teachers, and community members. Indian education ... has always been about cross-cultural negotiation and power differentials. It is a complex landscape of colliding interpretations of fundamental goals and purposes across cultural barricades ... Indian education is about Indian-White relations [which] are involved in a political economy that invisibly circumscribes and frames the language of educational possibility for First Nations.[17]

I have chosen to open the door of "environmental education" as an entry point for educational transformation because, at least initially, it opens more easily than other doors within Marker's "complex landscape." Please note that my concept of environmental education requires a different understanding of environment and place than the understanding held by the dominant society. Marilyn Dumont sensitively expresses this difference in her poem "Not Just a Platform for My Dance":[18]

> this land is not
> just a place to set my house my car my fence
>
> this land is not
> just a place to bury my dead my seed
>
> this land is
> my tongue   my eyes   my mouth
>
> this headstrong grass and relenting willow
> these flat-footed fields and applauding leaves
> these frank winds and electric sky

are my prayer
they are my medicine
and they become my song

this land is not
just a platform for my dance

In the remote Anishnabe community where I teach, many of the prisoners of colonization, Christianization and assimilation have learned to act as their own prison guards and the prison guards of their children and their tribal future. For example, although the Anishnabe express an intense wish for their children to keep their language and culture, instruction in the local school is still strongly entrenched in the language, curriculum and pedagogy of the dominant outsider. While "local control" initiatives have seen more community people employed at the school and speaking their own language within the confines of the classrooms, fear still abounds about the current and future success of the children if they are not marinated[19] in the language and culture of the colonizer.

In her review of language initiatives in Indigenous communities across North America, Barbara Burnaby writes of the difficulties in transforming the language, curriculum and pedagogy of schooling, noting that "Indigenous control has to do with getting both [I]ndigenous and non-[I]ndigenous people to act on their words rather than letting things slide along as usual because the usual way is most often in the direction of the mainstream way."[20] Environmental education offers an arena within which many people may more easily "act on their words" without "interpretations of fundamental goals and purposes" openly colliding.

As concerns about the environment mount within the larger "White" culture, teaching about the environment is seen as an imperative by many and at least recognized as politically correct by the rest — particularly in an isolated setting. Teachers who are trained and influenced by the environmental pedagogy of "White privilege" will plan the lessons for students in the community.

Nonetheless, members of the Anishnabe community will be asked to assist, and they will naturally use their own language and ways of relating as they interact with the students and the land. In this way, the planned environmental education will transform into "learning *from* the land."[21] When the experiences are brought back to the classroom, there will be opportunities for transformation and for experiencing different understandings within the institution of the school. Without labelling and debating the issues, the relational land-based activities (reminiscent of traditional Indigenous education) provide all who are involved with the opportunity to experience education differently and to gradually re-evaluate the privileging of conventional "White" education.

Burnaby also suggests that "efforts to stabilize [I]ndigenous languages must be linked to work on healing in communities [so] we can uncover not only ways to soothe the pain and counteract negativity, but also ways to support, talent, skills, leadership, and wisdom that is so greatly needed for language, culture, and community survival and development."[22] Healing engages the spirit in connection with our physical, mental, emotional and social beings. Yet the tendency to connect "spirituality" with "religion" is the source of much debate in northern communities. Gregory Cajete points out that "[w]hat is called education today was, for American Indians, a journey for learning to be fully human. Learning about the nature of the spirit in relationship to community and the environment was considered central to learning the full meaning of life." A focus on "learning from the land" fosters such an education without invoking the problematics of religious debate. As Cajete suggests, "Nature is the true ground of spiritual reality."[23]

"Learning *from* the land" also provides a reason to approach Elders for teachings while allowing them to "teach" in a natural manner. Inuk Betsy Annahatak describes how schooling as an institution has interfered with the traditional ways of transferring knowledge:

> ... students have lost the initiative to want to learn. They wait to be taught, and on the other hand elders are also waiting to be watched as models. Having gone through a structured school system where most of what they learned was determined by the school, the students tend to wait for elders to teach them Inuit culture. But the elders also have their ways, wherein they expect Inuit students to come and watch them as they go about their duties.[24]

The introduction of land-based and land-sourced activities as a way of teaching environmental education can provide opportunities for Anishnabe youth to watch and learn from their elders as they go about their duties.

Transforming education requires consideration of the what, when, why, where and how of all that transpires in the name of "schooling." Different possibilities for learning and "coming to know" present themselves when the environment — the ecology of place — provides a focal point for schooling activities, particularly when the language of the school gives way to the language of place. Each new generation needs the time and space to listen to and be with the land as it speaks so they can absorb these learnings and knowledges, which have arisen from the land over countless generations. With repeated listenings, it may be possible to internalize the teachings of respect, relationships, reverence and responsibility.[25] Possibilities for a transformed education come alive as the community of individuals (students, elders, parents, teachers) brings this sense of living, this different way of being, into the school. If the school can embrace the vital energy of the land, a connection can be forged that draws the school towards the sense of place that helps define and nurture the community.

If approached with an "Indigenous mind," environmental education will respect the teachings of the land, will value the relationships of "all my relations," will walk with reverence and will take responsibility for all that is done in its name. "Learning from the land" offers a possible context for transformation in relations. Eber Hampton speaks eloquently to this act of transformation: "Standing on the earth with the smell of spring in the air, may we accept each other's right to live, to define, to think, and to speak."[26]

Notes

* An earlier version of this paper was presented at the BAITWorM 2001 Conference: Teaching as if the World Mattered, OISE/UT, Toronto, ON, May 11–15, 2001.

** Capital "E" Elders has been capitalized when referring to people who have been recognized as teachers. The small "e" elders refers to people who are Aboriginal seniors. See Kim Anderson, *A Recognition of Being: Reconstructing Native Womanhood* (Toronto: Sumach Press, 2001), 289n11.

*** Marilyn Dumont, "Not Just a Platform For My Dance," from *A Really Good Brown Girl* (1996), reprinted with permission of Brick Books, London, Ontario.

1. Celia Haig-Brown, "Choosing Border Work," *Canadian Journal of Native Education* 19, no.1 (1992), 109.
2. As a beneficiary of "White privilege," I have a responsibility to recognize the power differential between cultures and to conduct myself within this recognition. As the old adage says, "If you're not part of the solution, you're part of the problem."
3. Carl Urion described an "Indigenous mind" during a talk given at Spring Winds, a graduate student conference held at the First Nations House of Learning, University of British Columbia, Vancouver, BC, February 2, 2001.
4. Dennis McPherson and J. Douglas Rabb, "Some Thoughts on Articulating a Native Philosophy," *Ayaangwaamizin: International Journal of Indigenous Philosophy* 1, no.1 (1997), 9.
5. For more about the late Elder Tsimilano and his teachings, see "Tribute to Vincent Stogan," in *First Nations House of Learning, Annual Report: Longhouse Teachings* (September 1999–August 2000).
6. The thoughts in this chapter are a written representation of "spoken words." Personally, I view writing as a form of "speaking."
7. I heard Elder Bob George speaking at the Living in the Present Conference, co-sponsored by the Residential Schools Project and the Squamish Valley Elders

Circle Society in May 2001. When I later returned to Elder Bob George to seek his permission to share his words and his thoughts in this written and published format, he asked me first if I was doing so for financial gain. After I assured him this was not the case, he told me he trusted me and believed that I would not do anything to hurt him just as he would not do anything to hurt me. This responsibility to respect trust is now conferred to you, the reader.

8. In the northern community where my granddaughters live, people also speak of *menobihmajihowin* (the good things about survival) and *bihmajihowin* (how we survive from the land).

9. The fact that I did not establish the existing educational system does not absolve me of responsibility. As long as I continue to support without question the existing systems and the institutions and privileged knowledge base that continue to support those systems, I am accountable.

10. Dianne Longboat, "First Nations Control of Education: The Path to Our Survival as Nations," in A. McKay and B. McKay, eds., *Indian Education in Canada,* Volume 2: *The Challenge* (Vancouver: UBC Press, 1987), 23.

11. Marie Battiste, "Introduction," in Marie Battiste and Jean Barman, eds., *First Nations Education in Canada: The Circle Unfolds* (Vancouver: UBC Press, 1995), xi.

12. Stan Wilson, "Honouring Spiritual Knowledge," *Canadian Journal of Native Education* 21, Supplement (1995), 69; Peter Hanohano, "The Spiritual Imperative of Native Epistemology: Restoring Harmony and Balance to Education," *Canadian Journal of Native Education* 23, no.2 (1999), 215.

13. Verna Kirkness, "Giving Voice to Our Ancestors," *Canadian Journal of Native Education* 19, no. 2 (1999), 146; George Erasmus, in *Preface to Tradition and Education: Towards a Vision of Our Future (*Ottawa: Assembly of First Nations, 1988).

14. Marie Battiste, "You Can't Be the Global Doctor if You're the Colonial Disease: Post-Colonial remedies for Protecting Indigenous Knowledge and Heritage." Keynote Address, May 13, 2001. Delivered at the BAITWorM Conference, OISE/UT, Toronto, ON.

15. Chief Dan George and H. Hirnschall, *My Heart Soars* (Saanichton, BC: Hancock House, 1974), 33.

16. Graham and Linda Smith spoke with graduate students at the First Nations House of Learning, UBC, Vancouver on November 8, 2000.

17. Michael Marker, "Economics and Local Self-determination: Describing the Clash Zone in First Nations Education," *Canadian Journal of Native Education* 24, no.1 (2000), 31.

18. Marilyn Dumont, "Not Just a Platform for My Dance," in *A Really Good Brown Girl* (London, ON: Brick Books, 1996), 46.

19. In the keynote address mentioned earlier, Marie Battiste spoke frequently of how we have all been "marinated" in the dominant colonial doctrines.

20. Barbara Burnaby, "Personal Thoughts on Indigenous Language Stabilization," in Jon Reyhner, ed., *Teaching Indigenous Languages* (Flagstaff, AZ: Northern Arizona University Press, 1997), 295.

21. The preposition "from" is critical here as the magical ingredient in the transformation. It is the land that teaches us. Recall that *bihmajihowin* was translated to me as "how we survive from the land."

22. Burnaby, "Personal Thoughts," 300.

23. Gregory Cajete, *Look to the Mountain: An Ecology of Indigenous Education* (Durango, CO: Kivaki, 1994), 43, 44.

24. Betsy Annahantak, "Quality Education for Inuit Today? Cultural Strengths, New Things, and Working Out the Unknowns: A Story by an Inuk," *Peabody Journal of Education* 69, no. 2 (1994), 17.

25. After two years of community consultations, the First Nations House of Learning, UBC, has adopted these principles in their teachings.

26. Eber Hampton, "Redefinition of Indian Education," in Battiste and Barman, eds., *First Nations Education in Canada*, 42.

Chapter Fourteen

Reclaiming Identity:
Native Wombmyn's Reflections on Wombma-Based Knowledges and Spirituality

Barbara Waterfall

Booshoo. Waabkishki-Bzhkikii-Kwe n'dizhnikaas. Jijaak n'doodem. I have given you a customary greeting in one of the languages of my lineages. I have stated that my spirit name is *White Buffalo Woman* and I am from the *Crane Clan*. I come from the Great Lakes Métis people. I grew up on the land, living in accordance with the rhythms and cycles of the natural environment. I feel very privileged to have grown up in this way as it has given me a strong foundation on which to base my life. I tell you all of this so that you know who I am, where I come from and how I am connected or related to you. I am an Indigenous woman on the land that we now know as Turtle Island. I speak to African women and to the Indigeniety that is in all of us. From an Indigenous standpoint, I speak to you as a Native sister within a universal system of kinship ties.

I want to begin this essay by stating what an honour it is for me to speak in this Black women's space. I respect that I am a guest in this space and feel grateful that I have been asked to contribute in this way. I believe that the collaboration between Native women and Black women in reclaiming identity and defining feminisms can be a very powerful endeavour. My personal connections with Black women and the writings of Black women have informed my way of thinking and have helped me to see who I am in the world, as if I was holding a mirror in front of my face. Most profound has been my interactions with Dr. Njoki Wane and other African women in the Ontario Institute for Studies in Education of the University of Toronto community. I have also been profoundly inspired by the writings of Queen Afua in *Sacred Woman*, and by Caroline Arewa in *Opening to Spirit*, as they have articulated an Indigenous Earth-based perspective that centres women's role and particularly women's spiritual powers.[1] Through these associations I have been able to see how colonialism has silenced or taken away our sense of self and attempted to change the ways we define and sustain that sense of self in our everyday lives.

In Canada, the colonizer has left both Native women and Black women with a legacy of a patriarchal ordering of things that has suppressed our power and our identity.[2] Over time, we have internalized our oppressor's ways and in so doing our experiences of oppression have come to be hegemonic and taken for granted. As Kim Anderson writes in *A Recognition of Being*, "Many of the 'traditions' we know stem from Euro-Canadian patriarchal ideals, and many of our own Indigenous traditions have been twisted to meet western patriarchal hegemony."[3] Ifi Amadiume makes a similar case in her book *African Matriarchal Foundations*.[4] It is, therefore, necessary that we interrogate what we refer to as "tradition." My experiences of coming to know and befriend my African sisters has helped me do this. My African sisters have also given me the courage to speak the unspeakable and to act on that understanding. Allow me to elaborate further to explain my point. Understandably this discussion will be Native-specific. However, if the reader will bear with me, I am sure that you will see similarities with non-Native women's experiences.

The function of Native tradition is to preserve our cultural identity and maintain our traditions through societal protocols. Social relations within Native systems serve the purpose of ensuring that these traditions are maintained and preserved. As indicated above, the notion of tradition becomes problematic when our understanding is skewed by patriarchal bias. In this essay, I will speak about the present-day taboos against menstruating women as an example of one of these traditions. When Native women challenge the authenticity of these menstrual taboos, we might be fiercely criticized by grandmothers, grandfathers, aunties, uncles, sisters, brothers or cousins for both speaking out and attempting to create a dialogue.

It is at this juncture where the meeting of like-minded African women can be most timely and liberating. Indeed, my being asked to contribute an essay to this book is an example of a timely encounter. I was speaking one day with Njoki about how within my Native culture there are strict taboos about menstruating women being in public and participating in cultural events. Njoki responded by saying, "We have the same taboos in my culture." We then proceeded to have a dialogue enabling both of us to articulate our own Indigenous-centred perspectives on women and on women's spiritual powers as central to Indigenous modes of knowledge production.[5] This was very liberating for me and I hope it had the same effect for Njoki. I say *chi meegwetch* (a big thank you) to the forces that brought Njoki and my other African sisters into my intimate circle.

The perspective I present in this essay represents one Native woman's voice. I do not speak for other Native women as I am only an authority on myself. Yet the words that I speak represent the teachings I have learned from the Native Elders I have had the good fortune of knowing. I willingly share my Elders teachings with you as I believe there is great power in creating a dialogue in a broader Indigenous context. Perhaps the most profound were those teachings of one of my Elders, the late Dr. Arthur Soloman. One day when I was over at his home, he asked me this question: "When are the women going to pick up their power?" I didn't have an answer for him at the time. In fact, I was shocked and startled by the abruptness of his question, but I knew that Art believed very strongly in the power of women and that he believed women are the key to unlocking the chains of our own oppression. He waited his whole life to see evidence of Native women recognizing our power and acting upon it. It is my hope that Art can see through the realm of the spirit that Native women today are seeking our rightful place in the circle of humanity. I consider the words in this essay to be an example of one such woman picking up her power.

I speak from my own subjective experience, an experience that reflects an epistemology of inner knowing. I do so to disrupt the Eurocentric notion that for knowledges to be legitimate they must come from abstract and objective observations of the natural world.[6] Likewise, Kaylynn Two Trees, an educator of mixed ancestry (African and Native American), speaks to the importance of centring subjective knowledge as a legitimate pedagogical approach.[7]

This essay is the result of my own epistemological process of seeking direction and guidance from the grandmother spirits. The primary methodological process for obtaining this direction and guidance has been through picking up the ancestral practice of retreating at the time of menses, or menstruation, to attend to and meditate on the messages from our grandmother spirits.[8] I have been heartened by the knowledge that Black women have been writing and encouraging women to do likewise. Queen Afua acknowledges the importance of reclaiming a womb-based epistemological practice. She states, "You must be open in your spirit, because, as women, our strength is the spiritual realm.

You know we always feel things from our wombs. We make our decisions from there."[9]

Native teachings acknowledge that wombmyn are granted at the time of our menses or "moon time" a more-attuned ability to communicate with the grandmother spirits within. In the old times, Native wombmyn would go to the moon lodge at the time of menses where they would fast and pray. They would be still and listen to the wisdoms within. This was a time when many wombmyn received prophetic visions about the changing times that were to come. It was wombmyn in moon lodges who saw the coming of giant silver birds flying overhead and great spider webs covering the land. Within our present-day context we understand these images as the foretelling of the technologies of airplanes and power lines.[10]

Today wombmyn are being called to once again return to the moon lodge because the grandmothers wish to communicate with us. The grandmothers have spoken to many women — Queen Afua, Paula Gunn Allen, Jane Caputi, Brooke Medicine Eagle and Jamie Sams — telling them they need to wake up to their destiny.[11] The grandmothers are asking all women who live on this land to wake up and realize the vast knowledge and power that we have within ourselves. We are being asked to take ourselves and our own authority seriously, to embrace our diversity and to learn from one another. Indeed, as Cherokee Grandmother Dhyanni Ywahoo has written, "For human beings right now, it is wise to look at the common threads ... and to know that we have nothing to argue or fight about."[12]

This Mother Planet of ours is off balance, and she is working hard to re-balance herself. Marilou Awiakta reminds us in her essay "Mother Nature Sends a Pink Slip" that we will be given ample warning.[13] If we as human beings, wish to reside on this Earth, we must make major changes in the way we live. We must learn to harmonize with the spirits of this land so that we can maintain our right to live here. In my journeying at "moon time" with the grandmothers, I have begun to understand this calling.

In this discussion I refer to woman as "wombma," and to women as "wombmyn." I do this for the purpose of centring and accentuating the womb and wombmyn's life giving and nurturing powers. It is not my intent to contribute to the biology as destiny theory, which has been criticized within White feminist discourse. I am well aware that patriarchy has controlled women's wombs and, within a Native perspective, has distorted the spiritual connection and interpretation of wombma-based spirituality. I contend that strict social taboos for menstruating women is one example of this distortion. What I am doing in this essay is presenting a Native feminist perspective on reclaiming spirituality, knowledge and identity that is consistent with other feminisms.[14] I have strategically accepted the offer to contribute to this book as I believe that Native women and Black women have a lot to teach one another. I present teachings that come from my own Indigeniety. Given the universality of wombmyn's moon-time experience, I trust that these teachings are relevant to all wombmyn.

The Centring and Celebration of Wombmyn's Knowledges and Ceremonies

This discussion is intended to be celebratory. In spite of colonial imposition and repression, wombmyn's knowledges and ways of being in the world are very much alive. My journeying has lead me to believe that wombmyn are an embodiment of this knowledge. As indicated above, the grandmothers are asking wombmyn to bring these knowledges into the forefront of our lives and into everything that we do. What I speak of here is a very ancient knowing that represents an ancient epistemological understanding. We do not have to go very far to experience this knowing, for it is contained within us. It comes from the womb, from the place of creation. This is the starting point where all life begins and it is the place where wombmyn's powers and wombmyn's knowledges originate.

The womb is wombmyn's domain and birthright. Wombmyn possess mysterious knowledge that comes from this place and it is wombmyn who transmit this knowledge. This is a fact of life that colonization has not changed. Yet it is a fact of life that many of us have forgotten. Today, many of us are reclaiming or picking up the pieces of our cultural practices that were disrupted through colonialism. Many wombmyn, however, fail to make the picking up, the nurturing and the celebrating of wombmyn's knowledges and wombmyn-centred cultural practices a priority in our lives. Rather, we find ourselves picking up Native men's knowledges and, in so doing, we pick up men's ceremonies. We have forgotten that the men's ceremonies, such as the sweat lodge ceremony, emulate wombmyn's domain. The sweat lodge represents a pregnant wombmyn and we go into the sweat lodge for healing and rebirth. This ceremony is a recreation of processes of wombmyn's knowledge production. We have forgotten that the processes of creation, menstruation, childbirth, breast-feeding and menopause are living ceremonies. Diane Mariechild defines birth, lactation and menstruation as an "incredible means for resourcing power."[15] We have forgotten for a reason. We were made to forget that wombmyn's knowledges were and continue to be a threat to the colonial ordering of things.[16]

I want to be clear that I am not advocating that wombmyn abstain from participating in such beautiful ceremonies as the sweat lodge. What I am saying is that we must not place our focus solely on these male-centred ceremonies. Indeed, the late Anishnabe Third Degree *Medewiwin-Kwe* (Grand Medicine Society Woman) Lilly Borgeoise stated that historically Native women did not have to attend the sweat lodge but it is advisable to make use of the sweat lodge today. Because of pollution and chemicals that are put in our foods, we require the ceremony of the sweat lodge for additional purification and cleansing. In the busyness that is our lives today we must find time to attend to wombmyn's ceremonies, mysteries and ceremonial processes. In the busyness of getting children ready to go to school, going to work, cooking, feeding our families, cleaning, picking up after children, teaching, writing, driving children to various activities, doing laundry, caring for our elderly and our sick, attending community meetings, attending men's ceremonies, we must remember wombmyn's mysteries so we can enhance and develop these traditions.

We must command our families and our communities to help us do so. When we fully engage and celebrate in the living experiences of being wombmyn, we are making a paradigmatic shift back to wombmyn-centred epistemological and methodological understandings. It is important to remember that long before colonization, in Canada and Africa, our wombmyn ancestors used wombmyn's knowledges to build and maintain sustainable societies.[17] It is paramount that we nurture and centre these knowledges in our everyday lives and teach our people the value that can be gained by respecting them.

Wombma's spirituality is the antithesis of colonialism. It is based upon the centrality and sacredness of life itself. It is a spirituality that values life and values the diversity in life. This spirituality does not see us as separate from the Earth nor as separate from other living beings. It understands that we belong to and are one within a universal system of kinship ties, a cosmology that could not justify a colonial agenda and was perceived by the colonizer as a threat. That which was a threat was to be stamped out or eradicated.[18] We no longer believed that wombmyn's powers needed to be active in our liberation or salvation. Instead, we came to associate wobmyn's role as one of servitude and patient waiting, no longer seeing how dynamic and volatile wombmyn's powers are. We forgot to see and learn from the wombmyn-based powers in the natural environment — Niagara Falls, the mighty tides of the Bay of Fundy, the power in thunder storms or earthquakes.

As a consequence, we came to devalue and fear wombma's bodily processes and our teachings became devalued or misconstrued when they came to be taught in a colonized context. We were taught from our own people that the energies from our womb could hurt others. Many of us were taught by our mothers and grandmothers to be careful not to step over shoes or clothing. We were taught to wash our clothes separately from the men's. These teachings once taught us to respect our power, but in a colonized context they were distorted and our power came to be associated with fear. We became more careful, not wanting to hurt others by the power of our wombs. If anyone became sick in the community, menstruating wombmyn were blamed. People assumed a menstruating wombma must have touched that person. Yet where in our natural teachings were we told that our wombmyn at the time of menses were toxic and could harm others?

These fears remain in Native communities today. People fail to consider how the stress of our oppression, refined foods and pollution in our environment have affected our health and well-being. Hence, the colonized teachings about menstruation prevail. We continue to see ourselves at moon time to be potentially toxic and thus to be feared. The result is that we live with a legacy of strict menstrual taboos that serves to diminish and limit us in our daily lives. According to Jane Caputi in *Gossips, Gorgons and Crones,* the origin of these taboos was not to protect society from a "feminine evil" but to "explicitly protect the perceived creative spirituality of menstruous women from the influence of others in a more neutral state." [19]

We are told we cannot attend ceremonies or public gatherings when we are menstruating. True, it is wise for us to retreat from the work of "do-ing" during our moon time for the purpose of being receptive. However, the present-day menstrual taboos often extend to our being told that we are not to drum, or sing with other wombmyn, or make our own offerings in wombma's ceremonies. Deep within, many of us feel that this does not make sense. Yet when we question where these teachings come from, we are often told that we are being disrespectful, that we have assimilated Eurocentric values.

I believe it is healthy to ask these questions, because we need to think through our menstrual taboos. In our Native tradition, the *Drum Is Wombmyn's Principle. Wombmyn's Ceremonies Venerate Wombmyn's Power and Wombmyn's Principles.* Why then should we be excluded from drumming and being around other wombmyn when we are menstruating? Many of our Native grandmothers tell us we should be in the moon lodge, but what is being done by our families and communities to help us revive this vital wombmyn's practice? Furthermore, how many of us who are fortunate enough to have paid employment, have the luxury of taking time off work to retreat at moon time? When Native wombmyn attempt to be doing something nurturing and healing for ourselves, why is it met with fear and restrictive teachings?

The late Lilly Bourgeois often spoke about the present-day interpretations of our menstrual taboos as a means to keep Native wombmyn oppressed. Indeed, if we are understood to be powerful, why then are we not in positions of power within our communities? Do not the present-day teachings about menstruation and wombmyn's responsbilities during menstruation come from colonialism? Who is benefiting by wombmyn's creativity and knowledge being restricted, thwarted or oppressed? I have come to believe that our fear of our wombs also serves the colonial pur-pose of keeping wombmyn in a state of fearing and constantly questioning our own power and authority. Lilly had very kind, respectful, nurturing and empowering teachings for wombmyn. She encouraged us to understand our Native culture as living and dynamic, as that which changes and adapts through time. She thus encouraged us to not rigidly accept practices if they do not make sense in this present-day context.

Today we are being asked by the feminine aspect of Creation to live according to the rhythms and cycles of nature. There is a time to be active and there is a time to be still. I believe that all menstruating wombmyn are being called into the moon lodge to attend to wombma's wisdoms. This calling can be felt by fatigue, irritability, bloating and other symptoms that are associated with the time before menstruation. Brooke Medicine Eagle, in *Buffalo Woman Comes Singing*, points out that rather than trying to cure our PMS, it is imperative that we begin to honour our bodies and follow our natural cycles and rhythms.[20] We are not robots or machines. We can't continue to drink coffee all day long and push our bodies into accepting the contemporary societal ordering of our lives. It is unnatural to do the same things day after day, at the same time, week after week. This is a linear understanding of the world and our bodies are not linear.

The question is, How can we bring the ancient practice of the moon lodge into our present-day lives? In my own life I have found ways to make this possible — I have made choices informed by my own cultural context. I have created a room in my home that is my moon lodge. Sometimes I merely slow down the pace and spend time in there. I take the time to rest and drink soothing wombmyn's medicines or teas. I often don't answer the phone or respond to e-mail. I retreat from television and keep the lights low at night. Soft lighting such as candle light helps me attend to the grandmothers' bidding. I more naturally move into a reflective state and find myself recording my reflections, insights and awarenesses in a personal journal. At other times, I might retreat from the busyness of life by fasting and meditating. At the very least I structure retreat time for one day of each month. This requires that I say no to other obligations at work, at home and in the community. Saying "No" when others would rather have us do otherwise can result in unpleasant reactions from others. Yet saying "No" to others outweighs the effects of these immediate reactions. In time, if we are persistent the people around us will learn to respect our moon time practice.

I acknowledge that I am privileged to be in a profession where I can take time off work. I feel that those of us who have this privilege have a responsibility to assert this practice so that wombmyn's time away from work for the purpose of moon-time questing will once again become a taken-for-granted way of doing things. Initially it required discipline on my part to take this needed time for myself. However, once I began to experience the benefits of my moon-time practice this became an easier commitment to live up to. I find the grandmothers have their own unique way of ensuring that the demands of our work world are taken care of when we are taking time out for ourselves. It also is quite common to gain insights about how to approach problems at home or issues at work or in the community during our retreat. Indeed, I find that when I return to work from my moon lodge I am that much more productive.

Reconnecting with our natural rhythms and honouring our inner wisdom will help us to live in harmony with Mother Earth. If we want to continue life on Earth we must return to the life-sustaining ways of our grandmothers and undo the destructive ways of colonialism. Wombmyn possess knowledges and energies that are central to a sustainable future. These knowledges can most readily be accessed at the time of menstruation. We need to believe in ourselves and take ourselves seriously. We must be our own authority in our lives and not defer to the power of our men. It is our responsibility as wombmyn to develop our spiritual practices so that we gain access to these wisdoms within. In my Native culture we have mother lodges and grandmother lodges. As I am not a grandmother yet, I do not have an intimate understanding about the grandmother lodges. It is our responsibility to bring the spirit of our lodges, however changed, back into the centre of our daily lives and create wombmyn-centred knowledges and understandings.

Seven Living Principles

I have presented a Native feminist perspective that centres and reclaims the womb as the source of creation. I argue that it is imperative that wombmyn attend to the womb of creation through the revival of wombma-based epistemological practices. I present an example of how this can be accomplished by portraying how I have reclaimed the ancestral practices of the Native moon lodge in my own life. In our essay "Renewing the Hoop of Creation in Science and Technology," Njoki Wane and I speak of the womb as the starting place for Indigenous Earth-centred sciences and technologies. We also state, "Grounded in a woman-centred ethic of nurturance and life giving, (Indigenous) science and technology develop to preserve and maintain a sustainable future for the seven generations to come."[21] Queen Afua also supports this premise. She says, "We must move out and harness all of our power, which has been dormant, locked away in our wombs, for we are at the crossroads of life on this planet."[22]

I contend that it is imperative that we return to the Indigenous wombmyn-centred methodologies of our ancestors. When we bring our wombmyn's lodges and wombmyn's ceremonial practices into the centre of our lives we are able to reclaim our identity and our modes of knowledge production, and we are able to achieve spiritual wellness. As we centre these knowledges and practices in our daily lives we are actively using our powers to create a sustainable future. I also state that it is the responsibility of all wombmyn to pick up wombma-based methods of knowledge production and that there is great power and utility when Indigenous wombmyn share their wombma-based grandmother teachings with wombmyn from other cultures.

What I am proposing here is not a theory. It is a sustainable way of life that is very possible to accomplish in the times we are living in. I say this, because I have found ways to be a whole wombmyn in my daily life. I am not saying that I do this perfectly. Yet we can find ways to listen to our own inner wisdoms. We must re-learn to consciously be in wombmyn-centred space and to speak from this place. We must consciously be in relationship with others in this space. We must do this for our

Mother Earth, our children, our families and for the future generations to come. The ancestors and the future generations are looking to us. Mother Earth is looking to us. I ask you, my sisters, are we going to answer this call?

In closing I would like to share seven living principles that have become evident through my questing with the grandmothers. I sense from the grandmothers that these principles have universal qualities. These are:

1. When we attend to the womb of be-ing we understand in a profound way that all human beings are interconnected and as such we are all related. This is not merely an ideological concept. We know it from our own inner truth, or be-ing.

2. From this understanding we are to understand that we are all One Human Family. We must treat each other as such and, in so doing, we will understand that there is strength in diversity and diverse perspective. We are encouraged to embrace our diversity.

3. As wombmyn we have positive personal power that is about empowerment of the self in flow with the elemental powers of Creation. Power in flow is not imposing or dominating. Power in flow is in harmony with other powers.

4. We are here as wombmyn to bring into the centre of our lives that which is nurturing and life-giving.

5. The primary principle from which we are to live our lives should be based on the primacy of wombmyn and on the wombmyn-centred principle of respectful co-existence. We are here as wombmyn to teach our children, our men and the rest of humanity the fundamental basis of this understanding.

6. Within Indigenous Earth-based traditions are methodological practices for the attainment of wombmyn's knowledges and mystery traditions. It is imperative that we pick up these as a part of our everyday practices as they will enable us to build a sustainable future on Earth.

7. Our teaching practices and everyday way of life can be based on the maintenance and development of these life-sustaining principles and methodologies. We must never underestimate the vast power within wombmyn and the practical understanding that wombmyn are the key to building this sustainable future.

These seven core messages have come as a direct result of my journeying with the grandmothers. I say *chi meegwetch* to the grandmothers for their wisdom. I say *chi meegwetch* to grandmother Mae-Louise Campbell in Manitoba for encouraging me to speak and for validating the truth in this essay. I say *chi meewetch* to you the reader for listening! I say *chi meegwetch* to All My Sisters! *Chi Meegwetch* All My Relations! *Chi Meegwetch! Chi Meegwetch! Chi Meegwetch!*

NOTES

1. Caroline S. Arewa, *Opening to Spirit: Contacting the Healing Power of the Chakras and Honoring African Spirituality* (London: Thoisons, 1988); Queen Afua, *Sacred Woman: A Guide to Healing the Feminine Body, Mind and Spirit* (New York: Ballantine Publishing, 2000).

2. See, for example, Paula Gunn Allen, *The Sacred Hoop: Recovering the Feminine in American Indian Traditions* (Boston: Beacon Press, 1998); Ifi Amadiume, *African Matriarchal Foundations: The Igbo Case* (Karnak House, 1987).

3. Kim Anderson, *A Recognition of Being: Reconstructing Native Womanhood* (Toronto: Sumach Press, 2001), 36.

4. Amadiume, *African Matriarchal Foundations.*
5. Njoki Nathani Wane and Barbara Waterfall, "Renewing the Hoop of Creation in Science and Technology: Pedagogical Implications" (paper in progress, 2002), 11.
6. Marie Battiste and James Youngblood Henderson, *Indigenous Knowledge and Heritage: A Global Challenge* (Toronto: University of Toronto Press, 2000), 23–5.
7. Kaylynn Two Trees, "Mixed Blood, New Voice," in Joy James and Ruth Farmer, eds., *Spirit, Space and Survival: African American Women in (White) Academe* (New York: Routledge, 1993).
8. See Amy Lee, "The Sacred Roles of Women and Men," in S. McFadden, ed., *Profiles of Wisdom: Native Elders Speak about the Earth* (Sante Fe: Bear and Co., 1991), 193; Brooke Medicine Eagle, *Buffalo Woman Comes Singing* (New York: Ballentine Books, 1992), 327–43; Jamie Sams, *The 13 Original Clan Mothers* (New York: Harper SanFranciso, 1993), 12–13.
9. Queen Afua, *Sacred Woman*, 48.
10. Medicine Eagle, *Buffalo Woman Comes Singing*, 330.
11. See Queen Afua, *Sacred Woman,* 32; Paula Gunn Allen, *Off the Reservation: Reflections on Boundary-Busting, Border-Crossing Loose Canons* (Boston: Beacon Press, 1998), 88–9; Jane Caputi, *Gossips, Gorgons and Crones: The Fates of the Earth,* (Sante Fe: Bear and Co., 1993), 270; Medicine Eagle, *Buffalo Woman Comes Singing*, 13; Sams, *The 13 Original Clan Mothers*, 19.
12. Dyhanni Ywahoo "Adventures Along the Beauty Road," in McFadden, ed., *Profiles in Wisdom,* 55.
13. Marilou Awiakta, "Mother Nature Sends a Pink Slip," *Appalachian Heritage* (Winter 1991).
14. Wane and Waterfall, "Renewing the Hoop of Creation in Science and Technology," 11.
15. Diane Mariechild, *The Inner Dance: A Guide to Spiritual and Psychological Unfolding* (Freedom, CA: The Crossing Press, 1987), 169.
16. See Gunn Allen, *The Sacred Hoop*, 3; Caputi, *Gossips, Gorgons and Crones,* 3–17.
17. Wane and Waterfall, "Renewing the Hoop of Creation in Science and Technology," 3.
18. See Gunn Allen, *The Sacred Hoop,* 37; Winona Stevenson, "Colonialism and First Nations Women in Canada," in Enakshi Dua and Angela Robertson, eds., *Scratching the Surface: Canadian Anti-Racist Feminist Thought* (Toronto: Women's Press, 1999), 61.
19. Caputi, *Gossips, Gorgons and Crones,* 164.

20. Medicine Eagle, *White Buffalo Woman Comes Singing,* 329.
21. Wayne and Waterfall, “Renewing the Hoop of Creation in Science and Technology,” 12.
22. Queen Afua, *Sacred Woman,* 32.

Bibliography

Agnew, Vijay. *Resisting Discrimination: Women from Asia, Africa, and the Caribbean and the Women's Movement in Canada.* Toronto: University of Toronto Press, 1996.

Agustin, N.A. "Learnfare and Black Motherhood: The Social Construction of Deviance." In Adrien Katherine Wing, ed. *Critical Race Feminism: A Reader*, 144-50. New York: New York University Press, 1997.

Aidoo Ama, Ata. "To Be a Woman." In Robin Morgan, ed. *Sisterhood is Global*, 258-65. New York: Anchor Books, 1994.

—. "The African Woman Today." In Obioma Nnaemeka, ed. *Sisterhood, Feminism and Power: From Africa to the Diaspora*, 39-50. Trenton: Africa World Press, 1997.

Allen, Paula Gunn. *The Sacred Hoop: Recovering the Feminine in American Indian Traditions.* Boston: Beacon Press, 1986.

—. *Off the Reservation: Reflections on Boundary-Busting, Border-Crossing Loose Canons.* Boston: Beacon Press, 1998.

Amadiume, Ifi. *Reinventing Africa: Matriarchy, Religion and Culture.* London: Zed Books Ltd., 1997.

Anderson, Kim. *A Recognition of Being: Reconstructing Native Womanhood.* Toronto: Sumach Press, 2001.

Aptheker, Bettina. *Woman's Legacy: Essays on Race, Sex, and Class in American History.* Amherst: The University of Massachusetts Press, 1982.

Arbor, Ruth. "Defining Positioning within Politics of Difference: Negotiating Spaces 'in between.'" *Race Ethnicity and Education* 3, no. 1 (2000).

Ashcroft, B., G. Griffiths, and H. Thiophene. *The Post-Colonial Studies Reader.* London: Routledge, 1995.

Awiakta, Marilou. "A Mother Nature Sends a Pink Slip." *Appalachian Heritage* (Winter 1991).

Backhouse, Constance. *Petticoats & Prejudice: Women and Law in Nineteenth-Century Canada.* Toronto: Women's Press, 1991.

—. *Colour-Coded: A Legal History of Racism in Canada 1900-1950.* Toronto: University of Toronto Press, 1999.

Bannerji, Himani. "Racism, Sexism, Knowledge and the Academy." *Resources for Feminist Research* 20, no. (1991): 5-11.

—, ed. *Returning the Gaze: Essays on Racism, Feminism and Politics.* Toronto: Sister Vision Press, 1993.

—, ed. *Thinking Through: Essays on Feminism, Marxism, and Anti-Racism.* Toronto: Women's Press, 1995.

—. "Politics and the Writing of History." In Ruth Roach Pierson and Nupur Chaudhuri, eds., With the Assistance of Beth McAuley. *Nation, Empire, Colony: Historicizing Gender and Race.* Bloomington: Indiana University Press, 1998.

Battiste, Marie, and J. Barman, eds. *First Nations Education in Canada: The Circle Unfolds.* Vancouver: University of British Columbia Press, 1995.

Battiste, Marie, and James Youngblood Henderson. *Protecting Indigenous Knowledge and Heritage: A Global Challenge.* Saskatoon: Purich Publishing, 2000.

Beale, Frances. "Double Jeopardy: To Be Black and Female." In Toni Cade Bambara, ed. *The Black Woman: An Anthology*, 90-100. Toronto: New American Library of Canada Ltd., 1970.

Beckles, Hilary Mcd. "Historicizing Slavery in West Indian Feminisms." *Feminist Review: Rethinking Caribbean Difference*, no. 59 (Summer 1998): 34-56.

Bederman, Gail. *Manliness and Civilization: A Cultural History of Gender and Race in the United States, 1880-1917.* Chicago: The University of Chicago Press, 1995.

Benjamin, Lois, ed. *Black Women in the Academy: Promises and Perils.* Gainesville: University Press of Florida, 1997.

Bernard, Wanda, and Candace Bernard. "Passing the Torch: A Mother and Daughter Reflect on their Experiences Across Generations." *Canadian Woman Studies* 18, nos. 2/3 (Summer/Fall 1998).

Bhopal, Kalwant. "The Influence of Feminism on Black Women in the Higher Education Curriculum." In Sue Davies et al., eds. *Changing the Subject: Women in Higher Education*, 124-37. Portsmouth: Taylor and Francis, 1994.

Bock, Gisella. "Women's History and Gender History: Aspects of an International Debate." *Gender and History* 1, no. 1 (Spring 1989).

Brand, Dionne. *No Burden to Carry: Narratives of Black Working Women in Ontario, 1920s to 1950s*. Toronto: Women's Press, 1991.

Brereton, Bridget. "Autobiographies, Diaries and Letters by Women as Sources for Caribbean History." *Feminist Review: Rethinking Caribbean Difference*, no. 59 (Summer 1998): 143-63.

Brewer, Dionne. "Giving Name and Voice: Black Women Scholars, Research and Knowledge Transformation." In Lois Benjamin, ed., *Black Women in the Academy: Promises and Perils*, 68-80. Tampa: University of Florida, 1997.

Brewer, Rose. "Theorizing Race, Class and Gender: The New Scholarship of Black Feminist Intellectuals and Black Women's Labour." In Stanlie M. James and P.A. Busia Abena, eds. *Theorizing Black Feminisms: The Visionary Pragmatism of Black Women*, 13-30. New York: Routledge, 1993.

Bristow, Peggy, Dionne Brand, Linda Carty, Afua Cooper, Sylvia Hamilton and Adrienne Shadd. *"We're Rooted Here and They Can't Pull Us Up": Essays in African-Canadian Women's History*. Toronto: University of Toronto Press, 1994.

Butler, Judith. *Gender Trouble: Feminism and the Subversion of Identity*. New York: Routledge, 1990.

——. "Endangered/Endangering: Schematic Racism and White Paranoia." In Robert Gooding-Williams, ed. *Reading Rodney King, Reading Urban Uprising*, 15-22. London: Routledge, 1993.

Cajete, Gregory. 1994. *Look to the Mountain: An Ecology of Indigenous Education*. Durango, CO: Kivaki, 1994.

Calliste, A., and George Dei, eds. *Anti-Racist Feminism: Critical Race and Gender Studies*. Halifax: Fernwood Publishing, 2000.

Candace, Wanda Thomas Bernard, Chioma Ekpo, Josephine Enang, Bertlyn Joseph and Njoki Nathani Wane. "'She Who Learns Teaches': Othermothering in the Academy." *Journal of the Association for Research on Mothering* 2, no. 2 (Fall/Winter 2000): 66-84.

Caputi, Jane. *Gossips, Gorgons and Crones: The Fates of the Earth*. Sante Fe: Bear and Co., 1993.

Carby, Hazel V. "The Multicultural Wars." In Gina Dent, ed. *Black Popular Culture*, 187-99. Seattle: Bay Press, 1992.

——. *Cultures of Babylon: Black Britain and African America.* London: Verso, 1999.

——. "White Women, Listen." In Les Back and John Solomos, eds. *Theories of Race and Racism: A Reader*, 389-403. New York: Routledge, 2000.

Carty, Linda. "Black Women in Academia: A Statement from the Periphery." In Himani Bannerji, et al., eds. *Unsettling Relations: The University as a Site of Feminist Struggle*, 13-41. Toronto: Women's Press, 1991.

——. "Women's Studies in Canada: A Discourse and Praxis of Exclusion." *Resources for Feminist Research* 20, nos. 3/4 (1991): 12-18.

——. "Combining Our Efforts: Making Feminism Relevant to the Changing Sociality." In Linda Carty, ed. *And Still We Rise: Feminist Political Mobilizing in Contemporary Canada*, 7-21. Toronto: Women's Press, 1993.

——. "African Canadian Women and the State: Labour Only Please." In Peggy Bristow et al. *"We're Rooted Here and They Can't Pull Us Up": Essays in African Canadian Women's History*, 193-229. Toronto: University of Toronto Press, 1994.

——. "Seeing Through the Eye of Difference: A Reflection on Three Research Journeys." In Heidi Gottfried, ed. *Feminism and Social Change: Bridging, Theory and Practice*, 123-42. Urbana: University of Illinois Press, 1996.

Carty, Linda, and Dionne Brand. "Visible Minority Women: A Creation of the Canadian State." In Himani Bannerji, ed. *Returning the Gaze: Essays on Racism, Feminism and Politics*, 207-22. Toronto: Sister Vision Press, 1993.

Christensen, Kimberly. "'With Whom Do You Believe Your Lot is Cast?' White Feminists and Racism." *Signs: Journal of Women in Culture and Society* 22, no. 3 (1997).

Christian, Barbara. "The Race for Theory." In Bill Ashcroft, ed. *The Post-Colonial Studies Reader*, 457-60. London: Routledge, 1987.

——. "The Truth That Never Hurts: Black Lesbians in Fiction in the 1980s." In Chandra T. Mohanty, Ann Russo and Lourdes Torres, eds. *Third World Women and the Politics of Feminism*, 101-29. Bloomington: Indiana University Press, 1991.

Collins, Patricia Hill. "Learning from the Outsider Within: The Sociological Significance of Black Feminist Thought." *Social Problems 33*, no. 6 (1986): 514-34.

——. "The Social Construction of Black Feminist Thought." In N. Tuana and R. Tong, eds. *Feminism and Philosophy: Essential Readings in Theory, Reinterpretation, and Application*, 526-47. Boulder: Westview Press, 1995.

——. *Fighting Words: Black Woman and the Search For Justice.* Minneapolis: University of Minnesota Press, 1998.

——. *Black Feminist Thought: Knowledge, Consciousness, and the Politics of Empowerment.* Second Edition. New York: Routledge, 2000.

Clark-Hine, Darlene. "We Specialize in the Wholly Impossible: The Philanthropic Work of Black Women." In Kathleen D. McCarthy, ed. *Lady Bountiful Revisited*, 70-93. New Brunswick, NJ: Rutgers University Press, 1990.

Code, Lorraine. "Feminist Theory." In Sandra Burt, Lorraine Code and Lindsay Dorney, eds. *Changing Patterns: Women in Canada.* Toronto: McClelland and Stewart Inc., 1993.

Combahee River Collective, The. "A Black Feminist Statement." In Gloria T. Hull, Patricia Bell-Scott and Barbara Smith, eds. *All the Women Are White, All the Blacks Are Men, But Some of Us Are Brave*, 13-22. New York: Feminist Press, 1982.

Cooper, Afua. "The Search for Mary Bibb, Black Woman Teacher in Nineteenth-Century Canada West." *Ontario History* 83, no. 1 (March 1991): 39–54.

Daniels, Jessie. *White Lies: Race, Class, Gender and Sexuality in White Supremacist Discourse.* New York: Routledge, 1997.

Das Gupta, Tania. *Racism and Paid Work.* Toronto: Garamond Press, 1996.

Davies, Carole Boyce. *Black Women, Writing and Identity: Migration of the Subject.* London: Routledge, 1994.

Davis, Angela. *Women, Race and Class.* New York: Vintage Books, 1983.

Davy, Kate. "Outing Whiteness." *Theater Journal* 47 (1995): 189-205.

Dei, George. *Anti-Racism Education: Theory and Practice.* Halifax: Fernwood Publications, 1996.

——. "Why Write 'Black': Reclaiming African Cultural Resource Knowledges in Diasporic Contexts." In Frank Columbus, ed. *Advances in Psychology Research*, 201-18. New York: Nova Science Publishers, 2000.

Dei, George, Bud Hall, and Dorothy Rosenberg. *Indigenous Knowledges in Global Contexts: Multiple Readings of Our World.* Toronto: University of Toronto Press, 2000.

Dei, George, and Agnes Calliste. *Power, Knowledge and Anti-Racism Education: A Reader*. Halifax: Fernwood Publishing, 1996.

de Lauretis, Teresa. "Upping the Anti (sic) in Feminist Theory." In Marianne Hirsh and Evelyn Fox Keller, eds. *Conflicts in Feminism*, 255-70. New York: Routledge, 1995.

Deliovsky, Katerina. "Jungle Fever: The Social Construction of Six White Women in Interracial Relationship with Black Men." MA thesis, McMaster University, 1999.

Dua, Enakshi, and Angela Robertson, eds. *Scratching the Surface: Canadian Anti-Racist Feminist Thought*. Toronto: Women's Press, 1999.

Dubois, W.E.B. "The Souls of Black Folks." In John Hope Franklin, ed., *Three Negro Classics*, 207-389. New York: Avon Books, 1965.

duCille, Anne. "The Occult of True Black Womanhood: Critical Demeanor and Black Feminist Studies." *Signs: Journal of Women in Culture and Society* 19, no. 3 (Spring 1994): 591-629.

Dyer, Richard. *White*. New York: Routledge, 1997.

Eichelberger, Brenda. 1977. "Voices of Black Feminism." *Quest* 111, no. 4 (Spring 1977): 17-33.

Essed, Philomena. *Understanding Everyday Racism: An Interdisciplinary Theory*. Newbury Park, CA: Sage, 1991.

——. *Diversity: Gender, Color, and Culture*. Trans. Rita Gircour. Amherst: University of Massachusetts Press, 1996.

Etter-Lewis, Gwendolyn, and Michelle Foster, eds. *Unrelated Kin: Race and Gender in Women's Personal Narratives*. New York: Routledge, 1996.

Fanon, Franz. *Black Skin White Mask*. New York: Grove Press Inc., 1967.

Farmer, Ruth, and James Joy, eds. *Spirit, Space and Survival: African American Women in (White) Academe*. New York: Routledge, 1993 .

Few, April L. "The (Un)Making of Martyrs: Black Mothers, Daughters, and Intimate Violence." *Journal of the Association for Research on Mothering* 1, no. 1 (Spring/Summer 1999): 68-75.

Ford-Smith, Honor, and the Sistren Collective. *Lionheart Gal: The Life Stories of Jamaican Women*. Toronto: Sister Vision Press, 1987.

Frankenberg, Ruth. *White Women, Race Matters: The Social Construction of Whiteness*. Minneapolis: University of Minnesota Press, 1993.

——, ed. *Displacing Whiteness: Essays in Social and Cultural Criticism.* Durham, NC: Duke University Press, 1997.

Freire, Paulo. *Pedagogy of the Oppressed.* New York: Bergin and Garvey Publishers, Inc., 1970; New York: Continuum, 1993.

——, ed. *Mentoring the Mentor: A Critical Dialogue with Paulo Freire.* New York: Peter Lang, 1997.

Frye Jacobson, Matthew. *Whiteness of a Different Color: European Immigrants and the Alchemy of Race.* Cambridge: Harvard University Press, 1998.

Frye, Marilyn. "On Being White: Toward A Feminist Understanding of Race and Race Supremacy." In Frye, ed. *The Politics of Reality: Essays in Feminist Theory,* 110-27. Freedom, CA: The Crossing Press, 1983.

Gabriel, John. *Whitewashed.* London: Routledge, 1998.

George, Chief Dan, and H. Hirnschall. *My Heart Soars.* Saanichton, BC: Hancock House, 1974.

Goffman, Erving. *Stigma: Notes on the Management of Spoiled Identity.* New York: Prentice-Hall, Inc., 1963.

Grenier, Louise. *Working with Indigenous Knowledge: A Guide for Researchers.* Ottawa: International Development Research Centre, 1998.

Grillo, Trina, and Stephanie Wildman. "Obscuring the Importance of Race: The Implications of Making Comparisons between Racism and Sexism (or other isms)." In Adrien Katherine Wing, ed. *Critical Race Feminism: A Reader,* 44-50. New York University Press, 1997.

——. "Sexism, Racism, and the Analogy Problem in Feminist Thought." In Jeannee Adleman and Gloria Enguidanoes, eds. *Racism in the Lives of Women: Testimony, Theory and Guides to Anti-Racist Practice,* 171-78. New York: Harrington Park Press, 1997.

Haig-Brown, Celia. "Choosing Border Work." *Canadian Journal of Native Education* 19, no. 1 (1992).

Hamilton, Sylvia. "Our Mothers Grand and Great: Black Women of Nova Scotia." In *Canadian Woman Studies* 11, no. 3 (Spring 1991).

——. "African Nova Scotian Women: Mothering Across the Generations." In Sharon Abbey and Andrea O'Reilly, eds. *Redefining Motherhood: Changing Identities and Patterns,* 256. Toronto: Second Story Press, 1998; now available from Sumach Press, Toronto.

Hanohano, P. "The Spiritual Imperative of Native Epistemology: Restoring Harmony and Balance to Education." *Canadian Journal of Native Education* 23, no. 2 (1999): 206-19.

Henry, Annette. "Missing: Black Self-Representation in Canadian Educational Research." In Suzanne de Castell and Mary Bryson, eds. *Radical Interventions: Identity, Politics and Difference/s in Educational Praxis*, 131-45. Albany: State University of New York Press, 1997.

——. *Taking Back Control: African Canadian Women Teachers' Lives and Practices.* Albany: State University of New York Press, 1998.

Henry, F., and C. Tator. *Racist Discourse in Canada's English Print Media.* Toronto: Canadian Race Relations Foundation, 2000.

Henry, Frances et al., eds. *The Colour of Democracy: Racism in Canadian Society.* Toronto: Harcourt Brace, 2000.

Henry, Millsom. "Ivory Towers and Ebony Women: The Experiences of Black Woman." In Sue Davies et al., eds. *Changing the Subject: Women in Higher Education*, 42-57. Portsmouth, UK: Taylor and Francis, 1994.

Higginbotham, Evelyn Brooks. "African-American Women's History and the Metalanguage of Race." *Signs: Journal of Women in Culture and Society* 17, no. 2 (1992): 251-74.

Hoch, Paul. *White Hero Black Beast: Racism, Sexism and the Mask of Masculinity.* London: Pluto Press, 1979.

Hodes, Martha. *White Women, Black Men: Illicit Sex in the Nineteenth-Century South.* New Haven: Yale University Press, 1997.

hooks, bell. *Ain't I A Woman: Black Women and Feminism.* Boston: South End Press, 1981.

——. *Feminist Theory: From Margin to Center.* Boston: South End Press, 1984.

——. *Talking Back: Thinking Feminist-Thinking Black.* Boston: South End Press, 1989.

——. *Yearning: Race, Gender, and Cultural Politics.* Toronto: Between the Lines, 1990.

——. "Black Women Intellectuals." In bell hooks and Cornel West, *Breaking Bread: Insurgent Black Intellectual Life.* Toronto: Between the Lines, 1991.

——. *Black Looks: Race and Representation.* Toronto: Between the Lines, 1992.

——. *Outlaw Culture: Resisting Representations.* New York: Routledge, 1994.

——. *Teaching to Transgress: Education as the Practice of Freedom.* New York: Routledge, 1994.

——. *Killing Rage: Ending Racism.* New York: Henry Holt and Company, 1995.

——. *Reel to Real: Race, Sex, and Class at the Movies.* New York: Routledge, 1996.

——. "Representing Whiteness in the Black Imagination." In Ruth Frankenberg, ed. *Displacing Whiteness: Essays in Social and Cultural Criticism,* 165-79. Durham, NC: Duke University Press, 1997.

Hudson-Weems, Clenora. "Africana Womanism." In Obioma Nnaemeka, ed. *Sisterhood, Feminism and Power: From Africa to the Diaspora,* 149-62. Trenton: Africa World Press, 1997.

Hull, Gloria T., Patricia Bell Scott, and Barbara Smith, eds. *All the Women Are White, All the Blacks Are Men, But Some of Us Are Brave: Black Women's Studies.* New York: The Feminist Press, 1982.

James, Joy. *Shadowboxing: Representations of Black Feminist Politics.* New York: St. Martin's Press, 1999.

James, Stanlie M., and P.A. Busia Abena, eds. *Theorizing Black Feminisms: The Visionary Pragmatism of Black Women.* New York: Routledge, 1993.

Kabira, Wanjiku Mukabi, and Elizabeth Akinyi Nzioki. "Women's Groups Movement Activities: Achievements and Obstacles." In *Celebrating Women's Resistance,* 41-66. Nairobi: African Women's Perspective, 1993.

Kemdirm, Protus. "African Culture and Womanhood: The Issue of Single Parenthood." In Obioma Nnaemeka, ed. *Sisterhood, Feminism and Power: From Africa to the Diaspora,* 453-56. Trenton: Africa World Press, 1997.

Kemp, Sandra, and Judith Squires, eds. *Feminisms.* Oxford: Oxford University Press. 1997.

Kincheloe, Joe L, Shirley R. Steinberg, Nelson M. Rodriguez and Ronald E. Chennault, eds. *White Reign: Deploying Whiteness in America.* New York: St. Martin's Press, 1998.

King, Deborah. "Multiple Jeopardy, Multiple Consciousness: The Context of a Black Feminist Ideology." *Signs: Journal of Women in Culture and Society* 19, no. 3 (1994).

Kirby, Sandra, et al., eds. *Women Changing Academe: The Proceedings of the 1990 Canadian Women's Studies Association Conference.* Winnipeg: Sororal Publishing, 1991.

Kline, Marleee. "Women's Oppression and Racism: Critique of the 'Feminist Standpoint.'" In Jesse Vorst et al., eds. *Race, Class, Gender: Bonds and Barriers.* Toronto: Garamond Press; Winnipeg: Society for Socialist Studies, 1991.

Lather, Patti. *Getting Smart: Feminist Research and Pedagogy Within the Postmodern.* New York: Routledge, 1991.

Lawson, Erica. "Black Women's Mothering in a Historical Perspective: Understanding the Past, Forging the Future." *Journal of the Association for Research on Mothering* 2, no. 2 (Fall/Winter 2000): 21-30.

Leah, Ronnie Joy. "Do You Call Me 'Sister?': Women of Colour and the Canadian Labour Movement." In Enakshi Dua and Angela Robertson, eds. *Scratching the Surface: Canadian Anti-Racist Feminist Thought*, 97-126. Toronto: Women's Press, 1999.

Longboat, D. "First Nations Control of Education: The Path to Our Survival as Nations." In A. McKay and B. McKay, eds. *Indian Education in Canada.* Volume 2: *The Challenge.* Vancouver: University of British Columbia Press, 1987.

Loomba, Ania. "Colonial and Postcolonial Identities." In *Colonialism/Post-colonialism*, 104-73. New York: Routledge, 1998.

Lorber, Judith. *Gender Inequality: Feminist Theories and Politics.* Los Angeles: Roxbury Publishing Company, 2001.

Lorde, Audre. *Sister Outsider: Essays and Speeches.* Trumansburg, NY: Crossing Press, 1984.

——. "I Am Your Sister: Black Women Organizing Across Sexualities." In Makeda Silvera, ed. *Piece of My Heart: A Lesbian of Colour Anthology*, 94-99. Toronto: Sister Vision Press, 1991.

Luebke, Barbara F., and Mary Ellen Reilly. *Women Studies: The First Generation.* New York: Routledge, 1995.

Lugones, Maria C., and Elizabeth Spelman. "Have We Got a Theory for You! Feminst Theory, Cultural Imperialism, and the Demand for 'The Woman's Voice.'" In N. Tuana and R. Tong, eds., *Feminism and Philosophy: Essential Readings in Theory, Reinterpretation, and Application*, 494-507. Boulder: Westview Press, 1995.

Maher, Frances A., and Mary Kay Tetreault Thompson. *The Feminist Classroom: An Inside Look at How Professionals and Students are Transforming Higher Education for a Diverse Society.* New York: Basic Books, 1994.

Mama, Amina. "Sheroes and Villains: Conceptualizing Colonial and Contemporary Violence Against Women in Africa." In M. Jacqui Alexander and Chandra Talpade Mohanty, eds. *Feminist Geneologies, Colonial Legacies, Democratic Futures*, 46-63. New York: Routledge, 1998.

Margolis, Eric, and Mary Romero. "The Department is Very Male, Very White, Very Old, and Very Conservative: The Functioning of the Hidden Curriculum in Graduate Sociology Departments." *Harvard Educational Review* 68, no. 1 (1998): 1-32.

Mariechild, Diane. *The Inner Dance: A Guide to Spiritual and Psychological Unfolding.* Freedom, CA: The Crossing Press, 1987.

Marker, M. "Economics and Local Self-determination: Describing the Clash Zone in First Nations Education." *Canadian Journal of Native Education* 24, no. 1 (2000): 30-44.

Maynard, Mary. "Challenging the Boundaries: Towards an Anti-Racist Women's Studies." In Mary Maynard and June Purvis, eds. *New Frontiers in Women's Studies: Knowledge, Identity and Nationalism.* Portsmouth, UK: Taylor and Francis, 1996.

McKay, Nellie Y. "A Troubled Peace: Black Women in the Halls of the White Academy." In Louis Benjamin, ed. *Black Women in the Academy: Promises and Perils.* Gainesville: University Press of Florida, 1997.

McPherson, D., and Rabb, D.J. "Some Thoughts on Articulating a Native Philosophy." *Ayaangwaamizin: International Journal of Indigenous Philosophy* 1, no. 1 (1997): 11-21.

Medicine Eagle, Brooke. *Buffalo Woman Comes Singing.* New York: Ballantine Books, 1991.

Mirza, Heidi Safia. "Black Women in Higher Education: Defining a Space/Finding a Place." In Lousie Morley and Val Walsh, eds. *Feminist Academics: Creative Agents for Change*, 145-55. Portsmouth, UK: Taylor and Francis, 1995.

——, ed. *Black British Feminism: A Reader.* London: Routledge, 1997.

Mogadime, Dolana. "Black Girls/ Black Women-Centred Texts and Black Teachers as Othermothers." *Journal of the Association for Research on Mothering* 2, no. 2 (Fall/Winter 2000): 222-33.

——. "Contradictions in Feminist Pedagogy: Black Students' Perspectives." *Resources for Feminist Research.* Forthcoming.

Mohanty, Chandra T. " On Race and Voice: Challenges for Liberal Education in the 1990s." In Becky Thompson and Sangeeta Tyagi, eds. *Beyond a Dream Deferred*, 1-61. Minneapolis: University of Minnesota Press, 1989.

——. "Under Western Eyes." In Les Back and John Solomos, eds. *Theories of Race and Racism: A Reader*, 203-23. New York: Routledge, 2000.

Mohanty, Chandra T., Ann Russo and Lourdes Torres, eds. *Third World Women and the Politics of Feminism.* Bloomington: Indiana University Press, 1991.

Mojab, Shahrzad. "Speaking of Our Lives: Minority Women in Academe." *Convergence* 30, nos. 2/3 (1997): 115-25.

Monture-Angus, Patricia. *Thunder in My Soul: A Mohawk Woman Speaks.* Halifax: Fernwood Publishing, 1995.

——. *Journeying Forward: Dreaming First Nations' Independence.* Halifax: Fernwood Publishing, 1999.

Moraga, Cherrie, and Gloria Anzaldúa, eds. *This Bridge Called My Back: Writings by Radical Women of Color.* New York: Kitchen Table: Women of Color Press, 1981.

Morrison, Toni, and Claudia Brodsky Lacour, eds. *Birth of a Nation'hood: Gaze, Script and Spectacle in the O.J. Simpson Trial.* New York: Pantheon Books, 1998.

Morton, Patricia. *Disfigured Images: The Historical Assault on Afro-American Women.* New York: Praeger Publishers, 1991.

Moses, Yohanda. "Black Women in Academe: Issues and Strategies." In Lois Benjamin, ed. *Black Women in the Academy: Promises and Perils*, 23-37. Gainesville: University Press of Florida, 1997.

Mukherjee, Arun. "A House Divided: Women of Colour and American Feminist Theory." In Constance Backhouse and David H. Flaherty, eds. *Challenging Times: The Women's Movement in Canada and the United States.* Montreal: McGill-Queen's, 1992.

Nelson, Dana D. *National Manhood: Capitalist Citizenship and the Imagined Fraternity of White Men.* Durham, NC: Duke University Press, 1998.

Nfah-Abbenyi, Juliana Makuchi. "Why (What) Am I (Doing) Here: A Cameroonian Woman?" In Margaret Gillett and Ann Beer, eds. *Our Own Agenda: Autobiographical Essays by Women Associated with McGill University*, 250-61. Montreal: McGill-Queen's University Press, 1995.

——. *Gender in African Women's Writing: Identity, Sexuality, and Difference.* Bloomington: Indiana University Press, 1997.

Ng, Roxana. "Teaching against the Grain: Contradictions and Possibilities." In Roxana Ng et al., eds. *Anti-Racism, Feminism, and Critical Approaches to Education*, 129-50. New York: Bergin and Garvey, 1991.

Nnaemeka, Obioma, ed. *Sisterhood, Feminism and Power: From Africa to the Diaspora.* Trenton: Africa World Press, 1997.

N'Zengou-Tayo, Marie-Jose. " 'Fanm se poto mitan': Hatian Woman, the Pillar of Society." *Feminist Review: Rethinking Caribbean Difference,* no. 59 (Summer 1998): 118-42.

O'Grady, Lorraine. "Olympia's Maid: Reclaiming Black Female Subjectivity." In Joanna Fruen et al., eds. *New Feminist Criticism: Art, Identity, Action,* 152-70. New York: HarperCollins, 1994.

Ogundipe-Leslie, Molara. "African Women, Culture and Another Development." In *Recreating Ourselves: African Women and Critical Transformations,* 21-42. Trenton: Africa World Press, 1994.

Omolade, Barbara. "'Making Sense': Notes for Studying Black Teen Mothers." In Martha A. Fineman and Isabel Karpin, eds. *Mothers in Law: Feminist Theory and the Legal Regulation of Motherhood,* 270-85. New York: Columbia University Press, 1995.

Palmer, Phyllis Marynick. "White Women/Black Women: The Dualism of Female Identity and Experience in the United States." *Feminist Studies* 9, no. 1 (Spring 1983): 151-70.

Patai, Daphane, and Noretta Koertge. *Professing Feminism: Cautionary Tales from the Strange World of Feminist Studies.* New York: Basic Books, 1994.

Peake, Linda, and Brian Ray. "Racializing the Canadian Landscape: Whiteness, Uneven Geographies and Social Justice." *Canadian Geography* 45, no. 1 (Spring 2001).

Pence, Jean L. "Learning Leadership Through Mentorships." In M. Dunlap and P. A. Schmuck, eds. *Women Leading in Education,* 125-44. Albany: State University of New York Press, 1995.

Philip, Nourbese. *A Genealogy of Resistance and Other Essays.* Toronto: The Mercury Press, 1997.

Pierson, Ruth Roach, and Nupur Chaudhuri, eds., With the Assistance of Beth McAuley. *Nation, Empire, Colony: Historicizing Gender and Race.* Bloomington: Indiana University Press, 1998.

Pratt, Mary Louise. *Imperial Eyes Travel Writing and Transculturation.* London: Routledge, 1992.

Rassol, Naz. "Black Women as the 'Other' in the Academy." In Louise Morley and Val Walsh, eds. *Feminist Academics: Creative Agents for Change,* 22-41. Portsmouth, UK: Taylor and Francis, 1995.

Razack, Sherene. *Looking White People in the Eye: Gender, Race, and Culture in Courtrooms and Classrooms.* Toronto: University of Toronto Press, 1998.

——."Race, Space, and Prostitution: The Making of the Bourgeois Subject." *Canadian Journal of Women and the Law* 10 (1998): 1-39.

——, ed. *Race, Space, and the Law: Unmapping a White Settler Society.* Toronto: Between the Lines, 2002.

Rich, Adrienne. "Disloyal to Civilization: Feminism, Racism, Gynephobia. " In *On Lies, Secrets, and Silence.* New York: Norton, 1979.

Roberts, Dorothy. "Racism and Patriarchy in the Meaning of Motherhood" In Martha A. Fineman and Isabel Karpin, eds. *Mothers in Law: Feminist Theory and the Legal Regulation of Motherhood,* 224-49. New York: Columbia University Press, 1995.

Rodriguez, Nelson, M. "Emptying the Content of Whiteness: Toward an Understanding of the Relation between Whiteness and Pedagogy." In Joe L. Kincheloe, Shirley R. Steinberg, Nelson M. Rodriguez and Ronald E. Chennault, eds. *White Reign: Deploying Whiteness In America.* New York: St. Martin's Press, 1998.

Rodriguez, N.M., and L.E. Villaverde. *Dismantling White Privilege: Pedagogy, Politics, and Whiteness.* New York: P. Lang, 2000.

Romero, Mary, and Debbie Storrs. "Is That Sociology? The Accounts of Women of Color Graduate Students in Ph.D. Programs." In D. M. Dunlap and P. A. Schmuck, eds. *Women Leading in Education,* 71-85. Albany: State University of New York Press, 1995.

Sams, Jamie. *The 13 Original Clan Mothers.* New York: Harper San Francisco, 1993.

Scheurich, James Joseph. "Toward a White Discourse on White Racism." *Educational Researcher* (November 1993).

Schiebinger, Londa. "Theories of Gender and Race." In Janet Price and Margrit Shildrick, eds. *Feminist Theory and the Body: A Reader,* 21-31. New York: Routledge, 1999.

Shelby, Lewis. "Africana Feminism: An Alternative Paradigm for Black Women in the Academy." In Lois Benjamin, ed. *Black Women in the Academy: Promises and Perils.* Gainesville: University Press of Florida, 1997.

Silvera, Makeda. *Silenced: Talks with Working-class Caribbean Women about their Lives and Struggles as Domestic Workers in Canada.* Second Edition. Toronto: Sister Vision Press, 1995.

Simms, Glenda. "Racism as a Barrier to Canadian Citizenship." In William Kaplan, ed. *Belonging: The Meaning and Future of Canadian Citizenship*, 333-48. Montreal: McGill-Queen's University Press, 1993.

Smith, Barbara. *The Truth that Never Hurts: Writings on Race, Gender, and Freedom.* New Brunswick, NJ: Rutgers University Press, 1998.

Smith, Christian. "Black Feminism and the Academy." In Les Back and John Solomos, eds. *Theories of Race and Racism: A Reader*, 462-72. New York: Routledge, 2000.

Smith, Dorothy E. *The Everyday World as Problematic: A Feminist Sociology.* Boston: Northeastern University Press, 1987.

Smith, Sidonie, and Julia Watson, eds. *De/colonizing the Subject: The Politics of Gender in Women's Autobiography.* Minneapolis: University of Minnesota Press, 1992.

Sofola, Zulu. "Feminism and African Womanhood." In Obioma Nnaemeka, ed. *Sisterhood, Feminism and Power: From Africa to the Diaspora*, 51-64. Trenton: Africa World Press, 1997.

Spelman, Elizabeth. *Inessential Woman: Problems of Exclusion in Feminist Thought.* Boston: Beacon Press, 1996.

Steady, Philomena Chioma. "African Feminism: A Worldwide Perspective." In Rosalyn Terborg-Penn, ed. *Women in Africa and the African Diaspora*, 3-24. Boston: Harvard University Press, 1989.

——, ed. *The Black Woman Cross-Culturally.* Rochester: Schenkman Books, 1992.

Stevenson, Winona. "Colonialism and First Nations Women in Canada." In Enakshi Dua and Angela Robertson, eds. *Scratching the Surface: Canadian Anti-Racist Feminist Thought.* Toronto: Women Press, 1999.

Stoler, Ann. "Making Empire Respectable: The Politics of Race and Sexual Morality in Twentieth-Century Colonial Cultures." *American Ethnologist* 16, no. 4 (1989).

Sudbury, Julia. *Other Kinds of Dreams: Black Women's Organizations and the Politics of Transformation.* London: Routledge, 1998.

Tatum, Beverely. "Lighting Candles in the Dark: One Black Woman's Response to White Antiracist Narratives." In C. Clark and J. O'Donnell, eds. *Becoming and Unbecoming White: Owning and Disowning a Racial Identity.* Westport: Bergin and Garvey, 1999.

Terborg-Penn, Rosalyn. "Through an African Feminist Theoretical Lens: Viewing Caribbean Women's History Cross-Culturally." In Verene Shepherd, Bridget Brereton and Barbara Bailey, eds. *Engendering History: Caribbean Women in Historical Perspective*, 3-19. Kingston, Jamaica: Ian Randle Publishers, 1995.

Thiongo, Ngugi Wa. *Decolonizing the Mind: The Politics of Language in African Literature.* Oxford: Heinemann, 1986.

Thomson, Colin. *Blacks in Deep Snow: Black Pioneers in Canada.* Don Mills, ON: J.M. Dent and Sons, 1997.

Thompson, Becky. "Home/Work: Antiracism, Activism and the Meaning of Whiteness." In Michelle Fine, Lois Weis, Linda C. Powell and L. Mun Wong, eds. *Off White: Readings On Race, Power, and Society.* New York: Routledge, 1997.

Turner, Caroline Sotello Viernes, and Judith Rann Thompson. "Socializing Women Doctoral Students: Minority and Majority Experiences." *The Review of Higher Education* 16, no. 3 (1993): 355-70.

Turner, Caroline Sotello Viernes, and Samuel L. Myers Jr. *Faculty of Color in Academe: Bittersweet Success.* Boston: Allyn and Bacon, 2000.

Valverde, Mariana. "Racism and Anti-Racism in Feminist Research." In Constance Backhouse and David H. Flaherty, eds. *Challenging Times: The Women's Movement in Canada and the United States.* Montreal: McGill-Queen's Press, 1992.

——. "'When the Mother of the Race is Free': Race, Reproduction, and Sexuality in First-Wave Feminism." In Franca Iacovetta and Mariana Valverde, eds. *Gender Conflicts: New Essays in Women's History*, 3-26. Toronto: University of Toronto Press, 1992.

Van Dijk, Tuen. *Elite Discourse and Racism. Sage Series on Race and Ethnic Relations.* Newbury Park, CA: Sage, 1993.

Wallace, Michelle. "A Black Feminist 's Search for Sisterhood." In Gloria T. Hull, Patricia Bell-Scott and Barbara Smith, eds. *All the Women Are White, All the Blacks Are Men, But Some of Us Are Brave*, 5-12. New York: Feminist Press, 1982.

Wane, Njoki, Nathani. "Indigenous Knowledges: Lessons from the Elders." In George Dei, Bud Hall and Dorothy Rosenberg, eds. *Indigenous Knowledges in Global Contexts: Multiple Readings of Our World*, 54-69. Toronto. University of Toronto Press, 2000.

——. "Reflections on the Mutuality of Mothering: Women, Children, and Othermothering." *Journal of the Association for Research on Mothering* 2, no. 2

(Fall/Winter 2000): 105-16.

——. "African Women and Spirituality: Connection Between Thought and Education." In Edmund O'Sullivan, Amish Morrell and Mary O'Connor, eds. *Expanding the Boundaries of Transformative Learning: Essays on Theory and Praxis*, 135-50. New York: Palgrave Macmillan, 2002.

Wane, Njoki Nathani, and Barbara Waterfall. "The Spirals of Spirituality: Renewing the Hoop of Creation in Science and Technology — Pedagogical Implications." In Linda Muzzin and Peggy Tripp, eds. *Teaching as if the World Mattered: Intersections of Race, Gender, Class and Species*. Forthcoming.

Ware, Vron. *Beyond the Pale: White Women, Racism and History*. London: Verso, 1992.

Werbner, Richard. "Multiple Identities, Plural Arenas." In R. Werbner and T. Roger, eds. *Postcolonial Identities in Africa*, 1-25. London: Zed Books, 1996.

Williams, Patricia J. *The Alchemy of Race and Rights: Diary of a Law Professor*. Cambridge: Harvard University Press, 1991.

Wing, Adrien Katherine, ed. *Critical Race Feminism: A Reader*. New York: New York University Press, 1997.

Winks, Robin. *The Blacks in Canada: A History*. New Haven: Yale University Press, 1971.

Yee, Shirley J. "Gender Ideology and Black Women as Community-Builders in Ontario, 1850-70." *The Canadian Historical Review* 75, no. 1 (March1994).

Zinn, Maxine Baca, and Bonnie Dill Thornton. "Theorizing Difference from Multiracial Feminism." *Feminist Studies* 22, no. 2 (1996): 321-31.

Contributors

Afua Cooper is a historian and a poet. She recently graduated from the University of Toronto with a PhD in history, where she has also taught.

Katerina Deliovsky is a sociology PhD candidate at McMaster University. She is an anti-racist feminist whose research areas of interest include feminist theory, the sociology of gender, race and class, interracial relationships and how these issues contribute to social justice.

Brenda Firman has lived and worked in various capacities in remote First Nations' communities for close to fifteen years. Her teaching experience spans kindergarten to adult and includes the training of community educators. She is currently a doctoral student in Curriculum and Instruction at the University of British Columbia.

Tamari Kitossa is completing his PhD in the Department of Sociology and Equity Studies at OISE/UT. His primary interests are exploring the experiences of African-Canadian men and women; racial representation, masculinity and the media; and implications of class, gender and race analysis in research relating to sociology, history and political economy. His essay "Same Difference: Biocentric Imperialism and the

Assault on Indigenous Culture and Hunting" has been published in the journal *Environments.*

Erica Lawson is a PhD candidate in the Department of Sociology and Equity Studies at OISE/UT. Her research focuses on Black mothers and daughters, health and racism. Her work is informed by anti-racism theory and practice, Black feminist thought and Indigenous knowledge. Erica holds a BA from Carleton University and an MA from OISE/UT. In addition to pursuing academic studies, Erica works in the areas of policy and critical race research for a legal organization.

Grace Mathieson is a teacher in Ontario's elementary school system. An underlying dissatisfaction with the school system and her teaching practice led her to return to university to study in the Department of Sociology and Equity Studies in Education at OISE/UT. Her personal challenge is to transform her classroom curriculum and practice so that it reflects her beliefs in social and racial justice. Although it is easy to be discouraged by the Dracon-ian measures being applied to education by government, her passion and vision fuel her classroom work with young students, and she believes that White educators have much to contribute to rethinking education.

Dolana Mogadime is a PhD student in the Department of Sociology and Equity Studies in Education at OISE/UT. Her research interests centre on investigating the lived realities of Black women's lives and their contribution to the education of children in Africa and the African Diaspora. Dolana began this work by writing about her mother's life and work as a political activist and teacher in both South Africa and Canada, which has been published in various feminist journals such as *Canadian Woman Studies,* Special Issues, "Women in Education" and "Looking Back, Looking Forward: Mothers, Daughters and Feminism," and in the *Journal of the Association of Research on Mothering,* Special Issue, "Mothering in the African Diaspora."

NJOKI NATHANI WANE is Assistant Professor in the Department of Sociology and Equity Studies in Education at OISE/UT. Her areas of research interest are African and Black feminisms, spirituality, Indigenous knowledges, African women and the question of development, and anti-racist and anti-colonial studies. Her most recent publications are "African Women and Spirituality: Connections between Thought and Education" in *Expanding the Boundaries of Transformative Learning;* "Narratives of Embu Rural Women: Gender Roles and Indigenous Knowledge," *Gender Technology and Development Journal;* "Indigenous Knowledges, Lessons from Elders: A Kenyan Case Study" in *Indigenous Knowledges in Global Contexts;* "African Women and Mothering. African Women's Technologies: Applauding the Self, Reclaiming Indigenous Space," *Journal of Postcolonial Education;* "Reflections in Mutuality in Mothering and Othermothering," *Journal of the Association for Research on Mothering;* "'She Who Learns Teaches': Othermothering in the Academy," *Journal of the Association for Research on Mothering;* and, "Grandmothers Called out of Retirement: The Challenges of African Women Facing AIDS Today," *Canadian Woman Studies.* She is the co-editor of *Equity in School and Society.*

BARBARA WATERFALL is a member of the Faculty of Social Work at Wilfrid Laurier University. Prior to this, she was an assistant professor in the Native Human Services Program at Laurentian University. She is a PhD candidate in the Department of Sociology and Equity Studies at OISE/UT and is working on her dissertation that focuses on decolonizing Native social work education. Her article entitled "Native People and the Social Work Profession: Critical Exploration of Colonizing Problematics and the Development of Decolonized Thought" is to be published in *The Journal of Educational Thought.*

Patricia J. Williams is a lawyer and Associate Professor of Law at the University of Wisconsin. She is the author of *The Alchemy of Race and Rights: Diary of a Law Professor.*

Adrien Katherine Wing is a professor in the College of Law at the University of Iowa. She is the editor of *Critical Race Feminism: A Reader.*